HOLT SCIENCE & TECHNOLOGY

Sound and Light

ANNOTATED TEACHER'S EDITION

HOLT, RINEHART AND WINSTON

A Harcourt Classroom Education Company

Austin · New York · Orlando · Atlanta · San Francisco · Boston · Dallas · Toronto · London

Staff Credits

Editorial

Robert W. Todd, Executive Editor

Anne Earvolino, Senior Editor

Michael Mazza, Ken Shepardson, Kelly Rizk, Bill Burnside, Editors

ANCILLARIES

Jennifer Childers, Senior Editor

Chris Colby, Molly Frohlich, Shari Husain, Kristen McCardel, Sabelyn Pussman, Erin Roberson

COPYEDITING

Dawn Spinozza, Copyediting Supervisor

EDITORIAL SUPPORT STAFF

Jeanne Graham, Mary Helbling, Tanu'e White, Doug Rutley

EDITORIAL PERMISSIONS

Cathy Paré, Permissions Manager

Jan Harrington, Permissions Editor

Art, Design, and Photo

BOOK DESIGN

Richard Metzger, Design Director

Marc Cooper, Senior Designer

Ron Bowdoin, Designer

Alicia Sullivan, Designer (ATE), **Cristina Bowerman,** Design Associate (ATE)

Eric Rupprath, Designer (Ancillaries)

Holly Whittaker, Traffic Coordinator

IMAGE ACQUISITIONS

Joe London, Director

Elaine Tate, Art Buyer Supervisor

Tim Taylor, Photo Research Supervisor

Stephanie Morris, Assistant Photo Researcher

PHOTO STUDIO

Sam Dudgeon, Senior Staff Photographer

Victoria Smith, Photo Specialist

Lauren Eischen, Photo Coordinator

DESIGN NEW MEDIA

Susan Michael, Design Director

Production

Mimi Stockdell, Senior Production Manager

Beth Sample, Senior Production Coordinator

Suzanne Brooks, Sara Carroll-Downs

Media Production

Kim A. Scott, Senior Production Manager

Adriana Bardin-Prestwood, Senior Production Coordinator

New Media

Armin Gutzmer, Director

Jim Bruno, Senior Project Manager

Lydia Doty, Senior Project Manager

Jessica Bega, Project Manager

Cathy Kuhles, Nina Degollado, Technical Assistants

Design Implementation and Production

The Quarasan Group, Inc.

Acknowledgments

Chapter Writers

Christie Borgford, Ph.D.
Professor of Chemistry
University of Alabama
Birmingham, Alabama

Andrew Champagne
Former Physics Teacher
Ashland High School
Ashland, Massachusetts

Mapi Cuevas, Ph.D.
Professor of Chemistry
Santa Fe Community College
Gainesville, Florida

Leila Dumas
Former Physics Teacher
LBJ Science Academy
Austin, Texas

William G. Lamb, Ph.D.
Science Teacher and Dept. Chair
Oregon Episcopal School
Portland, Oregon

Sally Ann Vonderbrink, Ph.D.
Chemistry Teacher
St. Xavier High School
Cincinnati, Ohio

Lab Writers

Phillip G. Bunce
Former Physics Teacher
Bowie High School
Austin, Texas

Kenneth E. Creese
Science Teacher
White Mountain Junior High School
Rock Springs, Wyoming

William G. Lamb, Ph.D.
Science Teacher and Dept. Chair
Oregon Episcopal School
Portland, Oregon

Alyson Mike
Science Teacher
East Valley Middle School
East Helena, Montana

Joseph W. Price
Science Teacher and Dept. Chair
H. M. Browne Junior High School
Washington, D.C.

Denice Lee Sandefur
Science Teacher and Dept. Chair
Nucla High School
Nucla, Colorado

John Spadafino
Mathematics and Physics Teacher
Hackensack High School
Hackensack, New Jersey

Walter Woolbaugh
Science Teacher
Manhattan Junior High School
Manhattan, Montana

Academic Reviewers

Paul R. Berman, Ph.D.
Professor of Physics
University of Michigan
Ann Arbor, Michigan

Russell M. Brengelman, Ph.D.
Professor of Physics
Morehead State University
Morehead, Kentucky

John A. Brockhaus, Ph.D.
Director, Mapping, Charting and Geodesy Program
Department of Geography and Environmental Engineering
United States Military Academy
West Point, New York

Walter Bron, Ph.D.
Professor of Physics
University of California
Irvine, California

Andrew J. Davis, Ph.D.
Manager, ACE Science Center
Department of Physics
California Institute of Technology
Pasadena, California

Peter E. Demmin, Ed.D.
Former Science Teacher and Department Chair
Amherst Central High School
Amherst, New York

Roger Falcone, Ph.D.
Professor of Physics and Department Chair
University of California
Berkeley, California

Cassandra A. Fraser, Ph.D.
Assistant Professor of Chemistry
University of Virginia
Charlottesville, Virginia

L. John Gagliardi, Ph.D.
Associate Professor of Physics and Department Chair
Rutgers University
Camden, New Jersey

Gabriele F. Giuliani, Ph.D.
Professor of Physics
Purdue University
West Lafayette, Indiana

Roy W. Hann, Jr., Ph.D.
Professor of Civil Engineering
Texas A&M University
College Station, Texas

John L. Hubisz, Ph.D.
Professor of Physics
North Carolina State University
Raleigh, North Carolina

Samuel P. Kounaves, Ph.D.
Professor of Chemistry
Tufts University
Medford, Massachusetts

Karol Lang, Ph.D.
Associate Professor of Physics
The University of Texas
Austin, Texas

Gloria Langer, Ph.D.
Professor of Physics
University of Colorado
Boulder, Colorado

Phillip LaRoe
Professor
Helena College of Technology
Helena, Montana

Joseph A. McClure, Ph.D.
Associate Professor of Physics
Georgetown University
Washington, D.C.

LaMoine L. Motz, Ph.D.
Coordinator of Science Education
Department of Learning Services
Oakland County Schools
Waterford, Michigan

R. Thomas Myers, Ph.D.
Professor of Chemistry, Emeritus
Kent State University
Kent, Ohio

Hillary Clement Olson, Ph.D.
Research Associate
Institute for Geophysics
The University of Texas
Austin, Texas

David P. Richardson, Ph.D.
Professor of Chemistry
Thompson Chemical Laboratory
Williams College
Williamstown, Massachusetts

John Rigden, Ph.D.
Director of Special Projects
American Institute of Physics
Colchester, Vermont

Peter Sheridan, Ph.D.
Professor of Chemistry
Colgate University
Hamilton, New York

Vederaman Sriraman, Ph.D.
Associate Professor of Technology
Southwest Texas State University
San Marcos, Texas

Jack B. Swift, Ph.D.
Professor of Physics
The University of Texas
Austin, Texas

Atiq Syed, Ph.D.
Master Instructor of Mathematics and Science
Texas State Technical College
Harlingen, Texas

Leonard Taylor, Ph.D.
Professor Emeritus
Department of Electrical Engineering
University of Maryland
College Park, Maryland

Virginia L. Trimble, Ph.D.
Professor of Physics and Astronomy
University of California
Irvine, California

Acknowledgments (cont.)

Martin VanDyke, Ph.D.
Professor of Chemistry, Emeritus
Front Range Community
  College
Westminster, Colorado

**Gabriela Waschewsky,
  Ph.D.**
Science and Math Teacher
Emery High School
Emeryville, California

Safety Reviewer

Jack A. Gerlovich, Ph.D.
Associate Professor
School of Education
Drake University
Des Moines, Iowa

Teacher Reviewers

Barry L. Bishop
Science Teacher and Dept. Chair
San Rafael Junior High School
Ferron, Utah

Paul Boyle
Science Teacher
Perry Heights Middle School
Evansville, Indiana

Kenneth Creese
Science Teacher
White Mountain Junior High
  School
Rock Springs, Wyoming

Vicky Farland
Science Teacher and Dept. Chair
Centennial Middle School
Yuma, Arizona

Rebecca Ferguson
Science Teacher
North Ridge Middle School
North Richland Hills, Texas

Laura Fleet
Science Teacher
Alice B. Landrum Middle
  School
Ponte Vedra Beach, Florida

Jennifer Ford
Science Teacher and Dept. Chair
North Ridge Middle School
North Richland Hills, Texas

Susan Gorman
Science Teacher
North Ridge Middle School
North Richland Hills, Texas

C. John Graves
Science Teacher
Monforton Middle School
Bozeman, Montana

Dennis Hanson
Science Teacher and Dept. Chair
Big Bear Middle School
Big Bear Lake, California

David A. Harris
Science Teacher and Dept. Chair
The Thacher School
Ojai, California

Norman E. Holcomb
Science Teacher
Marion Local Schools
Maria Stein, Ohio

Kenneth J. Horn
Science Teacher and Dept. Chair
Fallston Middle School
Fallston, Maryland

Tracy Jahn
Science Teacher
Berkshire Junior-Senior High
  School
Canaan, New York

Kerry A. Johnson
Science Teacher
Isbell Middle School
Santa Paula, California

Drew E. Kirian
Science Teacher
Solon Middle School
Solon, Ohio

Harriet Knops
Science Teacher and Dept. Chair
Rolling Hills Middle School
El Dorado, California

Scott Mandel, Ph.D.
*Director and Educational
  Consultant*
Teachers Helping Teachers
Los Angeles, California

Thomas Manerchia
Former Science Teacher
Archmere Academy
Claymont, Delaware

Edith McAlanis
Science Teacher and Dept. Chair
Socorro Middle School
El Paso, Texas

Kevin McCurdy, Ph.D.
Science Teacher
Elmwood Junior High School
Rogers, Arkansas

Alyson Mike
Science Teacher
East Valley Middle School
East Helena, Montana

Donna Norwood
Science Teacher and Dept. Chair
Monroe Middle School
Charlotte, North Carolina

Joseph W. Price
Science Teacher and Dept. Chair
H. M. Browne Junior High
  School
Washington, D.C.

Terry J. Rakes
Science Teacher
Elmwood Junior High School
Rogers, Arkansas

Beth Richards
Science Teacher
North Middle School
Crystal Lake, Illinois

Elizabeth J. Rustad
Science Teacher
Crane Middle School
Yuma, Arizona

Rodney A. Sandefur
Science Teacher
Naturita Middle School
Naturita, Colorado

Helen Schiller
Science Teacher
Northwood Middle School
Taylors, South Carolina

Bert J. Sherwood
Science Teacher
Socorro Middle School
El Paso, Texas

Patricia McFarlane Soto
Science Teacher and Dept. Chair
G. W. Carver Middle School
Miami, Florida

David M. Sparks
Science Teacher
Redwater Junior High School
Redwater, Texas

Larry Tackett
Science Teacher and Dept. Chair
Andrew Jackson Middle School
Cross Lanes, West Virginia

Elsie N. Waynes
Science Teacher and Dept. Chair
R. H. Terrell Junior High School
Washington, D.C.

Sharon L. Woolf
Science Teacher
Langston Hughes Middle
  School
Reston, Virginia

Alexis S. Wright
Middle School Science Coordinator
Rye Country Day School
Rye, New York

Lee Yassinski
Science Teacher
Sun Valley Middle School
Sun Valley, California

John Zambo
Science Teacher
Elizabeth Ustach Middle School
Modesto, California

Sound and Light

Skills Development

Process Skills

QuickLabs

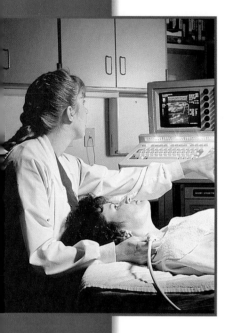

Chapter Labs

Research and Critical Thinking Skills

Apply

Feature Articles

Science, Technology, and Society

Across the Sciences

Science Fiction

Eureka!

Eye on the Environment

Connections

Astronomy Connection

Biology Connection

Environment Connection

Geology Connection

Mathematics

Program Scope and Sequence

Selecting the right books for your course is easy. Just review the topics presented in each book to determine the best match to your district curriculum.

	A MICROORGANISMS, FUNGI, AND PLANTS	**B** ANIMALS
CHAPTER 1	**It's Alive!! Or, Is It?** ❏ Characteristics of living things ❏ Homeostasis ❏ Heredity and DNA ❏ Producers, consumers, and decomposers ❏ Biomolecules	**Animals and Behavior** ❏ Characteristics of animals ❏ Classification of animals ❏ Animal behavior ❏ Hibernation and estivation ❏ The biological clock ❏ Animal communication ❏ Living in groups
CHAPTER 2	**Bacteria and Viruses** ❏ Binary fission ❏ Characteristics of bacteria ❏ Nitrogen-fixing bacteria ❏ Antibiotics ❏ Pathogenic bacteria ❏ Characteristics of viruses ❏ Lytic cycle	**Invertebrates** ❏ General characteristics of invertebrates ❏ Types of symmetry ❏ Characteristics of sponges, cnidarians, arthropods, and echinoderms ❏ Flatworms versus roundworms ❏ Types of circulatory systems
CHAPTER 3	**Protists and Fungi** ❏ Characteristics of protists ❏ Types of algae ❏ Types of protozoa ❏ Protist reproduction ❏ Characteristics of fungi and lichens	**Fishes, Amphibians, and Reptiles** ❏ Characteristics of vertebrates ❏ Structure and kinds of fishes ❏ Development of lungs ❏ Structure and kinds of amphibians and reptiles ❏ Function of the amniotic egg
CHAPTER 4	**Introduction to Plants** ❏ Characteristics of plants and seeds ❏ Reproduction and classification ❏ Angiosperms versus gymnosperms ❏ Monocots versus dicots ❏ Structure and functions of roots, stems, leaves, and flowers	**Birds and Mammals** ❏ Structure and kinds of birds ❏ Types of feathers ❏ Adaptations for flight ❏ Structure and kinds of mammals ❏ Function of the placenta
CHAPTER 5	**Plant Processes** ❏ Pollination and fertilization ❏ Dormancy ❏ Photosynthesis ❏ Plant tropisms ❏ Seasonal responses of plants	
CHAPTER 6		
CHAPTER 7		

Life Science

C — CELLS, HEREDITY, & CLASSIFICATION

Cells: The Basic Units of Life
- ❏ Cells, tissues, and organs
- ❏ Populations, communities, and ecosystems
- ❏ Cell theory
- ❏ Surface-to-volume ratio
- ❏ Prokaryotic versus eukaryotic cells
- ❏ Cell organelles

The Cell in Action
- ❏ Diffusion and osmosis
- ❏ Passive versus active transport
- ❏ Endocytosis versus exocytosis
- ❏ Photosynthesis
- ❏ Cellular respiration and fermentation
- ❏ Cell cycle

Heredity
- ❏ Dominant versus recessive traits
- ❏ Genes and alleles
- ❏ Genotype, phenotype, the Punnett square and probability
- ❏ Meiosis
- ❏ Determination of sex

Genes and Gene Technology
- ❏ Structure of DNA
- ❏ Protein synthesis
- ❏ Mutations
- ❏ Heredity disorders and genetic counseling

The Evolution of Living Things
- ❏ Adaptations and species
- ❏ Evidence for evolution
- ❏ Darwin's work and natural selection
- ❏ Formation of new species

The History of Life on Earth
- ❏ Geologic time scale and extinctions
- ❏ Plate tectonics
- ❏ Human evolution

Classification
- ❏ Levels of classification
- ❏ Cladistic diagrams
- ❏ Dichotomous keys
- ❏ Characteristics of the six kingdoms

D — HUMAN BODY SYSTEMS & HEALTH

Body Organization and Structure
- ❏ Homeostasis
- ❏ Types of tissue
- ❏ Organ systems
- ❏ Structure and function of the skeletal system, muscular system, and integumentary system

Circulation and Respiration
- ❏ Structure and function of the cardiovascular system, lymphatic system, and respiratory system
- ❏ Respiratory disorders

The Digestive and Urinary Systems
- ❏ Structure and function of the digestive system
- ❏ Structure and function of the urinary system

Communication and Control
- ❏ Structure and function of the nervous system and endocrine system
- ❏ The senses
- ❏ Structure and function of the eye and ear

Reproduction and Development
- ❏ Asexual versus sexual reproduction
- ❏ Internal versus external fertilization
- ❏ Structure and function of the human male and female reproductive systems
- ❏ Fertilization, placental development, and embryo growth
- ❏ Stages of human life

Body Defenses and Disease
- ❏ Types of diseases
- ❏ Vaccines and immunity
- ❏ Structure and function of the immune system
- ❏ Autoimmune diseases, cancer, and AIDS

Staying Healthy
- ❏ Nutrition and reading food labels
- ❏ Alcohol and drug effects on the body
- ❏ Hygiene, exercise, and first aid

E — ENVIRONMENTAL SCIENCE

Interactions of Living Things
- ❏ Biotic versus abiotic parts of the environment
- ❏ Producers, consumers, and decomposers
- ❏ Food chains and food webs
- ❏ Factors limiting population growth
- ❏ Predator-prey relationships
- ❏ Symbiosis and coevolution

Cycles in Nature
- ❏ Water cycle
- ❏ Carbon cycle
- ❏ Nitrogen cycle
- ❏ Ecological succession

The Earth's Ecosystems
- ❏ Kinds of land and water biomes
- ❏ Marine ecosystems
- ❏ Freshwater ecosystems

Environmental Problems and Solutions
- ❏ Types of pollutants
- ❏ Types of resources
- ❏ Conservation practices
- ❏ Species protection

Energy Resources
- ❏ Types of resources
- ❏ Energy resources and pollution
- ❏ Alternative energy resources

Scope and Sequence *(continued)*

	F INSIDE THE RESTLESS EARTH	**G** EARTH'S CHANGING SURFACE
CHAPTER 1	**Minerals of the Earth's Crust** ❏ Mineral composition and structure ❏ Types of minerals ❏ Mineral identification ❏ Mineral formation and mining	**Maps as Models of the Earth** ❏ Structure of a map ❏ Cardinal directions ❏ Latitude, longitude, and the equator ❏ Magnetic declination and true north ❏ Types of projections ❏ Aerial photographs ❏ Remote sensing ❏ Topographic maps
CHAPTER 2	**Rocks: Mineral Mixtures** ❏ Rock cycle and types of rocks ❏ Rock classification ❏ Characteristics of igneous, sedimentary, and metamorphic rocks	**Weathering and Soil Formation** ❏ Types of weathering ❏ Factors affecting the rate of weathering ❏ Composition of soil ❏ Soil conservation and erosion prevention
CHAPTER 3	**The Rock and Fossil Record** ❏ Uniformitarianism versus catastrophism ❏ Superposition ❏ The geologic column and unconformities ❏ Absolute dating and radiometric dating ❏ Characteristics and types of fossils ❏ Geologic time scale	**Agents of Erosion and Deposition** ❏ Shoreline erosion and deposition ❏ Wind erosion and deposition ❏ Erosion and deposition by ice ❏ Gravity's effect on erosion and deposition
CHAPTER 4	**Plate Tectonics** ❏ Structure of the Earth ❏ Continental drifts and sea floor spreading ❏ Plate tectonics theory ❏ Types of boundaries ❏ Types of crust deformities	
CHAPTER 5	**Earthquakes** ❏ Seismology ❏ Features of earthquakes ❏ P and S waves ❏ Gap hypothesis ❏ Earthquake safety	
CHAPTER 6	**Volcanoes** ❏ Types of volcanoes and eruptions ❏ Types of lava and pyroclastic material ❏ Craters versus calderas ❏ Sites and conditions for volcano formation ❏ Predicting eruptions	

Earth Science

H WATER ON EARTH

The Flow of Fresh Water
- ❏ Water cycle
- ❏ River systems
- ❏ Stream erosion
- ❏ Life cycle of rivers
- ❏ Deposition
- ❏ Aquifers, springs, and wells
- ❏ Ground water
- ❏ Water treatment and pollution

Exploring the Oceans
- ❏ Properties and characteristics of the oceans
- ❏ Features of the ocean floor
- ❏ Ocean ecology
- ❏ Ocean resources and pollution

The Movement of Ocean Water
- ❏ Types of currents
- ❏ Characteristics of waves
- ❏ Types of ocean waves
- ❏ Tides

I WEATHER AND CLIMATE

The Atmosphere
- ❏ Structure of the atmosphere
- ❏ Air pressure
- ❏ Radiation, convection, and conduction
- ❏ Greenhouse effect and global warming
- ❏ Characteristics of winds
- ❏ Types of winds
- ❏ Air pollution

Understanding Weather
- ❏ Water cycle
- ❏ Humidity
- ❏ Types of clouds
- ❏ Types of precipitation
- ❏ Air masses and fronts
- ❏ Storms, tornadoes, and hurricanes
- ❏ Weather forecasting
- ❏ Weather maps

Climate
- ❏ Weather versus climate
- ❏ Seasons and latitude
- ❏ Prevailing winds
- ❏ Earth's biomes
- ❏ Earth's climate zones
- ❏ Ice ages
- ❏ Global warming
- ❏ Greenhouse effect

J ASTRONOMY

Observing the Sky
- ❏ Astronomy
- ❏ Keeping time
- ❏ Mapping the stars
- ❏ Scales of the universe
- ❏ Types of telescope
- ❏ Radioastronomy

Formation of the Solar System
- ❏ Birth of the solar system
- ❏ Planetary motion
- ❏ Newton's Law of Universal Gravitation
- ❏ Structure of the sun
- ❏ Fusion
- ❏ Earth's structure and atmosphere

A Family of Planets
- ❏ Properties and characteristics of the planets
- ❏ Properties and characteristics of moons
- ❏ Comets, asteroids, and meteoroids

The Universe Beyond
- ❏ Composition of stars
- ❏ Classification of stars
- ❏ Star brightness, distance, and motions
- ❏ H-R diagram
- ❏ Life cycle of stars
- ❏ Types of galaxies
- ❏ Theories on the formation of the universe

Exploring Space
- ❏ Rocketry and artificial satellites
- ❏ Types of Earth orbit
- ❏ Space probes and space exploration

Scope and Sequence *(continued)*

	K INTRODUCTION TO MATTER	**L** INTERACTIONS OF MATTER
CHAPTER 1	**The Properties of Matter** ❏ Definition of matter ❏ Mass and weight ❏ Physical and chemical properties ❏ Physical and chemical change ❏ Density	**Chemical Bonding** ❏ Types of chemical bonds ❏ Valence electrons ❏ Ions versus molecules ❏ Crystal lattice
CHAPTER 2	**States of Matter** ❏ States of matter and their properties ❏ Boyle's and Charles's laws ❏ Changes of state	**Chemical Reactions** ❏ Writing chemical formulas and equations ❏ Law of conservation of mass ❏ Types of reactions ❏ Endothermic versus exothermic reactions ❏ Law of conservation of energy ❏ Activation energy ❏ Catalysts and inhibitors
CHAPTER 3	**Elements, Compounds, and Mixtures** ❏ Elements and compounds ❏ Metals, nonmetals, and metalloids (semiconductors) ❏ Properties of mixtures ❏ Properties of solutions, suspensions, and colloids	**Chemical Compounds** ❏ Ionic versus covalent compounds ❏ Acids, bases, and salts ❏ pH ❏ Organic compounds ❏ Biomolecules
CHAPTER 4	**Introduction to Atoms** ❏ Atomic theory ❏ Atomic model and structure ❏ Isotopes ❏ Atomic mass and mass number	**Atomic Energy** ❏ Properties of radioactive substances ❏ Types of decay ❏ Half-life ❏ Fission, fusion, and chain reactions
CHAPTER 5	**The Periodic Table** ❏ Structure of the periodic table ❏ Periodic law ❏ Properties of alkali metals, alkaline-earth metals, halogens, and noble gases	
CHAPTER 6		

Physical Science

M FORCES, MOTION, AND ENERGY

Matter in Motion
- ❏ Speed, velocity, and acceleration
- ❏ Measuring force
- ❏ Friction
- ❏ Mass versus weight

Forces in Motion
- ❏ Terminal velocity and free fall
- ❏ Projectile motion
- ❏ Inertia
- ❏ Momentum

Forces in Fluids
- ❏ Properties in fluids
- ❏ Atmospheric pressure
- ❏ Density
- ❏ Pascal's principle
- ❏ Buoyant force
- ❏ Archimedes' principle
- ❏ Bernoulli's principle

Work and Machines
- ❏ Measuring work
- ❏ Measuring power
- ❏ Types of machines
- ❏ Mechanical advantage
- ❏ Mechanical efficiency

Energy and Energy Resources
- ❏ Forms of energy
- ❏ Energy conversions
- ❏ Law of conservation of energy
- ❏ Energy resources

Heat and Heat Technology
- ❏ Heat versus temperature
- ❏ Thermal expansion
- ❏ Absolute zero
- ❏ Conduction, convection, radiation
- ❏ Conductors versus insulators
- ❏ Specific heat capacity
- ❏ Changes of state
- ❏ Heat engines
- ❏ Thermal pollution

N ELECTRICITY AND MAGNETISM

Introduction to Electricity
- ❏ Law of electric charges
- ❏ Conduction versus induction
- ❏ Static electricity
- ❏ Potential difference
- ❏ Cells, batteries, and photocells
- ❏ Thermocouples
- ❏ Voltage, current, and resistance
- ❏ Electric power
- ❏ Types of circuits

Electromagnetism
- ❏ Properties of magnets
- ❏ Magnetic force
- ❏ Electromagnetism
- ❏ Solenoids and electric motors
- ❏ Electromagnetic induction
- ❏ Generators and transformers

Electronic Technology
- ❏ Properties of semiconductors
- ❏ Integrated circuits
- ❏ Diodes and transistors
- ❏ Analog versus digital signals
- ❏ Microprocessors
- ❏ Features of computers

O SOUND AND LIGHT

The Energy of Waves
- ❏ Properties of waves
- ❏ Types of waves
- ❏ Reflection and refraction
- ❏ Diffraction and interference
- ❏ Standing waves and resonance

The Nature of Sound
- ❏ Properties of sound waves
- ❏ Structure of the human ear
- ❏ Pitch and the Doppler effect
- ❏ Infrasonic versus ultrasonic sound
- ❏ Sound reflection and echolocation
- ❏ Sound barrier
- ❏ Interference, resonance, diffraction, and standing waves
- ❏ Sound quality of instruments

The Nature of Light
- ❏ Electromagnetic waves
- ❏ Electromagnetic spectrum
- ❏ Law of reflection
- ❏ Absorption and scattering
- ❏ Reflection and refraction
- ❏ Diffraction and interference

Light and Our World
- ❏ Luminosity
- ❏ Types of lighting
- ❏ Types of mirrors and lenses
- ❏ Focal point
- ❏ Structure of the human eye
- ❏ Lasers and holograms

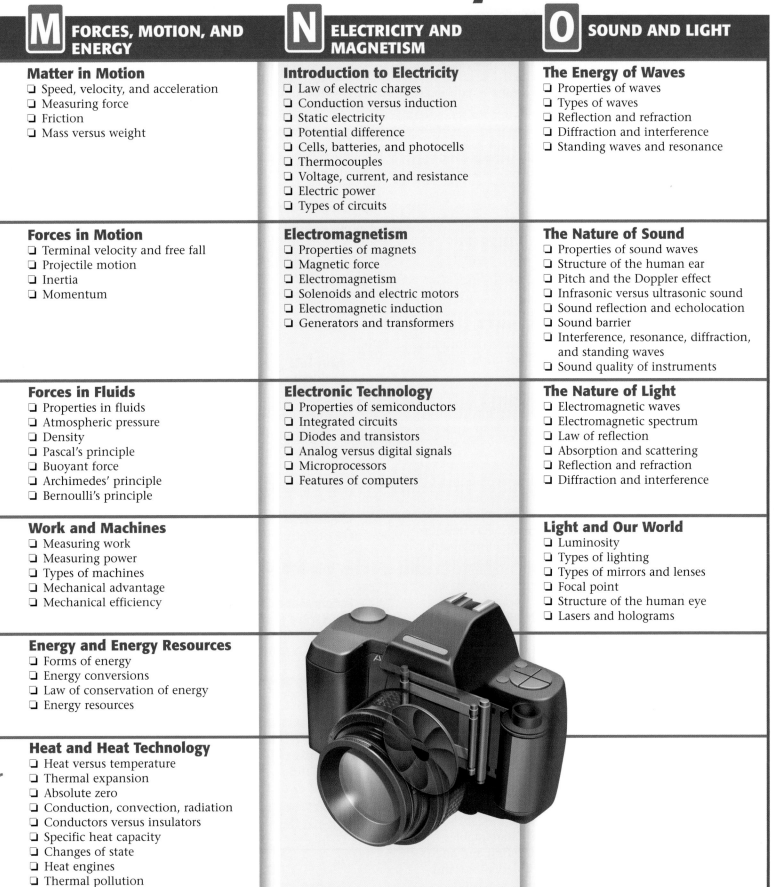

Components Listing

Effective planning starts with all the resources you need in an easy-to-use package for each short course.

Directed Reading Worksheets Help students develop and practice fundamental reading comprehension skills and provide a comprehensive review tool for students to use when studying for an exam.

Study Guide Vocabulary & Notes Worksheets and Chapter Review Worksheets are reproductions of the Chapter Highlights and Chapter Review sections that follow each chapter in the textbook.

Science Puzzlers, Twisters & Teasers Use vocabulary and concepts from each chapter of the Pupil's Editions as elements of rebuses, anagrams, logic puzzles, daffy definitions, riddle poems, word jumbles, and other types of puzzles.

Reinforcement and Vocabulary Review Worksheets Approach a chapter topic from a different angle with an emphasis on different learning modalities to help students that are frustrated by traditional methods.

Critical Thinking & Problem Solving Worksheets Develop the following skills: distinguishing fact from opinion, predicting consequences, analyzing information, and drawing conclusions. Problem Solving Worksheets develop a step-by-step process of problem analysis including gathering information, asking critical questions, identifying alternatives, and making comparisons.

Math Skills for Science Worksheets Each activity gives a brief introduction to a relevant math skill, a step-by-step explanation of the math process, one or more example problems, and a variety of practice problems.

Science Skills Worksheets Help your students focus specifically on skills such as measuring, graphing, using logic, understanding statistics, organizing research papers, and critical thinking options.

LAB ACTIVITIES

ALL LABS ARE CLASSROOM TESTED & APPROVED

Datasheets for Labs These worksheets are the labs found in the *Holt Science & Technology* textbook. Charts, tables, and graphs are included to make data collection and analysis easier, and space is provided to write observations and conclusions.

Whiz-Bang Demonstrations Discovery or Making Models experiences label each demo as one in which students discover an answer or use a scientific model.

Calculator-Based Labs Give students the opportunity to use graphing-calculator probes and sensors to collect data using a TI graphing calculator, Vernier sensors, and a TI CBL 2™ or Vernier Lab Pro interface.

EcoLabs and Field Activities Focus on educational outdoor projects, such as wildlife observation, nature surveys, or natural history.

Inquiry Labs Use the scientific method to help students find their own path in solving a real-world problem.

Long-Term Projects and Research Ideas Provide students with the opportunity to go beyond library and Internet resources to explore science topics.

ASSESSMENT

Chapter Tests Each four-page chapter test consists of a variety of item types including Multiple Choice, Using Vocabulary, Short Answer, Critical Thinking, Math in Science, Interpreting Graphics, and Concept Mapping.

Performance-Based Assessments Evaluate students' abilities to solve problems using the tools, equipment, and techniques of science. Rubrics included for each assessment make it easy to evaluate student performance.

TEACHER RESOURCES

Lesson Plans Integrate all of the great resources in the *Holt Science & Technology* program into your daily teaching. Each lesson plan includes a correlation of the lesson activities to the National Science Education Standards.

Teaching Transparencies Each transparency is correlated to a particular lesson in the Chapter Organizer.

Concept Mapping Transparencies, Worksheets, and Answer Key

Give students an opportunity to complete their own concept maps to study the concepts within each chapter and form logical connections. Student worksheets contain a blank concept map with linking phrases and a list of terms to be used by the student to complete the map.

TECHNOLOGY RESOURCES

One-Stop Planner CD-ROM

Finding the right resources is easy with the One-Stop Planner CD-ROM. You can view and print any resource with just the click of a mouse. Customize the suggested lesson plans to match your daily or weekly calendar and your district's requirements. Powerful test generator software allows you to create customized assessments using a databank of items.

The One-Stop Planner for each level includes the following:

- All materials from the Teaching Resources
- Bellringer Transparency Masters
- Block Scheduling Tools
- Standards Correlations
- Lab Inventory Checklist
- Safety Information
- Science Fair Guide
- Parent Involvement Tools
- Spanish Audio Scripts
- Spanish Glossary
- Assessment Item Listing
- Assessment Checklists and Rubrics
- Test Generator

sciLINKS

*sci*LINKS numbers throughout the text take you and your students to some of the best on-line resources available. Sites are constantly reviewed and updated by the National Science Teachers Association. Special "teacher only" sites are available to you once you register with the service.

go.hrw.com

To access Holt, Rinehart and Winston Web resources, use the home page codes for each level found on page 1 of the Pupil's Editions. The codes shown on the Chapter Organizers for each chapter in the Annotated Teacher's Edition take you to chapter-specific resources.

Smithsonian Institution

Find lesson plans, activities, interviews, virtual exhibits, and just general information on a wide variety of topics relevant to middle school science.

CNNfyi.com

Find the latest in late-breaking science news for students. Featured news stories are supported with lesson plans and activities.

CNN Presents Science in the News Video Library

Bring relevant science news stories into the classroom. Each video comes with a Teacher's Guide and set of Critical Thinking Worksheets that develop listening and media analysis skills. Tapes in the series include:

- Eye on the Environment
- Multicultural Connections
- Scientists in Action
- Science, Technology & Society

Guided Reading Audio CD Program

Students can listen to a direct read of each chapter and follow along in the text. Use the program as a content bridge for struggling readers and students for whom English is not their native language.

Interactive Explorations CD-ROM

Turn a computer into a virtual laboratory. Students act as lab assistants helping Dr. Crystal Labcoat solve real-world problems. Activities develop students' inquiry, analysis, and decision-making skills.

Interactive Science Encyclopedia CD-ROM

Give your students access to more than 3,000 cross-referenced scientific definitions, in-depth articles, science fair project ideas, activities, and more.

ADDITIONAL COMPONENTS

Holt Anthology of Science Fiction

Science Fiction features in the Pupil's Edition preview the stories found in the anthology. Each story begins with a Reading Prep guide and closes with Think About It questions.

Professional Reference for Teachers

Articles written by leading educators help you learn more about the National Science Education Standards, block scheduling, classroom management techniques, and more. A bibliography of professional references is included.

Holt Science Posters

Seven wall posters highlight interesting topics, such as the Physics of Sports, or useful reference material, such as the Scientific Method.

Holt Science Skills Workshop: Reading in the Content Area

Use a variety of in-depth skills exercises to help students learn to read science materials strategically.

Key
These materials are blackline masters.
All titles shown in green are found in the *Teaching Resources* booklets for each course.

Science & Math Skills Worksheets

The *Holt Science and Technology* program helps you meet the needs of a wide variety of students, regardless of their skill level. The following pages provide examples of the worksheets available to improve your students' science and math skills, whether they already have a strong science and math background or are weak in these areas. Samples of assessment checklists and rubrics are also provided.

In addition to the skills worksheets represented here, *Holt Science and Technology* provides a variety of worksheets that are correlated directly with each chapter of the program. Representations of these worksheets are found at the beginning of each chapter in this Annotated Teacher's Edition. Specific worksheets related to each chapter are listed in the Chapter Organizer. Worksheets and transparencies are found in the softcover *Teaching Resources* for each course.

Many worksheets are also available on the HRW Web site. The address is **go.hrw.com.**

Science Skills Worksheets: Thinking Skills

BEING FLEXIBLE

USING YOUR SENSES

THINKING OBJECTIVELY
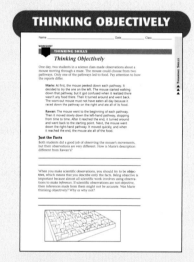

UNDERSTANDING BIAS
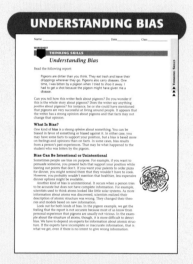

USING LOGIC

BOOSTING YOUR MEMORY

IMPROVING YOUR STUDY HABITS

READING A SCIENCE TEXTBOOK
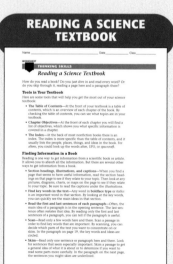

Science Skills Worksheets: **Experimenting Skills**

SAFETY RULES!

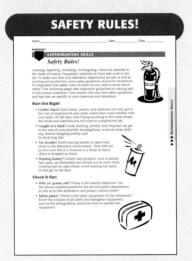

DOING A LAB WRITE-UP

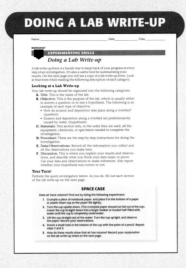

UNDERSTANDING VARIABLES

WORKING WITH HYPOTHESES

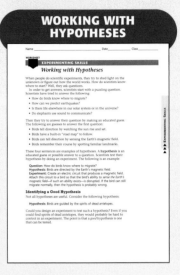

DESIGNING AN EXPERIMENT

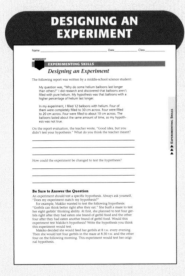

USING THE INTERNATIONAL SYSTEM OF UNITS (SI)

MEASURING

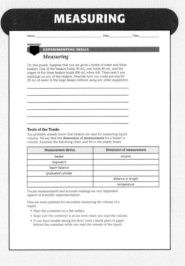

Science Skills Worksheets: **Researching Skills**

CHOOSING YOUR TOPIC

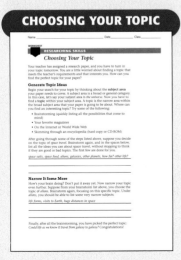

ORGANIZING YOUR RESEARCH

FINDING USEFUL SOURCES

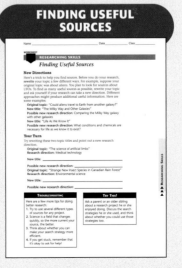

RESEARCHING ON THE WEB

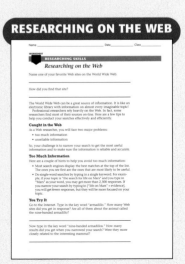

Science Skills Worksheets: Researching Skills (continued)

IDENTIFYING BIAS

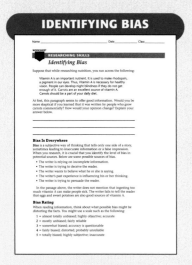

Name_____ Date_____ Class_____

WORKSHEET
RESEARCHING SKILLS
Identifying Bias

Suppose that while researching nutrition, you run across the following:

Vitamin A is an important nutrient. It is used to make rhodopsin, a pigment in our eyes. Thus, Vitamin A is necessary for healthy vision. People can develop night blindness if they do not get enough of it. Carrots are an excellent source of vitamin A. Carrots should be a part of your daily diet.

At first, this paragraph seems to offer good information. Would you be more skeptical if you learned that it was written by people who grow carrots commercially? How would your opinion change? Explain your answer below.

Bias Is Everywhere
Bias is a subjective way of thinking that tells only one side of a story, sometimes leading to inaccurate information or a false impression. When you research, it is crucial that you identify the level of bias in potential sources. Below are some possible sources of bias.
• The writer is relying on incomplete information.
• The writer is trying to deceive the reader.
• The writer wants to believe what he or she is saying.
• The writer's past experience is influencing his or her thinking.
• The writer is trying to persuade the reader.

In the passage above, the writer does not mention that ingesting too much vitamin A can make people sick. The writer fails to tell the reader that egg and sweet potatoes are also good sources of vitamin A.

Bias Rating
When reading information, think about what possible bias might be distorting the facts. You might use a scale such as the following:
1 = almost totally unbiased; highly objective; accurate
2 = mostly unbiased; fairly reliable
3 = somewhat biased; accuracy is questionable
4 = fairly biased; distorted; probably unreliable
5 = totally biased; highly subjective; inaccurate

TAKING NOTES

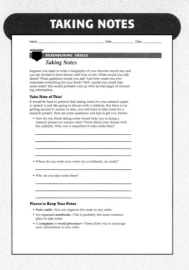

Name_____ Date_____ Class_____

WORKSHEET
RESEARCHING SKILLS
Taking Notes

Suppose you want to write a biography of your favorite movie star and you are invited to have dinner with him or her. What would you talk about? What questions would you ask? And how could you ever remember everything for your book? Well, maybe you could take some notes! You would probably end up with several pages of interesting information.

Take Note of This!
It would be hard to pretend that taking notes for your research paper or speech is just like going to dinner with a celebrity. But there is no getting around it: sooner or later, you will have to take notes for a research project. Here are some questions and tips to get you started.
• How do you think taking notes would help you in doing a research project for science class? Think about your dinner with the celebrity. Why was it important to take notes then?

_____
_____
_____

• Where do you write your notes (in a notebook, on cards)?

_____
_____

• Why do you take notes there?

_____
_____

Places to Keep Your Notes
• **Note cards**—You can organize the cards in any order.
• An organized **notebook**—This is probably the most common place to take notes.
• A **computer** or **word processor**—These allow you to rearrange your information in any order.

SCIENCE WRITING

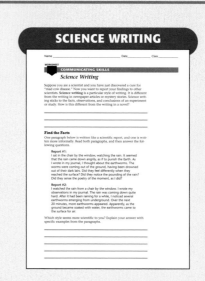

Name_____ Date_____ Class_____

WORKSHEET
COMMUNICATING SKILLS
Science Writing

Suppose you are a scientist and you have just discovered a cure for "mad cow disease." Now you want to report your findings to other scientists. **Science writing** is a particular style of writing. It is different from the writing in newspaper articles and mystery stories. Science writing sticks to the facts, observations, and conclusions of an experiment or study. How is this different from the writing in a novel?

Find the Facts
One paragraph below is written like a scientific report, and one is written more informally. Read both paragraphs, and then answer the following questions.

Report #1:
I sat in the chair by the window, watching the rain. It seemed that the rain came down angrily, as if to punish the Earth. As I wrote in my journal, I thought about the earthworms. The worms were coming out of the ground, having been drowned out of their dark lairs. Did they feel differently when they reached the surface? Did they sense the poetry of the moment, as I did?

Report #2:
I watched the rain from a chair by the window. I wrote my observations in my journal. The rain was coming down quite hard. After it had been raining for a while, I noticed several earthworms emerging from underground. Over the next 20 minutes, more earthworms appeared. Apparently, as the ground became soaked with water, the earthworms came to the surface for air.

Which style seems more scientific to you? Explain your answer with specific examples from the paragraphs.

_____
_____
_____

Science Skills Worksheets: Communicating Skills

SCIENCE DRAWING

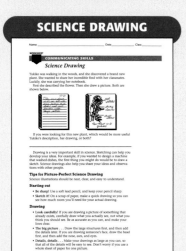

Name_____ Date_____ Class_____

WORKSHEET
COMMUNICATING SKILLS
Science Drawing

Yukiko was walking in the woods, and she discovered a brand new plant. She wanted to share her incredible find with her classmates. Luckily, she was carrying her notebook.
First she described the flower. Then she drew a picture. Both are shown below.

If you were looking for this new plant, which would be more useful, Yukiko's description, her drawing, or both?

Drawing is a very important skill in science. Sketching can help you develop your ideas. For example, if you wanted to design a machine that washed dishes, the first thing you might do would be to draw a sketch. Science drawings also help you share your ideas and observations with other people.

Tips for Picture-Perfect Science Drawing
Science illustrations should be neat, clear, and easy to understand.

Starting out
• **Be sharp!** Use a soft lead pencil, and keep your pencil sharp.
• **Sketch it!** On a scrap of paper, make a quick drawing so you can see how much room you'll need for your actual drawing.

Drawing
• **Look carefully!** If you are drawing a picture of something that already exists, carefully draw what you actually see, not what you think you should see. Be as accurate as you can, and make your lines clear.
• **The big picture** . . . Draw the large structures first, and then add the details later. If you are drawing someone's face, draw the head first, and then add the nose, ears, and eyes.
• **Details, details** . . . Make your drawings as large as you can, so that all of the details will be easy to see. Don't worry if you use a whole sheet of paper for one picture.

USING MODELS TO COMMUNICATE

Name_____ Date_____ Class_____

WORKSHEET
COMMUNICATING SKILLS
Using Models to Communicate

A **model** is a picture or representation of a real object or idea that is supported by observations and inferences. Models are often used to explain a scientific event or principle, as in the following example:

To show how Earth revolves around the sun, hold a volleyball 1m away from a table lamp with its light bulb exposed. Turn the volleyball on its axis, and move in a large circle around the light bulb.

1. How does this model demonstrate Earth's motion around the sun?

_____
_____

2. Based on this example, define model in your own words.

_____
_____

3. All models are accurate in some ways and inaccurate in others.
   a. In what ways is the model above accurate?

_____
_____

   b. In what ways is the model above inaccurate?

_____
_____

4. Briefly describe another model that you have seen or used in science class.

_____
_____

INTRODUCTION TO GRAPHS

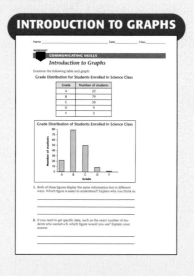

Name_____ Date_____ Class_____

WORKSHEET
COMMUNICATING SKILLS
Introduction to Graphs

Examine the following table and graph:

Grade Distribution for Students Enrolled in Science Class

Grade	Number of students
A	22
B	79
C	50
D	9
F	2

Grade Distribution of Students Enrolled in Science Class

1. Both of these figures display the same information but in different ways. Which figure is easier to understand? Explain why you think so.

_____
_____

2. If you need to get specific data, such as the exact number of students who earned a B, which figure would you use? Explain your answer.

_____
_____

GRASPING GRAPHING

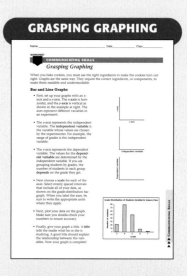

Name_____ Date_____ Class_____

WORKSHEET
COMMUNICATING SKILLS
Grasping Graphing

When you bake cookies, you must use the right ingredients to make the cookies turn out right. Graphs are the same way. They require the correct ingredients, or components, to make them readable and understandable.

Bar and Line Graphs
• First, set up your graphs with an x-axis and a y-axis. The **x-axis** is horizontal, and the **y-axis** is vertical as shown in the example at right. The axes represent different variables in an experiment.
• The x-axis represents the independent variable. The **independent variable** is the variable whose values are chosen by the experimenter. For example, the range of grades is the independent variable.
• The y-axis represents the dependent variable. The values for the **dependent variable** are determined by the independent variable. If you are grouping students by grades, the number of students in each group **depends** on the grade they get.
• Next choose a scale for each of the axes. Select evenly spaced intervals that include all of your data, as shown on the grade-distribution bar graph. When you label the axes, be sure to write the appropriate units where they apply.
• Next, plot your data on the graph. Always double-check your numbers to ensure accuracy.
• Finally, give your graph a title. A title tells the reader what he or she is studying. A good title should explain the relationship between the variables. Now your graph is complete!

INTERPRETING YOUR DATA

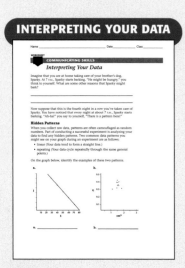

Name_____ Date_____ Class_____

WORKSHEET
COMMUNICATING SKILLS
Interpreting Your Data

Imagine that you are at home taking care of your brother's dog, Sparky. At 7 P.M., Sparky starts barking. "He might be hungry," you think to yourself. What are some other reasons that Sparky might bark?

Now suppose that this is the fourth night in a row you've taken care of Sparky. You've noticed that every night at about 7 P.M., Sparky starts barking. "Ah-ha!" you say to yourself, "There is a pattern here!"

Hidden Patterns
When you collect raw data, patterns are often camouflaged as random numbers. Part of conducting a successful experiment is analyzing your data to find any hidden patterns. Two common data patterns you might see on your graph during an experiment are as follows:
• linear (Your data tend to form a straight line.)
• repeating (Your data cycle repeatedly through the same general points.)

On the graph below, identify the examples of these two patterns.

RECOGNIZING BIAS IN GRAPHS

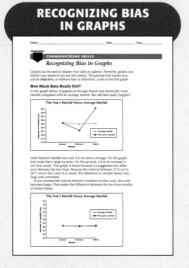

Name_____ Date_____ Class_____

WORKSHEET
COMMUNICATING SKILLS
Recognizing Bias in Graphs

Graphs can be used to display your data at a glance. However, graphs can distort your results if you are not careful. The picture that results may not be **objective**, or without bias or distortion. Look at the first graph.

How Much Rain Really Fell?
In the graph below, it appears as though March had drastically more rainfall compared with an average month. But did that really happen?

This Year's Rainfall Versus Average Rainfall

Wait! March's rainfall was only 0.4 cm above average. On the graph, that looks like a large increase. On the ground, a 0.4 cm increase is not that much. This graph is *biased* because it exaggerates the difference between the two lines. Because the interval between 27.8 cm to 28.7 cm on the y-axis is so small, the difference in rainfall seems very large and misleading.

If you increase the interval between numbers on the y-axis, the scale becomes larger. That makes the difference between the two lines smaller, as shown below.

This Year's Rainfall Versus Average Rainfall

MAKING DATA MEANINGFUL

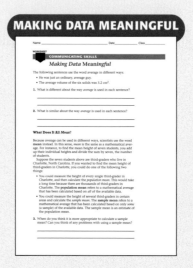

Name_____ Date_____ Class_____

WORKSHEET
COMMUNICATING SKILLS
Making Data Meaningful

The following sentences use the word average in different ways:
• He was just an ordinary, average guy.
• The average volume of the six solids was 3.2 cm³.

1. What is different about the way *average* is used in each sentence?

_____
_____

2. What is similar about the way *average* is used in each sentence?

_____
_____

What Does It All Mean?
Because average can be used in different ways, scientists use the word **mean** instead. In this sense, *mean* is the same as a mathematical average. For instance, to find the mean height of seven students, you add up their individual heights and divide the sum by seven, the number of students.
Suppose the seven students are third-graders who live in Charlotte, North Carolina. If you wanted to find the mean height of third-graders in Charlotte, you could do one of the following two things:
• You could measure the height of every single third-grader in Charlotte, and then calculate the *population mean*. This would take a long time because there are thousands of third-graders in Charlotte. The **population mean** refers to a mathematical average that has been calculated based on *all* of the available data.
• You could measure the height of several third-graders in certain areas and calculate the *sample mean*. The **sample mean** refers to a mathematical average that has been calculated based on only *some* (a sample) of the available data. The sample mean is an estimate of the population mean.

3. When do you think it is more appropriate to calculate a sample mean? Can you think of any problems with using a sample mean?

_____
_____

HINTS FOR ORAL PRESENTATIONS

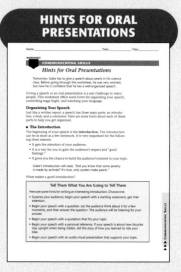

Name_____ Date_____ Class_____

WORKSHEET
COMMUNICATING SKILLS
Hints for Oral Presentations

Tomorrow, Gabe has to give a speech about pearls in his science class. Before going through this worksheet, he was very worried, but now he is confident that he has a well-organized speech.

Giving a speech or an oral presentation is a real challenge to many people. This worksheet offers some hints for organizing your speech, controlling stage fright, and watching your language.

Organizing Your Speech
Just like a written report, a speech has three main parts: an introduction, a body, and a conclusion. Here are some hints about each of these parts to help you get organized.

■ **The Introduction**
The beginning of your speech is the **introduction**. The introduction can be as short as a few sentences. It is very important for the following three reasons:
• It gets the attention of your audience.
• It is a way for you to gain the audience's respect and "good feelings."
• It gives you the chance to build the audience's interest in your topic.

Gabe's introduction will read, "Did you know that some jewelry starts uptight when first worn? It's true, only oysters make pearls."

What makes a good introduction?

_____

Tell Them What You Are Going to Tell Them
Here are some hints for writing an interesting introduction. Choose one.
• Surprise your audience; begin your speech with a startling statement, get their attention.
• Begin your speech with a question. Let the audience think about it for a few moments, and then answer the question. The audience will be listening for your answer.
• Begin your speech with a quotation that fits your topic.
• Begin your speech with a personal reference. If your speech is about how bicycles stay upright when being ridden, tell the story of how you learned to ride your bike.
• Begin your speech with an audio-visual presentation that supports your topic.

Math Skills for Science

ADDITION AND SUBTRACTION

MULTIPLICATION

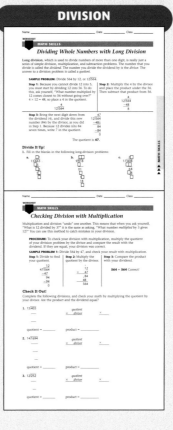

DIVISION

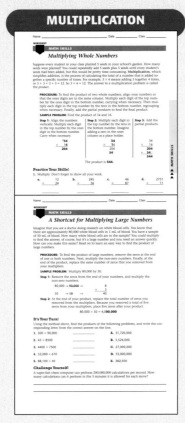

AVERAGES

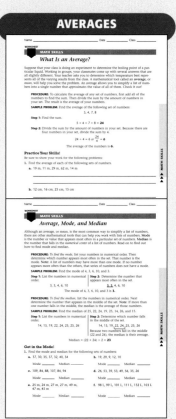

POSITIVE AND NEGATIVE NUMBERS

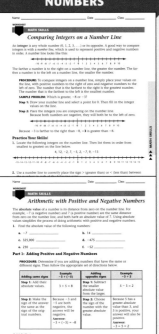

FRACTIONS

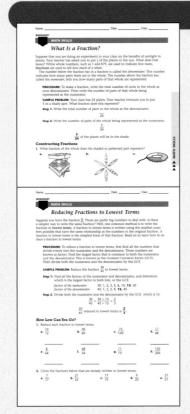

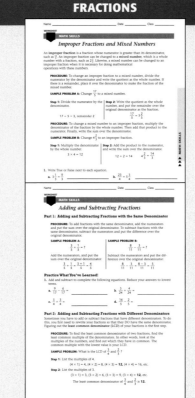

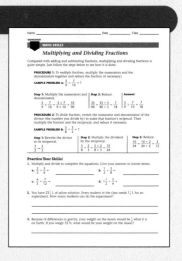

Math Skills for Science (continued)

RATIOS AND PROPORTIONS

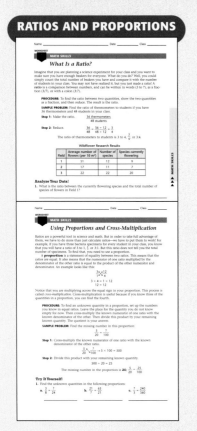

DECIMALS

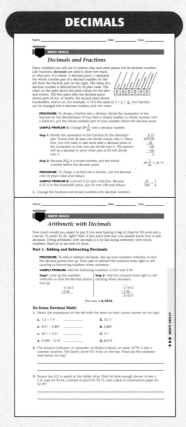

PERCENTAGES

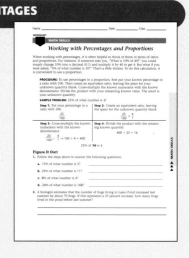
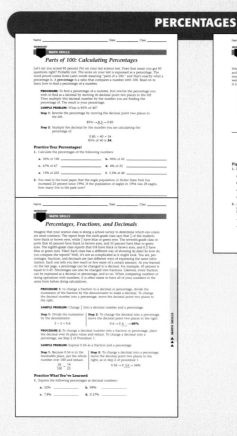

POWERS OF 10

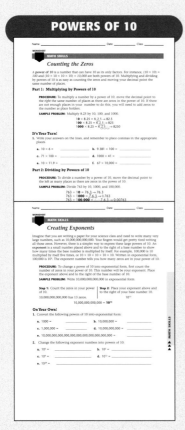

SCIENTIFIC NOTATION

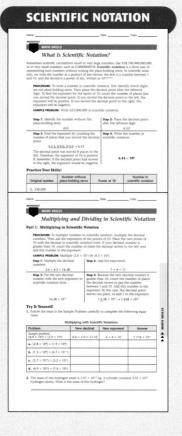

SI MEASUREMENT AND CONVERSION

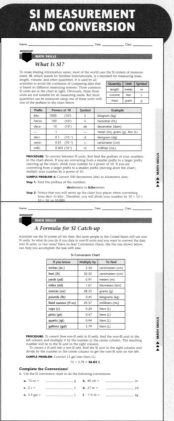

Math Skills for Science (continued)

GEOMETRY

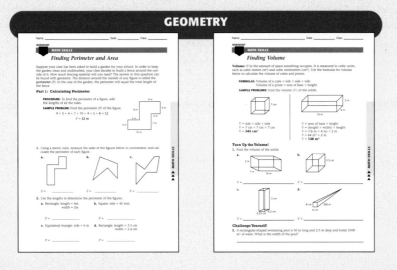

Finding Perimeter and Area

Finding Volume

THE UNIT FACTOR AND DIMENSIONAL ANALYSIS

The Unit Factor and Dimensional Analysis

MATH IN SCIENCE: INTEGRATED SCIENCE

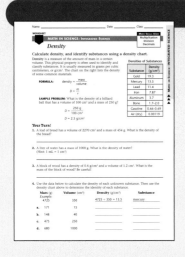

Density

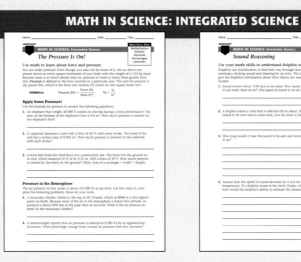

The Pressure Is On!

Sound Reasoning

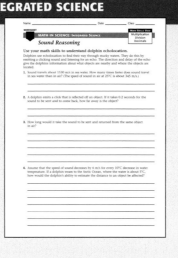

Using Temperature Scales

Radioactive Decay and the Half-life

Rain-Forest Math

Math Skills for Science (continued)

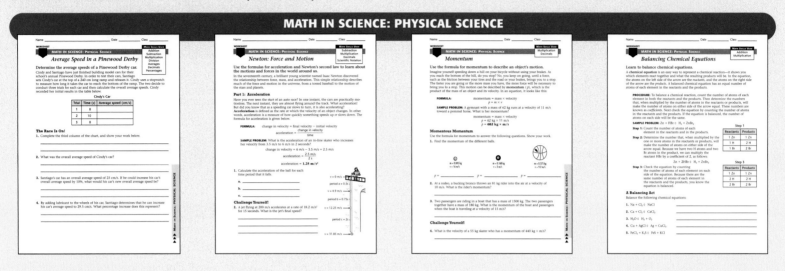

MATH IN SCIENCE: PHYSICAL SCIENCE

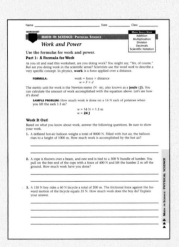
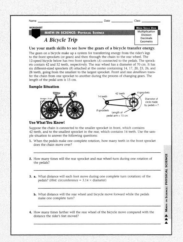
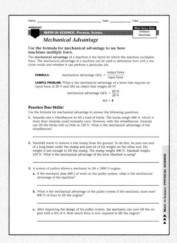
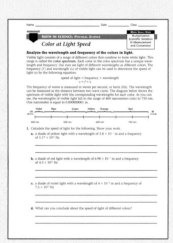

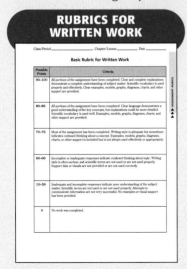
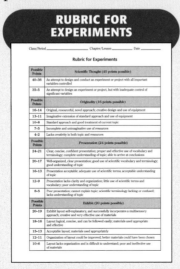

Assessment Checklist & Rubrics

The following is just a sample of over 50 checklists and rubrics contained in this booklet.

RUBRICS FOR WRITTEN WORK

RUBRIC FOR EXPERIMENTS

TEACHER EVALUATION OF COOPERATIVE LEARNING

TEACHER EVALUATION OF STUDENT PROGRESS

PHYSICAL SCIENCE NATIONAL SCIENCE EDUCATION STANDARDS CORRELATIONS

The following lists show the chapter correlation of **Holt Science and Technology: Sound and Light** with the *National Science Education Standards* (grades 5-8)

UNIFYING CONCEPTS AND PROCESSES

Standard	Chapter Correlation	
Systems, order, and organization Code: UCP 1	Chapter 1	1.1
	Chapter 2	2.1, 2.2, 2.3, 2.4
	Chapter 3	3.1
	Chapter 4	4.1
Evidence, models, and explanation Code: UCP 2	Chapter 1	1.1
	Chapter 2	2.1, 2.2, 2.3, 2.4
	Chapter 3	3.1, 3.2, 3.3, 3.4
	Chapter 4	4.1, 4.2, 4.3
Change, constancy, and measurement Code: UCP 3	Chapter 1	1.2, 1.3
	Chapter 2	2.2, 2.3
	Chapter 3	3.4
	Chapter 4	4.2
Form and function Code: UCP 5	Chapter 1	1.2
	Chapter 2	2.4
	Chapter 4	4.4

SCIENCE IN PERSONAL AND SOCIAL PERSPECTIVES

Standard	Chapter Correlation	
Personal health Code: SPSP 1	Chapter 2	2.1, 2.4
	Chapter 3	3.2
	Chapter 4	4.3
Populations, resources, and environments Code: SPSP 2	Chapter 2	2.4
	Chapter 4	4.4
Natural hazards Code: SPSP 3	Chapter 2	2.4
	Chapter 3	3.2
Risks and benefits Code: SPSP 4	Chapter 3	3.2
Science and technology in society Code: SPSP 5	Chapter 2	2.1, 2.2, 2.3
	Chapter 3	3.1, 3.2
	Chapter 4	4.1, 4.2, 4.4

SCIENCE AS INQUIRY

Standard	Chapter Correlation	
Abilities necessary to do scientific inquiry Code: SAI 1	Chapter 1	1.1, 1.2
	Chapter 2	2.1, 2.2, 2.3
	Chapter 3	3.2, 3.4
Understandings about scientific inquiry Code: SAI 2	Chapter 1	1.2
	Chapter 2	2.2, 2.3
	Chapter 3	3.2, 3.4

SCIENCE AND TECHNOLOGY

Standard	Chapter Correlation	
Understandings about science and technology Code: ST 2	Chapter 1	1.2, 1.3
	Chapter 2	2.1, 2.2, 2.3
	Chapter 4	4.4

HISTORY AND NATURE OF SCIENCE

Standard	Chapter Correlation	
Science as a human endeavor Code: HNS 1	Chapter 2	2.1, 2.2
	Chapter 3	3.2
	Chapter 4	4.1
Nature of science Code: HNS 2	Chapter 1	1.2
History of science Code: HNS 3	Chapter 2	2.2
	Chapter 4	4.1

PHYSICAL SCIENCE NATIONAL SCIENCE EDUCATION CONTENT STANDARDS

TRANSFER OF ENERGY	
Standard	**Chapter Correlation**
Energy is a property of many substances and is associated with heat, light, electricity, mechanical motion, sound, nuclei, and the nature of a chemical. Energy is transferred in many ways. Code: PS 3a	**Chapter 1** 1.1, 1.2 **Chapter 2** 2.1, 2.2, 2.3 **Chapter 3** 3.1, 3.2, 3.4 **Chapter 4** 4.1
Heat moves in predictable ways, flowing from warmer objects to cooler ones, until both reach the same temperature. Code: PS 3b	**Chapter 3** 3.4
Light interacts with matter by transmission (including refraction), absorption, or scattering (including reflection). To see an object, light from that object—emitted or scattered from it—must enter the eye. Code: PS 3c	**Chapter 1** 1.3 **Chapter 3** 3.3, 3.4 **Chapter 4** 4.1, 4.2, 4.3, 4.4
In most chemical and nuclear reactions, energy is transferred into or out of a system. Heat, light, mechanical motion, or electricity might all be involved in such transfers. Code: PS 3e	**Chapter 4** 4.1
The sun is a major source of energy for changes on the earth's surface. The sun loses energy by emitting light. A tiny fraction of that light reaches the earth, transferring energy from the sun to the earth. The sun's energy arrives as light with a range of wavelengths, consisting of visible light, infrared, and ultraviolet radiation. Code: PS 3f	**Chapter 1** 1.1 **Chapter 3** 3.2 **Chapter 4** 4.1

Master Materials List

For added convenience, Science Kit® provides materials-ordering software on CD-ROM designed specifically for *Holt Science and Technology*. Using this software, you can order complete kits or individual items, quickly and efficiently.

CONSUMABLE MATERIALS	AMOUNT	PAGE
Bean seedlings	5	132
Candle	1	114, 134
Cardboard tube	1	61
Clay, modeling	1 stick	93, 114, 134
Colored paper, black, blue, red, and white, 2 x 2 cm	1 each	133
Cup, plastic-foam	1	20
Index card, 3 x 5 in.	1	114, 134
Marker, permanent, black	1	132
Matches	1 box	114, 134
Milk	1 mL	75
Newspaper	2–3 pgs.	20
Paper, construction, black, approx. 8 x 9 cm	1	61
Paper, graphing	1 sheet	93, 128, 131, 133
Paper towel	3	132
Rubber band	1–2	29, 52
Shoe box	1	29
String, approx. 50 cm	1	52
Tape, masking, 20–30 cm	1	61, 84, 132
Tape, transparent, 20–30 cm	1	133
Watercolor paint	1 set	84

NONCONSUMABLE EQUIPMENT	AMOUNT	PAGE
Bottle, 2 L soda	1	75
Colored glass, approx. 20 x 20 cm	1	93
Colored plastic filter, blue, green, red, and yellow	1 each	82, 84
Cup, clear plastic	1–2	30, 52, 84, 133
Diffraction grating	1	61
Eraser, pink rubber	1	30, 52, 128, 131
Flashlight	1	75
Flashlight	3	84
Fluorescent light	1	61
Graduated cylinder, 100 mL	1	131
Lens, convex	1	134
Lid, jar	1	114, 134
Light bulb, incandescent	1	61
Light source	1	133
Lights, colored	1 each	132
Meterstick	1	84, 126, 128, 134
Mirror, concave and convex	1 each	114
Mirror, plane	1	93
Paintbrush	1	84
Pan, shallow, 20 x 30 cm	1	20
Pencil, colored	1 box	133
Petri dish with cover	3	132
Plastic tube, approx. 40 cm	1	131
Polarizing lens	2	113
Rope	1	3
Ruler, metric	1	39, 84, 93, 131
Spectroscope	1	61
Spring toy, coiled	1	12, 126
Stopwatch	1	20, 126
Thermometer	1	133
Tuning fork	1	30, 52
Tuning fork, different frequencies	4	128, 131
Tuning fork, same frequency	2	52

Answers to Concept Mapping Questions

The following pages contain sample answers to all of the concept mapping questions that appear in the Chapter Reviews. Because there is more than one way to do a concept map, your students' answers may vary.

CHAPTER 1 The Energy of Waves

18.

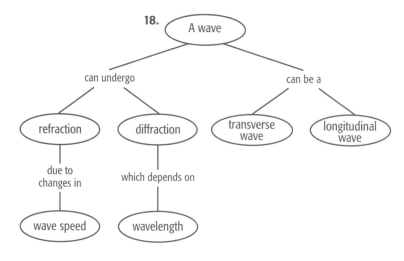

CHAPTER 2 The Nature of Sound

17.

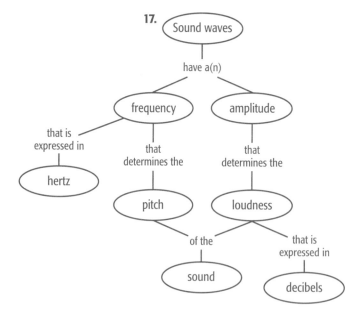

Concept Mapping Answers

CHAPTER 3 The Nature of Light

18.

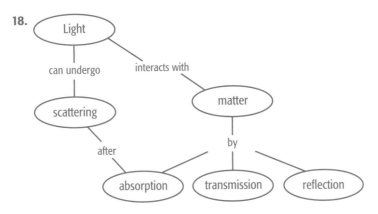

CHAPTER 4 Light and Our World

17.

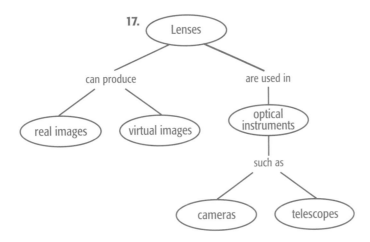

To the Student

This book was created to make your science experience interesting, exciting, and fun!

Go for It!

Science is a process of discovery, a trek into the unknown. The skills you develop using *Holt Science & Technology*— such as observing, experimenting, and explaining observations and ideas— are the skills you will need for the future. There is a universe of exploration and discovery awaiting those who accept the challenges of science.

Science & Technology

You see the interaction between science and technology every day. Science makes technology possible. On the other hand, some of the products of technology, such as computers, are used to make further scientific discoveries. In fact, much of the scientific work that is done today has become so technically complicated and expensive that no one person can do it entirely alone. But make no mistake, the creative ideas for even the most highly technical and expensive scientific work still come from individuals.

Activities and Labs

The activities and labs in this book will allow you to make some basic but important scientific discoveries on your own. You can even do some exploring on your own at home! Here's your chance to use your imagination and curiosity as you investigate your world.

Keep a ScienceLog

In this book, you will be asked to keep a type of journal called a ScienceLog to record your thoughts, observations, experiments, and conclusions. As you develop your ScienceLog, you will see your own ideas taking shape over time. You'll have a written record of how your ideas have changed as you learn about and explore interesting topics in science.

Know "What You'll Do"

The "What You'll Do" list at the beginning of each section is your built-in guide to what you need to learn in each chapter. When you can answer the questions in the Section Review and Chapter Review, you know you are ready for a test.

Check Out the Internet

You will see this  logo throughout the book. You'll be using *sci*LINKS as your gateway to the Internet. Once you log on to *sci*LINKS using your computer's Internet link, type in the *sci*LINKS address. When asked for the keyword code, type in the keyword for that topic. A wealth of resources is now at your disposal to help you learn more about that topic.

In addition to *sci*LINKS you can log on to some other great resources to go with your text. The addresses shown below will take you to the home page of each site.

This textbook contains the following on-line resources to help you make the most of your science experience.

Visit **go.hrw.com** for extra help and study aids matched to your textbook. Just type in the keyword HB2 HOME.

Visit **www.scilinks.org** to find resources specific to topics in your textbook. Keywords appear throughout your book to take you further.

 Smithsonian Institution® Internet Connections

Visit **www.si.edu/hrw** for specifically chosen on-line materials from one of our nation's premier science museums.

Visit **www.cnnfyi.com** for late-breaking news and current events stories selected just for you.

To the Student 1

Chapter Organizer

CHAPTER ORGANIZATION	TIME MINUTES	OBJECTIVES	LABS, INVESTIGATIONS, AND DEMONSTRATIONS
Chapter Opener pp. 2–3	45	National Standards: SAI 1, SPSP 3, PS 3a	**Start-Up Activity,** Energetic Waves, p. 3
Section 1 The Nature of Waves	90	▶ Describe how waves transfer energy without transferring matter. ▶ Distinguish between waves that require a medium and waves that do not. ▶ Explain the difference between transverse and longitudinal waves. UCP 1, 2, SAI 1, PS 3a, 3f	**Demonstration,** p. 4 in ATE **Demonstration,** p. 8 in ATE
Section 2 Properties of Waves	90	▶ Identify and describe four wave properties. ▶ Explain how amplitude and frequency are related to the energy of a wave. UCP 3, 5, SAI 1, ST 2, HNS 2, PS 3a; Labs UCP 5, SAI 1, 2, PS 3a	**Demonstration,** p. 10 in ATE **QuickLab,** Springy Waves, p. 12 **Discovery Lab,** Wave Energy and Speed, p. 20 **Datasheets for LabBook,** Wave Energy and Speed **Skill Builder,** Wave Speed, Frequency, and Wavelength, p. 126 **Datasheets for LabBook,** Wave Speed, Frequency, and Wavelength
Section 3 Wave Interactions	90	▶ Describe reflection, refraction, diffraction, and interference. ▶ Compare destructive interference with constructive interference. ▶ Describe resonance, and give examples. UCP 3, ST 2, PS 3c	**Demonstration,** p. 15 in ATE **Whiz-Bang Demonstrations,** Pitch Forks **Calculator-Based Labs,** In the Dog House **Long-Term Projects & Research Ideas,** It's a Whale of a Wave

See page **T23** for a complete correlation of this book with the

NATIONAL SCIENCE EDUCATION STANDARDS.

TECHNOLOGY RESOURCES

 Guided Reading Audio CD
English or Spanish, Chapter 1

 One-Stop Planner CD-ROM with Test Generator

 CNN **Science, Technology & Society,** Harnessing Sound Energy, Segment 24

CLASSROOM WORKSHEETS, TRANSPARENCIES, AND RESOURCES	SCIENCE INTEGRATION AND CONNECTIONS	REVIEW AND ASSESSMENT
Directed Reading Worksheet **Science Puzzlers, Twisters & Teasers**		
Directed Reading Worksheet, Section 1 **Transparency 131,** Primary and Secondary Waves **Transparency 280,** Transverse Waves **Transparency 280,** Longitudinal Waves	**Astronomy Connection,** p. 6 **Real-World Connection,** p. 6 in ATE **MathBreak,** Perpendicular Lines, p. 7 **Multicultural Connection,** p. 7 in ATE **Connect to Earth Science,** p. 7 in ATE **Connect to Life Science,** p. 8 in ATE **Real-World Connection,** p. 9 in ATE	**Self-Check,** p. 6 **Homework,** p. 8 in ATE **Section Review,** p. 9 **Quiz,** p. 9 in ATE **Alternative Assessment,** p. 9 in ATE
Directed Reading Worksheet, Section 2 **Transparency 281,** Wavelength **Transparency 281,** Frequency **Transparency 282,** Wave Speed, Wavelength, and Frequency **Reinforcement Worksheet,** Getting on the Same Frequency **Math Skills for Science Worksheet,** Dividing Whole Numbers with Long Division	**MathBreak,** Wave Calculations, p. 13 **Across the Sciences:** Sounds of Silence, p. 27	**Section Review,** p. 13 **Quiz,** p. 13 in ATE **Alternative Assessment,** p. 13 in ATE
Directed Reading Worksheet, Section 3 **Transparency 283,** Constructive and Destructive Interference **Reinforcement Worksheet,** Makin' Waves **Critical Thinking Worksheet,** The Case of the Speeding Ticket	**Real-World Connection,** p. 16 in ATE **Apply,** p. 17 **Multicultural Connection,** p. 18 in ATE **Science, Technology, and Society:** The Ultimate Telescope, p. 26	**Self-Check,** p. 15 **Homework,** p. 18 in ATE **Section Review,** p. 19 **Quiz,** p. 19 in ATE **Alternative Assessment,** p. 19 in ATE

  internet connect

Holt, Rinehart and Winston
On-line Resources

go.hrw.com

For worksheets and other teaching aids related to this chapter, visit the HRW Web site and type in the keyword: **HSTWAV**

National Science Teachers Association

www.scilinks.org

Encourage students to use the *sci*LINKS numbers listed in the internet connect boxes to access information and resources on the **NSTA** Web site.

END-OF-CHAPTER REVIEW AND ASSESSMENT

Chapter Review in Study Guide

Vocabulary and Notes in Study Guide

Chapter Tests with Performance-Based Assessment, Chapter 1 Test

Chapter Tests with Performance-Based Assessment, Performance-Based Assessment 1

Concept Mapping Transparency 20

Chapter Resources & Worksheets

Visual Resources

TEACHING TRANSPARENCIES

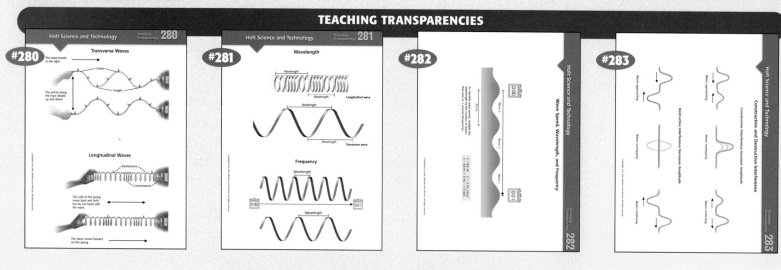

#280 — Holt Science and Technology — Teaching Transparency 280
Transverse Waves / Longitudinal Waves

#281 — Holt Science and Technology — Teaching Transparency 281
Wavelength / Frequency

#282 — Holt Science and Technology — Teaching Transparency 282
Wave Speed, Wavelength, and Frequency

#283 — Holt Science and Technology — Teaching Transparency 283
Constructive and Destructive Interference

TEACHING TRANSPARENCIES

#131 — Holt Science and Technology — Teaching Transparency 131
Primary Wave / Secondary Wave / Surface Wave

LINK TO EARTH SCIENCE

CONCEPT MAPPING TRANSPARENCY

#20 — Holt Science and Technology — Concept Mapping Transparency 20
The Energy of Waves
Use the following terms to complete the concept map below: transverse, frequency, waves, longitudinal, wave speed, amplitude, energy, medium

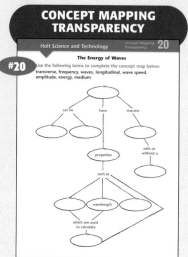

Meeting Individual Needs

DIRECTED READING

#1 — DIRECTED READING WORKSHEET
The Energy of Waves

Chapter Introduction
As you begin this chapter, answer the following.
1. Read the title of the chapter. List three things that you already know about this subject.

2. Write two questions about this subject that you would like answered by the time you finish this chapter.

Section 1: The Nature of Waves (p. 4)
3. Which of the following waves might your family have experienced after a day at the beach? (Circle all that apply.)
a. water waves
b. microwaves
c. light waves
d. sound waves

Waves Carry Energy (p. 4)
4. A wave can carry energy away from its source. True or False? (Circle one.)

REINFORCEMENT & VOCABULARY REVIEW

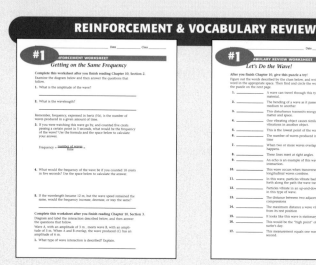

#1 — REINFORCEMENT WORKSHEET
Getting on the Same Frequency

Complete this worksheet after you finish reading Chapter 10, Section 2. Examine the diagram below and then answer the questions that follow.

1. What is the amplitude of the wave?

2. What is the wavelength?

Remember, frequency, expressed in hertz (Hz), is the number of waves produced in a given amount of time.

3. If you were watching this wave go by, and counted five crests passing a certain point in 5 seconds, what would be the frequency of the wave? Use the formula and the space below to calculate your answer.

$$\text{Frequency} = \frac{\text{number of waves}}{\text{time}}$$

4. What would the frequency of the wave be if you counted 10 crests in five seconds? Use the space below to calculate the answer.

5. If the wavelength became 12 m, but the wave speed remained the same, would the frequency increase, decrease, or stay the same?

Complete this worksheet after you finish reading Chapter 10, Section 3. Diagram and label the interaction described below, and then answer the questions that follow.
Wave A, with an amplitude of 3 m , meets wave B, with an amplitude of 3 m. When A and B overlap, the wave produced (C) has an amplitude of 6 m.
1. What type of wave interaction is described? Explain.

#1 — VOCABULARY REVIEW WORKSHEET
Let's Do the Wave!

After you finish Chapter 10, give this puzzle a try! Figure out the words described by the clues below, and write the word in the appropriate space. Then find and circle the words in the puzzle on the next page.

1. _____ A wave can travel through this type of material.
2. _____ The bending of a wave as it passes from one medium to another
3. _____ This disturbance transmits energy through matter and space.
4. _____ One vibrating object causes similar vibrations in another object.
5. _____ This is the lowest point of the wave.
6. _____ The number of waves produced in a given time
7. _____ When two or more waves overlap, this happens.
8. _____ These lines meet at right angles.
9. _____ An echo is an example of this wave interaction.
10. _____ This wave occurs when transverse and longitudinal waves combine.
11. _____ In this wave, particles vibrate back and forth along the path the wave travels.
12. _____ Particles vibrate in an up-and-down motion in this type of wave.
13. _____ The distance between two adjacent compressions
14. _____ The maximum distance a wave vibrates from its rest position
15. _____ It looks like this wave is stationary.
16. _____ This would be the "high point" of a surfer's day.
17. _____ This measurement equals one wave per second.

SCIENCE PUZZLERS, TWISTERS & TEASERS

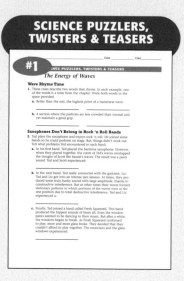

#1 — SCIENCE PUZZLERS, TWISTERS & TEASERS
The Energy of Waves

Wave Rhyme Time
1. These clues describe two words that rhyme. In each example, one of the words is a term from the chapter. Write both words in the space provided.
a. Better than the rest, the highest point of a transverse wave.

b. A section where the particles are less crowded than normal and yet maintain a good grip.

Saxophones Don't Belong in Rock 'n Roll Bands
2. Ted plays the saxophone and enjoys rock 'n roll. He joined some bands so he could perform on stage. But, things didn't work out. Tell what problems Ted encountered in each band.
a. In his first band, Ted played the baritone saxophone. However, when they played together, the crests of Ted's waves overlapped the trough of Scott the bassist's waves. The result was a puny sound. Ted and Scott experienced:

b. In the next band, Ted really connected with the guitarist, Liz. Ted and Liz got into an intense jam session. At times, they produced some truly funky sound with large amplitude, thanks to constructive interference. But at other times their waves formed stationary patterns in which portions of the waves were at the rest position due to total destructive interference. Ted and Liz experienced a:

c. Finally, Ted joined a band called Fresh Squeezed. This band produced the hippest sounds of them all. Even the window panes seemed to be dancing to their music. But after a while, the windows began to break. As Fresh Squeezed continued to play, more and more glass broke. They decided that they couldn't afford to play together. The musicians and the glass windows experienced:

Chapter 1 • The Energy of Waves

Review & Assessment

STUDY GUIDE

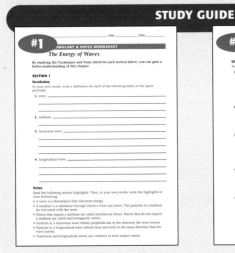

CHAPTER TESTS WITH PERFORMANCE-BASED ASSESSMENT

Lab Worksheets

WHIZ-BANG DEMONSTRATIONS

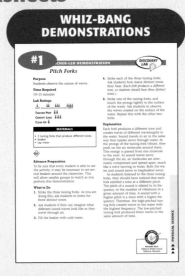

LONG-TERM PROJECTS & RESEARCH IDEAS

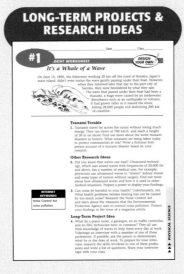

DATASHEETS FOR LABBOOK

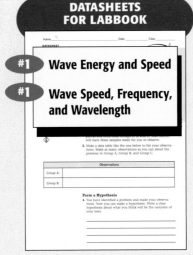

#1 Wave Energy and Speed

#1 Wave Speed, Frequency, and Wavelength

Applications & Extensions

CRITICAL THINKING & PROBLEM SOLVING

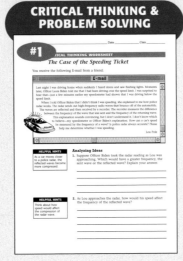

SCIENCE TECHNOLOGY

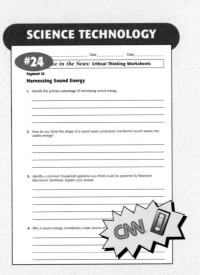

Chapter Background

SECTION 1

The Nature of Waves

▶ Tsunamis

What many people call tidal waves are not caused by the tides. They are usually caused by undersea earthquakes, volcanic eruptions, landslides, or violent windstorms that occur over the open sea. A large wave produced by any of these phenomena is called a *tsunami*.

- Tsunamis often begin as a series of small waves no larger than 1 m high but traveling at great speed (188 m/s) over deep water. In deep water, a tsunami may not even be seen. However, when the depth of the water becomes less than the height of the wave, the wave builds into a wall of water that can reach a height of 30 m.

▶ Mechanical Waves

Some scientists call waves "a wiggle in time and space." Mechanical waves are periodic disturbances that pass through matter. As a wave passes through matter, the material's particles vibrate about their rest positions and only the energy moves through. Some of the wave's energy is used to do work on the particles. Mechanical waves eventually die out as their energy is dissipated.

▶ Electromagnetic Waves

An electromagnetic wave is a transverse wave comprising vibrating electric and magnetic fields at right angles to each other. Electromagnetic waves, like mechanical waves, are described in terms of wavelength and frequency. Types of electromagnetic waves

(from longest wavelength to shortest) include radio waves, microwaves, infrared waves, visible light, ultraviolet light, X rays, and gamma rays.

SECTION 2

Properties of Waves

▶ Waves

A wave is produced by a vibrating object. For example, music is produced by vibrating strings or by vibrating columns of air.

- The frequency of the wave is equal to the frequency of the vibrating object. The square of the amplitude of the wave is proportional to the energy used to produce the wave.

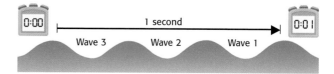

- The speed of a wave depends on the medium through which it travels. For mechanical waves, the density, elasticity, and temperature of the medium affect the speed. A mechanical wave's speed increases with elasticity and decreases with density. For example, the speed of sound at 0°C is 331.5 m/s in air and 5,200 m/s in steel.

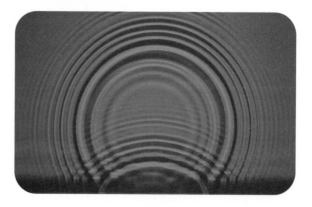

IS THAT A FACT!

➤ Heinrich Hertz (1857–1894) was a German physicist. The unit for describing frequency is named in his honor. Hertz's goal was to prove Maxwell's theory of electromagnetic radiation. While Hertz was performing his experiments, he discovered radio waves. This discovery led to the development of radio, radar, and television.

▶ Longitudinal Waves and Wavelength

Longitudinal waves do not have high and low points, but they do have regions of high pressure (compressions) and regions of low pressure (expansions). Sound waves are an example of longitudinal waves. When you strike a tuning fork, the prongs vibrate back and forth. Like a drum, the tuning fork sends out compressions when the prongs vibrate out and rarefactions when the prongs vibrate back. The compressions of the sound waves correspond to crests. Rarefactions of sound waves correspond to troughs. Therefore, the wavelength of a sound wave is the distance between adjacent compressions or adjacent expansions.

IS THAT A FACT!

➤ If you are listening to your favorite radio station, whose frequency is 96.1 MHz (96,100,000 Hz), the electrons in the radio antenna are vibrating at the same frequency—96,100,000 vibrations/second.

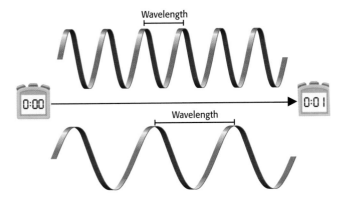

Wavelength

Wavelength

SECTION 3

Wave Interactions

▶ Christiaan Huygens

Christiaan Huygens (1629–1695) was a Dutch mathematician, astronomer, and physicist. His life overlapped that of Galileo (1564–1642) and of Newton (1642–1727). Many historians believe that Huygens's contributions to science were much broader than those of either Newton or Galileo.

• Huygens invented the pendulum clock and developed the first wave theory. Huygens's theory states that any point on a wave can be a source of a new disturbance.

▶ Lasers

In 1960, T. H. Maiman and others built the first successful laser. They used a large ruby crystal doped with chromium-ion impurities as the source of light. The electrons of the chromium ions were excited by a special flash lamp. The excited ions dropped to a lower energy level almost immediately and emitted photons of a single wavelength.

IS THAT A FACT!

➤ The word *refraction* comes from the Latin prefix *re-*, meaning "back," and *frangere*, meaning "to break."

> For background information about teaching strategies and issues, refer to the *Professional Reference for Teachers*.

The Energy of Waves

Pre-Reading Questions

Students may not know the answers to these questions before reading the chapter, so accept any reasonable response.

Suggested Answers

1. A wave is a disturbance that transmits energy through matter or space.

2. All waves have amplitude, wavelength, frequency, and wave speed.

3. Waves can reflect off barriers, can refract when passing into a new medium at an angle, can diffract around barriers or through openings, or can overlap and combine by interference.

The Energy of Waves

Sections

Pre-Reading Questions

1. What is a wave?
2. What properties do all waves have?
3. What can happen when waves interact?

2

 internet**connect**

 HRW On-line Resources

go.hrw.com
For worksheets and other teaching aids, visit the HRW Web site and type in the keyword: **HSTWAV**

 SCi**LINKS** NSTA

www.scilinks.com
Use the sci LINKS numbers at the end of each chapter for additional resources on the **NSTA** Web site.

Smithsonian Institution®

www.si.edu/hrw
Visit the Smithsonian Institution Web site for related on-line resources.

 CNN**fyi**.com

www.cnnfyi.com
Visit the CNN Web site for current events coverage and classroom resources.

CATCH THE WAVE!

A surfer takes advantage of a wave's energy to catch an exciting ride. The ocean wave that this surfer is riding is just one type of wave that you may encounter. You probably are very familiar with water waves, but did you know that waves are also responsible for light, sound, and even earthquakes? From music to television, waves play an important role in your life every day. In this chapter, you will learn about the properties of waves and how waves interact with each other and everything around them.

ENERGETIC WAVES

In this activity, you will observe the movement of a wave. Then you will determine the source of the wave's energy.

Procedure

1. Tie one end of a **piece of rope** to the back of a **chair.**

2. Hold the other end in one hand, and stand away from the chair so that the rope is almost straight but is not pulled tight.

3. Move the rope up and down quickly to create a single wave. Repeat this step several times. Record your observations in your ScienceLog.

Analysis

4. Which direction does the wave move?

5. How does the movement of the rope compare with the movement of the wave?

6. Where does the energy of the wave come from? Make an inference using direct evidence.

TRY at HOME

ENERGETIC WAVES

MATERIALS
FOR EACH GROUP:
• piece of rope, 1–2 m
• chair

Answers to START-UP Activity

4. The wave moves from one end of the rope to the other.

5. Each piece of rope moves up and down, that is, in a direction different from the wave. (If students have difficulty observing this, tie a piece of yarn to the rope, and have students watch only the yarn while waves are being made. The yarn will clearly move only up and down.)

6. The energy of the wave comes from shaking the rope. When I stop shaking the rope, the wave eventually stops moving.

Focus

The Nature of Waves

In this section, students learn that waves are a means of transmitting energy. Students learn about different types of waves and their properties.

 **Bellringer**

Have students answer the following question:

What do you think of when you hear the word *wave*? In your ScienceLog, write a brief description of what you think a wave is. Then write a short paragraph describing a time you might have experienced waves.

Discuss with students some of their answers.

1 Motivate

DEMONSTRATION

Show students a video or photographs of people surfing the giant waves of California, Hawaii, South Africa, or Australia. Explain that this section introduces basic concepts about waves but that the waves that "break" as surfers ride them are not covered—scientists still do not fully understand why waves break. Remind students that there are still natural phenomena that scientists do not fully understand. Studying waves around the world might make a fun career!

 Directed Reading Worksheet Section 1

Terms to Learn

wave	transverse wave
medium	longitudinal wave

What You'll Do

◆ Describe how waves transfer energy without transferring matter.
◆ Distinguish between waves that require a medium and waves that do not.
◆ Explain the difference between transverse and longitudinal waves.

The Nature of Waves

Imagine that your family has just returned home from a day at the beach. You had fun, but you are hungry from playing in the ocean under a hot sun. You put some leftover pizza in the microwave for dinner, and you turn on the radio. Just then, the phone rings. It's your best friend calling to find out if you've done your math homework yet.

In the events described above, how many different waves were present? Believe it or not, at least five can be identified! Can you name them? Here's a hint: A **wave** is any disturbance that transmits energy through matter or space. Okay, here are the answers: water waves in the ocean; microwaves inside the microwave oven; light waves from the sun; radio waves transmitted to the radio; and sound waves from the radio, telephone, and voices. Don't worry if you didn't get very many. You will be able to name them all after you read this section.

Waves Carry Energy

Energy can be carried away from its source by a wave. However, the material through which the wave travels does not move with the energy. For example, sound waves often travel through air, but the air does not travel with the sound. If air were to travel with sound, you would feel a rush of air every time you heard the phone ring! **Figure 1** illustrates how waves carry energy but not matter.

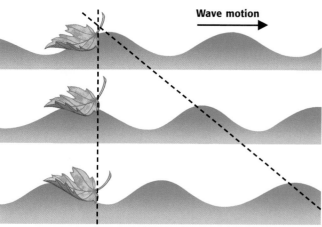

Figure 1 *Waves on a pond move toward the shore, but the water and the leaf floating on the surface do not move with the wave.*

As a wave travels, it uses its energy to do work on everything in its path. For example, the waves in a pond do work on the water to make it move up and down. The waves also do work on anything floating on the water's surface—for example, boats and ducks bob up and down with waves.

Energy Transfer Through a Medium Some waves transfer energy by the vibration of particles in a medium. A **medium** is a substance through which a wave can travel. A medium can be a solid, a liquid, or a gas. The plural of *medium* is *media*.

When a particle vibrates (moves back and forth, as in **Figure 2**), it can pass its energy to a particle next to it. As a result, the second particle will vibrate in a way similar to the first particle. In this way, energy is transmitted through a medium.

Sound waves require a medium. Sound energy travels by the vibration of particles in liquids, solids, and gases. If there are no particles to vibrate, no sound is possible. For example, if you put an alarm clock inside a jar and remove all the air from the jar to create a vacuum, you will not be able to hear the alarm.

Other waves that require a medium include ocean waves, which travel through water, and waves on guitar and cello strings. Waves that require a medium are called *mechanical waves*. **Figure 3** shows the effect of another mechanical wave.

Figure 2 *A vibration is one complete back-and-forth motion of an object.*

Figure 3 *Seismic waves travel through the ground. The 1964 earthquake in Alaska changed the features of this area.*

5

---

2) Teach

READING 📖 STRATEGY

Prediction Guide Before students read this section, ask them whether the following statements are true or false:

- Light waves are mechanical waves because they must travel in a medium. (false)
- In space, no one can hear an explosion. (true)
- Water waves are a combination of longitudinal and transverse waves. (true)

USING THE FIGURE

Discussion Encourage students to imagine that they are on the leaf shown in **Figure 1.** Ask them to describe their motions. Ask them how they could get to shore. (They would have to paddle.) Would the waves carry them to shore? (no)

Teacher Note: Explain to students that in **Figure 1** the diagonal line shows the motion of a wave as it travels across a pond, and the vertical line shows that the leaf does not move with the wave. Sheltered English

REAL-WORLD CONNECTION

Microwave Ovens Microwave ovens use electromagnetic waves to heat food. When the microwave energy penetrates a food item in a microwave oven, some of the energy from the waves causes water molecules to vibrate rapidly. The vibrating molecules are converting kinetic energy to thermal energy, which warms the rest of the particles in the food by conduction.

BRAIN FOOD

Albert Einstein, perhaps the world's most famous scientist, proposed that electromagnetic radiation could be viewed as a stream of particles, rather than as a wave of energy. He called these particles photons. In fact, Einstein proposed that energy has mass and that an electromagnetic wave can be viewed as a stream of particles that have mass. Experiments have proved that Einstein was right.

Answer to Self-Check

Mechanical waves require a medium; electromagnetic waves do not.

You can see distant objects in space using electromagnetic waves. Turn to page 26 to learn how.

Astronomy CONNECTION

Light waves from some stars and galaxies travel distances so great that they can be expressed only in light-years. A light-year is the distance that light travels in a year. Some of the light waves from these stars have traveled billions of light-years before reaching Earth. This means that the light that we see today from some distant stars left the star's surface before the Earth was formed.

Energy Transfer Without a Medium Some waves can transfer energy without traveling through a medium. Visible light is an example of a wave that doesn't require a medium. Other examples include microwaves produced by microwave ovens, TV and radio signals, and X rays used by dentists and doctors. Waves that do not require a medium are called *electromagnetic waves.*

Although electromagnetic waves do not require a medium, they can travel through substances such as air, water, and glass. However, they travel fastest through empty space. Light from the sun is a type of electromagnetic wave. **Figure 4** shows that light waves from the sun can travel through both space and matter to support life on Earth.

Figure 4 *Light waves from the sun travel more than 100 million kilometers through nearly empty space, then more than 300 km through the atmosphere, and then another 10 m through water to support life in and around a coral reef.*

Self-Check

How do mechanical waves differ from electromagnetic waves? *(See page 152 to check your answer.)*

internet connect

SCiLINKS
NSTA

TOPIC: The Nature of Waves
GO TO: www.scilinks.org
*sci*LINKS NUMBER: HSTP480

Types of Waves

Waves can be classified based on the direction in which the particles of the medium vibrate compared with the direction in which the waves travel. The two main types of waves are transverse waves and longitudinal (LAHN juh TOOD nuhl) waves. In certain conditions, a transverse wave and a longitudinal wave can combine to form another type of wave, called a surface wave.

Transverse Waves Waves in which the particles vibrate with an up-and-down motion are called **transverse waves.** *Transverse* means "moving across." The particles in a transverse wave move across, or perpendicular to, the direction that the wave is traveling. To be *perpendicular* means to be "at right angles." Try the MathBreak to practice identifying perpendicular lines.

A wave moving on a rope is an example of a transverse wave. In **Figure 5,** you can see that the points along the rope vibrate perpendicular to the direction the wave is traveling. The highest point of a transverse wave is called a *crest,* and the lowest point between each crest is called a *trough.* Although electromagnetic waves do not travel by vibrating particles in a medium, all electromagnetic waves are classified as transverse waves.

MATH BREAK

Perpendicular Lines

If the angle between two lines is 90°, the lines are said to be perpendicular. The figure below shows a set of perpendicular lines.

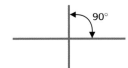

Look at the objects around you. Identify five objects with perpendicular lines or edges and five objects that do not have perpendicular lines. Sketch these objects in your ScienceLog.

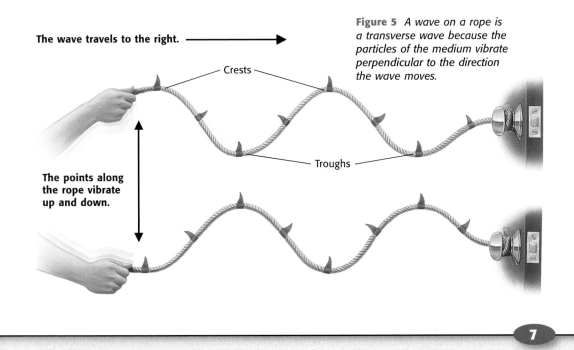

The wave travels to the right. ———→

Crests

Troughs

The points along the rope vibrate up and down.

Figure 5 *A wave on a rope is a transverse wave because the particles of the medium vibrate perpendicular to the direction the wave moves.*

7

Teaching Transparency 280
"Transverse Waves"

Answers to MATHBREAK

Accept all reasonable answers. Some possible answers:

perpendicular lines: corners of books, paper, the room, desks, and tiles on floors

no perpendicular lines: cups, globe, fruit, balls, plates

CONNECT TO EARTH SCIENCE

Use Teaching Transparency 131 to show students how earthquakes generate waves similar to transverse waves (called *secondary waves*) and longitudinal waves (called *primary waves*).

Teaching Transparency 131
"Primary and Secondary Waves"

LINK TO EARTH SCIENCE

USING THE FIGURE

Ask the students to look at **Figures 5** and **6.** Have them try to describe the similarities between a trough and a rarefaction and between a crest and compression. (A trough is the low point of a transverse wave, and a rarefaction is the area of least density in a longitudinal wave. A crest is the high point of a transverse wave, and a compression is the area of greatest density in a longitudinal wave.) **Sheltered English**

CONNECT TO
LIFE SCIENCE

Ears are pretty amazing. Sound waves (a type of longitudinal wave) travel down the ear canal, where they strike the eardrum, causing it to vibrate. Use the demonstration below to show what a longitudinal wave is.

DEMONSTRATION

1. Secure one end of a coiled spring toy. Either tape the end to a vertical surface or have a student hold it. Tie small pieces of yarn to a few of the coils (to make the wave motion more apparent).

2. Stretch the spring across a horizontal surface, such as a counter top.

3. Move the free end of the toy back and forth in a regular rhythm toward the secured end. Students should see compressions and rarefactions traveling down the spring.

Teaching Transparency 280
"Longitudinal Waves"

Longitudinal Waves In a **longitudinal wave,** the particles of the medium vibrate back and forth along the path that the wave travels. You can create a longitudinal wave on a spring, as shown in **Figure 6.**

When you push on the end of the spring, the coils of the spring are crowded together. A section of a longitudinal wave where the particles are crowded together is called a *compression.* When you pull back on the end of the spring, the coils are less crowded than normal. A section where the particles are less crowded than normal is called a *rarefaction* (RER uh FAK shuhn).

Compressions and rarefactions travel along a longitudinal wave much in the way the crests and troughs of a transverse wave move from one end to the other, as shown in **Figure 7.**

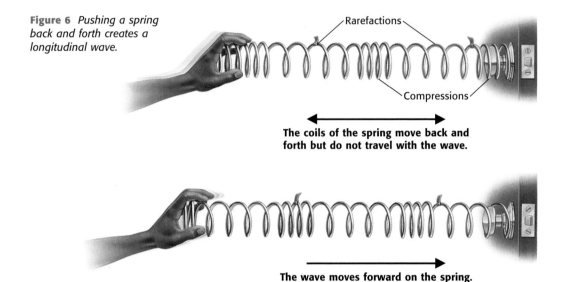

Figure 6 *Pushing a spring back and forth creates a longitudinal wave.*

Rarefactions

Compressions

The coils of the spring move back and forth but do not travel with the wave.

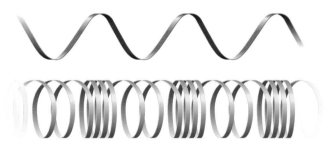

The wave moves forward on the spring.

Figure 7 *The compressions of a longitudinal wave are like the crests of a transverse wave, and the rarefactions are like troughs.*

Homework

Concept Mapping Have students create and label a concept map of longitudinal waves and transverse waves. Students should include the terms *compressions, rarefactions, crests,* and *troughs* in their concept map.

internetconnect

SCI**LINKS**
NSTA

TOPIC: Types of Waves
GO TO: www.scilinks.org
*sci***LINKS NUMBER:** HSTP490

A sound wave is an example of a longitudinal wave. Sound waves travel by compressions and rarefactions of air particles. **Figure 8** shows how a vibrating drumhead creates these compressions and rarefactions.

When the drumhead moves out after being hit, a compression is created in the air particles.

When the drumhead moves back in, a rarefaction is created.

Figure 8 *Sound energy is carried away from a drum in a longitudinal wave.*

Combinations of Waves When waves occur at or near the boundary between two media, a transverse wave and a longitudinal wave can combine to form a *surface wave*. An example is shown in **Figure 9.** Surface waves look like transverse waves, but the particles of the medium in a surface wave move in circles rather than up and down. The particles move forward at the crest of each wave and move backward at the trough. The arrows in Figure 9 show the movement of particles in a surface wave.

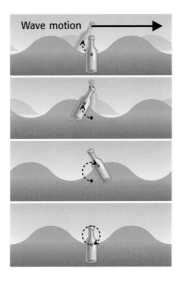

Wave motion

Figure 9 *Ocean waves are surface waves because they travel at the water's surface, where the water meets the air. A floating bottle shows the motion of particles in a surface wave.*

SECTION REVIEW

1. Describe how transverse waves differ from longitudinal waves.

2. Why can't you cause a floating leaf to move to the edge of a pond by throwing stones behind it?

3. Explain why supernova explosions in space can be seen but not heard on Earth.

4. **Applying Concepts** Sometimes people at a sports event do "the wave." Do you think this is a real example of a wave? Why or why not?

■ internet**connect**

sci*LINKS*
NSTA

TOPIC: The Nature of Waves, Types of Waves
GO TO: www.scilinks.org
*sci***LINKS NUMBER:** HSTP480, HSTP490

9

Answers to Section Review

1. As a transverse wave moves through a medium, the particles vibrate at right angles to the direction of the wave. In longitudinal waves, the particles vibrate back and forth along the wave's path.

2. Waves transfer energy but not matter. The leaf would just bob up and down; it would not move with the wave toward the shore.

3. Sound waves are mechanical waves and therefore cannot travel through space. However, visible light is an electromagnetic wave and therefore can travel through space.

4. No; the people stand up on their own and then sit down again. No energy is transmitted from one person to the next.

---

4) Close

Quiz

1. A wave is a disturbance that travels through _____ or _____. (space, matter)

2. A wave carries _____. (energy)

3. Waves that require a medium are called _____ waves. (mechanical)

4. Waves that do not require a medium are called _____ waves. (electromagnetic)

5. Waves produced by a combination of longitudinal and transverse waves are called _____ waves. (surface)

ALTERNATIVE ASSESSMENT

Provide students with markers, construction paper, yarn, glue, and scissors. Have students use these materials to illustrate the following three wave types: longitudinal, transverse, and surface. Students should label their waves and the medium (if any) through which the wave is moving and should indicate compressions, rarefactions, crests, and troughs.

REAL-WORLD CONNECTION

Seismic waves consist of longitudinal, transverse, and surface waves. Geophysicists searching for oil and gas deposits use seismic waves to study underground rock formations. A mechanical device produces seismic shock waves that reflect off the various layers of rock. These reflections produce a profile of the different layers. From the profiles, geophysicists can locate formations where oil and gas are usually found.

Focus

Properties of Waves

This section introduces properties common to all types of waves. Students explore frequency, wavelength, amplitude, energy content, and speed of waves.

Bellringer

Before class, draw a longitudinal wave and a transverse wave on the board or the overhead projector. Have students draw the waves and label the parts of each.

1 Motivate

DEMONSTRATION

Pluck a rubber band so that it makes a tone. Then change the length of the rubber band so that the tone changes pitch. Ask students to explain what caused the pitch change. Have them observe the wave (the vibration) in the rubber band as you repeat the demonstration. Lead students to the conclusion that the tone changes as the frequency of the wave changes. Explain that the frequency is the number of waves produced in a given amount of time. (You can also use a guitar for this demonstration.)

Directed Reading Worksheet Section 2

SECTION 2
READING WARM-UP

Terms to Learn

amplitude   frequency
wavelength   wave speed

What You'll Do

◆ Identify and describe four wave properties.

◆ Explain how amplitude and frequency are related to the energy of a wave.

Properties of Waves

Imagine that you are canoeing on a lake. You decide to stop paddling for a while and relax in the sunshine. The breeze makes small waves on the water. These waves are short and close together, and they have little effect on the canoe. Then a speedboat roars past you. The speedboat creates tall, widely spaced waves that cause your canoe to rock wildly. So much for relaxation!

Waves have properties that are useful for description and comparison. In this example, you could compare properties such as the height of the waves and the distance between the waves. In this section, you will learn about the properties of waves and how to measure them.

Amplitude

If you tie one end of a rope to the back of a chair, you can create waves by moving the other end up and down. If you move the rope a small distance, you will make a short wave. If you move the rope a greater distance, you will make a tall wave.

The property of waves that is related to the height of a wave is known as amplitude. The **amplitude** of a wave is the maximum distance the wave vibrates from its rest position. The rest position is where the particles of a medium stay when there are no disturbances. The larger the amplitude is, the taller the wave is. **Figure 10** shows how the amplitude of a transverse wave is measured.

Figure 10 *The amplitude of a transverse wave is measured from the rest position to the crest or to the trough of the wave.*

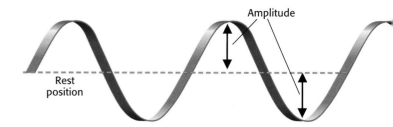

10

Larger Amplitude Means More Energy When using a rope to make waves, you have to work harder to create a wave with a large amplitude than to create one with a small amplitude. This is because it takes more energy to move the rope farther from its rest position. Therefore, a wave with a large amplitude carries more energy than a wave with a small amplitude, as shown in **Figure 11.**

Figure 11 *The amplitude of a wave depends on the amount of energy.*

| Small amplitude = low energy | Large amplitude = high energy |

Wavelength

Another property of waves is wavelength. A **wavelength** is the distance between any two adjacent crests or compressions in a series of waves. The distance between two adjacent troughs or rarefactions is also a wavelength. In fact, the wavelength can be measured from any point on one wave to the corresponding point on the next wave. All of the measurements will be equal, as shown in **Figure 12.**

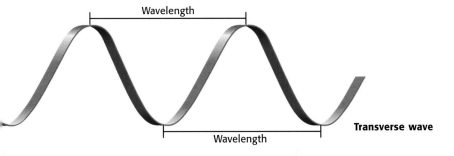

Wavelength

Wavelength

Figure 12 *Wavelengths measured from any two corresponding points are the same for a given wave.*

Longitudinal wave

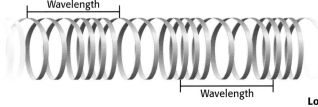

Wavelength

Wavelength

Transverse wave

11

2 Teach

READING STRATEGY

Prediction Guide Before students read this page, ask them:

Based on your experiences with water waves and from pictures of tsunamis, what do you think the height of a wave indicates?

Ask the students to explain their predictions.

MEETING INDIVIDUAL NEEDS

Learners Having Difficulty Provide students with yarn and tape. Have them use the yarn to construct a transverse wave similar to the one on these two pages. Ask them to increase the amplitude of the wave while keeping the frequency constant. (Students will need excess yarn for this step.) Have them explain what increasing the amplitude represents. Then have them change the frequency, and ask them what happened to the wavelength when they changed the frequency. (The wavelength decreased with an increase in frequency, and it increased with a decrease in frequency.)

Sheltered English

Teaching Transparency 281 "Wavelength"

3 Extend

QuickLab

MATERIAL

FOR EACH GROUP:
• coiled spring or piece of rope

Answers to QuickLab

3. To increase the amplitude of the wave, the spring must be shaken farther with bigger motions. That is, the student must provide more energy to the wave. There should be no effect on wavelength when amplitude increases. (It may be difficult to increase amplitude without increasing frequency. If students increase frequency significantly, wavelength will change.)

4. The wavelength should become shorter as the frequency is increased.

MISCONCEPTION ALERT

One hertz is often defined as one cycle per second. In this chapter, one hertz is defined as one wave per second. However, the unit expression is written 1 Hz = 1/s instead of 1 Hz = 1 wave/s to make the cancellation of units easier.

GOING FURTHER

Write the frequencies of local radio stations on the board. For example, 90.5 MHz is equal to 90,500,000 Hz. Ask students to calculate the wavelength of their favorite stations. Students will need to know the speed of light, $c = 3 \times 10^8$ m/s. The formula becomes $c = \lambda \times f$, where students know c and f and calculate λ. Have students rank the stations from lowest frequency to highest frequency and from longest wavelength to shortest wavelength.

QuickLab

Springy Waves

1. Hold a **coiled spring toy** on the floor between you and a classmate so that the spring is straight. This is the rest position.

2. Move one end of the spring from side to side at a constant rate. The number of times you move it in a complete cycle (back and forth) each second is the frequency.

3. Keeping the frequency the same, increase the amplitude. What did you have to do? How did the change in amplitude affect the wavelength?

4. Now shake the spring back and forth about twice as fast (to double the frequency). What happens to the wavelength?

5. Record your observations and answers in your ScienceLog.

Spring into action! Find the speed of waves on a spring toy. Turn to page 126 of the LabBook.

12

Teaching Transparency 281 "Frequency"

Frequency

Think about making rope waves again. The number of waves that you can make in 1 second depends on how quickly you move the rope. If you move the rope slowly, you make only a small number of waves each second. If you move it quickly, you make a large number of waves. The number of waves produced in a given amount of time is the **frequency** of the wave.

Measuring Frequency You can measure frequency by counting either the number of crests or the number of troughs that pass a point in a certain amount of time. If you were measuring the frequency of a longitudinal wave, you would count the number of compressions or rarefactions. Frequency is usually expressed in *hertz* (Hz). For waves, one hertz equals one wave per second (1 Hz = 1/s). The frequency of a wave is related to its wavelength, as shown in **Figure 13**.

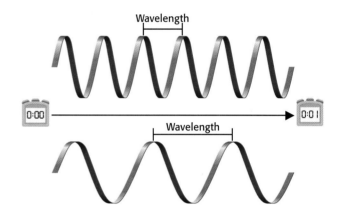

Figure 13 *At a given speed, the higher the frequency is, the shorter the wavelength.*

Higher Frequency Means More Energy It takes more energy to vibrate a rope quickly than to vibrate a rope slowly. If the amplitudes are equal, high-frequency waves carry more energy than low-frequency waves. In Figure 13, the top wave carries more energy than the bottom wave.

Because frequency and wavelength are so closely related, you can also relate the amount of energy carried by a wave to the wavelength. In general, a wave with a short wavelength carries more energy than a wave with a long wavelength.

IS THAT A FACT!

Humans normally hear sounds with frequencies from 20 to 20,000 Hz.

Wave Speed

Another property of waves is **wave speed**—the speed at which a wave travels. Speed is the distance traveled over time, so wave speed can be found by measuring the distance a single crest or compression travels in a given amount of time.

The speed of a wave depends on the medium in which the wave is traveling. For example, the wave speed of sound in air is about 340 m/s, but the wave speed of sound in steel is about 5,200 m/s.

Calculating Wave Speed   Wave speed can be calculated using wavelength and frequency. The relationship between wave speed (v), wavelength (λ, the Greek letter lambda), and frequency (f) is expressed in the following equation:

$$v = \lambda \times f$$

You can see in **Figure 14** how this equation can be used to determine wave speed. Try the MathBreak to practice using this equation.

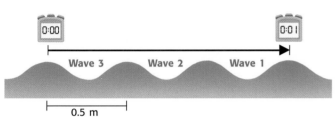

$$\lambda = 0.5 \text{ m} \qquad f = 3 \text{ Hz (3/s)}$$
$$v = 0.5 \text{ m} \times 3 \text{ Hz} = 1.5 \text{ m/s}$$

Figure 14 *To calculate wave speed, multiply the wavelength by the number of waves that pass in 1 second (frequency).*

SECTION REVIEW

1. Draw a transverse wave, and identify its amplitude and wavelength.

2. What is the speed (v) of a wave that has a wavelength (λ) of 2 m and a frequency (f) of 6 Hz?

3. **Inferring Conclusions** Compare the amplitudes and frequencies of the two types of waves discussed at the beginning of this section, and infer which type of wave carried the most energy. Explain your answer.

MATH BREAK

Wave Calculations

The equation for wave speed can be rearranged to determine wavelength (λ) or frequency (f).

$$\lambda = \frac{v}{f} \qquad f = \frac{v}{\lambda}$$

You can determine the wavelength of a wave with a speed of 20 m/s and a frequency of 4 Hz like this:

$$\lambda = \frac{v}{f}$$
$$\lambda = 20 \text{ m/s} \div 4 \text{ Hz}$$
$$\lambda = \frac{20 \text{ m}}{s} \times \frac{1 s}{4}$$
$$\lambda = 5 \text{ m}$$

Now It's Your Turn

1. What is the frequency of a wave if it has a speed of 12 cm/s and a wavelength of 3 cm?

2. A wave has a frequency of 5 Hz and a wave speed of 18 m/s. What is its wavelength?

internetconnect

SCI**LINKS**
NSTA

TOPIC: Properties of Waves
GO TO: www.scilinks.org
sciLINKS NUMBER: HSTP485

---

4 Close

Quiz

1. If wave speed is constant, as frequency increases, the _____ decreases. (wavelength)

2. _____ is the number of vibrations per second. (Frequency)

3. The distance between two corresponding points on consecutive waves is one _____. (wavelength)

4. As frequency increases, the _____ of the wave also increases. (energy)

ALTERNATIVE ASSESSMENT

Concept Mapping Have students make a concept map explaining how amplitude and frequency are related to the energy of a wave.

LabBook PG 126
Wave Speed, Frequency, and Wavelength

Answers to MATHBREAK

1. $f = \dfrac{v}{\lambda} = \dfrac{12 \text{ cm/s}}{3 \text{ cm}} = 4/s = 4 \text{ Hz}$

2. $\lambda = \dfrac{v}{f} = \dfrac{18 \text{ m/s}}{5 \text{ Hz}} = \dfrac{18 \text{ m/s}}{5/s}$
   $= 3.6 \text{ m}$

Teaching Transparency 282
"Wave Speed, Wavelength, and Frequency"

Reinforcement Worksheet
"Getting on the Same Frequency"

Math Skills Worksheet
"Dividing Whole Numbers with Long Division"

▼ Answers to Section Review

1.

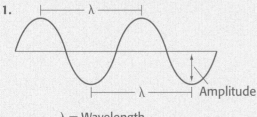

λ = Wavelength

2. $v = \lambda \times f = 2 \text{ m} \times 6 \text{ Hz} = 12 \text{ m/s}$

3. The amplitude of the speedboat waves was larger than that of the breeze waves. The frequency of the speedboat waves was lower than that of the breeze waves. However, the speedboat waves had more effect on the boat, so they most likely had more energy.

SECTION 3
READING WARM-UP

Focus

Wave Interactions

In this section, students explore how waves reflect, refract, or diffract when interacting with a different medium or barrier. Students also learn how waves interfere with other waves.

🔔 Bellringer

Write v, f, and λ on the board. Have students write each symbol, what each symbol stands for, and how each symbol relates to the other two.

1 Motivate

ACTIVITY

Use two different types of spring. A long, tightly coiled spring, often called a snake, and a large, coiled spring toy are ideal. Using a strong cord, tie one end of each spring together, forming a "spring rope." Have two volunteers sit about 3 m apart on the floor. Have one student hold the spring rope on the floor while the other creates transverse waves by moving the spring from side to side. Ask the class to observe what happens at the boundary between the two springs when a wave passes from one spring to the other spring. (Students should see a change in the wave's speed and wavelength.)

📄 **Directed Reading Worksheet** Section 3

Terms to Learn

reflection   interference
refraction   standing wave
diffraction   resonance

What You'll Do

◆ Describe reflection, refraction, diffraction, and interference.
◆ Compare destructive interference with constructive interference.
◆ Describe resonance, and give examples.

Wave Interactions

Imagine that you wake up early one morning before the sun has risen and go outside. You look up and notice that a full moon is high in the sky, and the stars are twinkling brilliantly, as shown in **Figure 15.** The sky is so clear you can find constellations (groupings of stars), such as the Big Dipper and Cassiopeia, and planets, such as Venus and Mars.

All stars, including the sun, produce light. But planets and the moon do not produce light. So why do they shine so brightly? Light from the sun *reflects* off the planets and the moon. Reflection is one of the wave interactions that you will learn about in this section.

Figure 15 *A wave interaction is responsible for this beautiful morning scene.*

Figure 16 *These water waves are reflecting off the side of the container.*

Reflection

Reflection occurs when a wave bounces back after striking a barrier. All waves—including water, sound, and light waves—can be reflected. The reflection of water waves is shown in **Figure 16.** Reflected sound waves are called *echoes,* and light waves reflecting off an object allow you to see that object. For example, light waves from the sun are reflected when they strike the surface of the moon. These reflected waves allow us to enjoy moonlit nights.

14

IS THAT A FACT!

The reflection of sound is called an *echo.* If you are closer than 15 m to a reflecting wall, you cannot hear an echo. The brain requires a 0.1 second delay to perceive an echo, and at less than 15 m, the sound wave would be reflected back from the wall in less than 0.1 second.

Refraction

Try this simple experiment: place a pencil in a half-filled glass of water. Now look at the pencil from the side. The pencil appears to be broken into two pieces! But when you take the pencil out of the water, it is perfectly fine.

What you observed in this experiment was the result of the refraction of light waves. **Refraction** is the bending of a wave as it passes at an angle from one medium to another.

Remember that the speed of a wave varies depending on the medium in which the wave is traveling. So when a wave moves from one medium to another, the wave's speed changes. When a wave enters a new medium at an angle, the part of the wave that enters first begins traveling at a different speed from the rest of the wave. This causes the wave to bend, as shown in **Figure 17**.

Wave crests

Figure 17 *Light waves passing at an angle into a new medium—such as water—are refracted because the speed of the waves changes.*

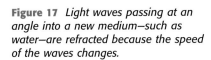
✓ Self-Check

Will a light wave refract if it enters a new medium perpendicular to the surface? Explain. *(See page 152 to check your answer.)*

Diffraction

Suppose you are walking down a city street and you hear music. The sound seems to be coming from around the corner, but you cannot see who is playing the music because the building on the corner blocks your view. Why is it that sound waves travel around a corner better than light waves do?

Most of the time, waves travel in straight lines. For example, a beam of light from a flashlight is fairly straight. But in some circumstances, waves curve or bend when they reach the edge of an object. The bending of waves around a barrier or through an opening is known as **diffraction**.

Activity

Light waves diffract around corners of buildings much less than sound waves. Imagine what would happen if light waves diffracted around corners much more than sound waves. Write a paragraph describing how this would change what you see and hear as you walk around your neighborhood.

TRY at HOME

15

---

② Teach

DEMONSTRATION

Display a large beaker half-filled with water. Place a ruler in the water, and rest it against the side. Have students observe the ruler from all sides. Have students record their observations and describe how the ruler appears to change when observed from different angles. Ask them to predict how the ruler would look if light entered the water perpendicular to the surface. (The light would not refract, and the pencil would not look bent.)

Answer to Self-Check

A light wave will not refract if it enters a new medium perpendicular to the surface because the entire wave enters the new medium at the same time.

USING THE FIGURE

Use **Figure 17** to show students how a wave bends during refraction. Point out that a wave that enters a new medium at a 90° angle will not refract because the entire wave enters the new medium at the same time. Therefore, the entire wave changes speed at the same time and does not bend. It may be helpful to draw a diagram similar to Figure 17 that shows a wave passing from one medium to another at a 90° angle.

⚠ MISCONCEPTION //// ALERT \\\\

Students may think that as a wave enters a different medium and its speed changes, its frequency also changes. Be sure students understand that when a wave changes speed, its wavelength changes but its frequency remains the same. Frequency is dependent on the source, not the medium.

Answer to Activity

Sample answer: I could see around corners, so I could avoid running into people. I could see oncoming traffic. I could look under or around furniture or other objects to find missing items. But I wouldn't be able to hear people calling me from another room. I wouldn't be able to hear oncoming traffic, such as the sirens of police cars, ambulances, or fire trucks.

In some occupations, workers are exposed to noise with amplitudes or frequencies that can be harmful. Now there are headphones available that create destructive interference to cancel the dangerous noise. These headphones receive the noise that the wearer hears, process the sounds, and then produce destructive interference to reduce or cancel the outside noise.

Have students think of and discuss situations in which these headphones would be useful.

Food heated in a microwave oven sometimes has hot spots and cold spots. This problem may be caused by *interference*. Constructive interference, which increases the amplitude of the microwaves, can cause hot spots. Destructive interference, which decreases the amplitude of the waves, can cause cold spots.

MEETING INDIVIDUAL NEEDS

Advanced Learners Have students research AM and FM radio waves. What are the differences between them? In terms of interference, why is it harder to receive FM broadcasts in some places? Why can AM broadcasts be heard for great distances under certain conditions?

Figure 18 Diffraction of Waves

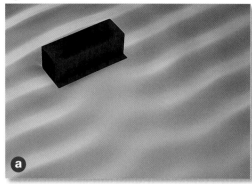

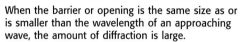

When the barrier or opening is the same size as or is smaller than the wavelength of an approaching wave, the amount of diffraction is large.

If the barrier or opening is larger than the wavelength of the wave, there is only a small amount of diffraction.

The amount of diffraction a wave experiences depends on its wavelength and the size of the barrier or opening the wave encounters, as shown in **Figure 18.** You can hear music around the corner of a building because sound waves have long wavelengths and are able to diffract around corners. However, you cannot see who is playing the music because the wavelengths of light waves are much smaller than the building, so light is not diffracted very much.

Interference

You know that all matter has volume. Therefore, objects cannot occupy the same space at the same time. But because waves are energy and not matter, more than one wave can exist in the same place at the same time. In fact, two waves can meet, share the same space, and pass through each other! When two or more waves share the same space, they overlap. The result of two or more waves overlapping is called **interference. Figure 19** shows one situation where waves occupy the same space.

Figure 19 *When sound waves from several instruments combine through interference, the result is a wave with a larger amplitude, which means a louder sound.*

16

MISCONCEPTION
**/// ALERT **

Interference only occurs in the region where the waves overlap. After the waves pass through this region, they continue on as if they never met.

Constructive Interference Increases Amplitude *Constructive interference* occurs when the crests of one wave overlap the crests of another wave or waves. The troughs of the waves also overlap. An example of constructive interference is shown in **Figure 20**. When waves combine in this way, the result is a new wave with higher crests and deeper troughs than the original waves. In other words, the resulting wave has a larger amplitude than the original waves had.

Figure 20 *When waves combine by constructive interference, the resulting wave has an amplitude that is larger than those of the original waves. After the waves interfere, they continue traveling in their original directions.*

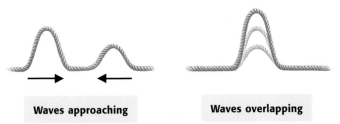

| Waves approaching | Waves overlapping | Waves continuing |

Destructive Interference Decreases Amplitude *Destructive interference* occurs when the crests of one wave and the troughs of another wave overlap. The resulting wave has a smaller amplitude than the original waves had. What do you think happens when the waves involved in destructive interference have the same amplitude? Find out in **Figure 21**.

Figure 21 *When two waves with the same amplitude combine by destructive interference, they cancel each other out. This is called* total destructive interference.

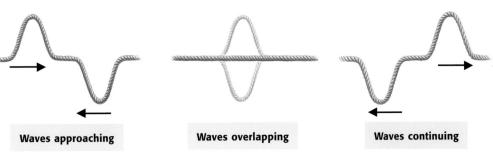

| Waves approaching | Waves overlapping | Waves continuing |

Sound Waves in Movie Theaters

Movie theaters use large screens and several speakers to make your moviegoing experience exciting. Theater designers know that increasing the amplitude of sound waves increases the volume of the sound. In terms of interference, how do you think the positioning of the speakers adds to the excitement?

Speakers

Speakers

17

IS THAT A FACT!

In 1962, New York City's Avery Fisher Hall opened, but there were problems with the hall's acoustics. There were too many echoes and dead spots caused by the interfering sound waves. In 1976, the hall's interior was removed and was replaced with an interior that produced better acoustics.

RESEARCH

Encourage students to use the Internet or library sources to research holograms and to prepare a report on their findings. Their reports should include who invented the hologram, how holograms are made using the interference of light, and how to view them.

Homework

Research Resonance is a very important concept in music. Have students conduct research to learn how resonance affects the sounds produced by different musical instruments. Students can share their results by writing a report, by making a poster, or by playing a musical instrument.

Multicultural CONNECTION

The marimba is an instrument of African origin that is similar to a xylophone.

MISCONCEPTION ALERT

The destruction of the Tacoma Narrows Bridge, as shown in **Figure 24,** is often given as an example of simple resonance. (The bridge's nickname was Galloping Gertie because it moved up and down in winds of just 5–7 km/h.) However, the destruction was actually caused by a much more complicated combination of vertical waves and twisting motions.

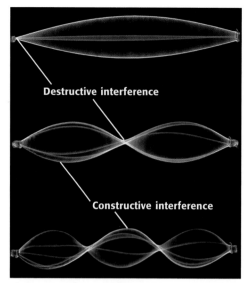

Figure 22 *When you move a rope at certain frequencies, you can create different standing waves.*

Interference Can Create Standing Waves

If you tie one end of a rope to the back of a chair and move the other end up and down, the waves you create travel down the rope and are reflected back. If you move the rope at certain frequencies, the rope appears to vibrate in loops, as shown in **Figure 22.** The loops result from the interference between the wave you created and the reflected wave. The resulting wave is called a standing wave. A **standing wave** is a wave that forms a stationary pattern in which portions of the wave are at the rest position due to total destructive interference and other portions have a large amplitude due to constructive interference. However, it only *looks* as if the wave is standing still. In reality, waves are traveling in both directions. Standing waves can be formed with transverse waves, as shown here, as well as with longitudinal waves.

One Object Causes Another to Vibrate During Resonance

As shown above, standing waves can occur at more than one frequency. The frequencies at which standing waves are produced are called *resonant frequencies*. When an object vibrating at or near the resonant frequency of a second object causes the second object to vibrate, **resonance** occurs. A resonating object absorbs energy from the vibrating object and therefore vibrates, too. An example of resonance is shown in **Figure 23.**

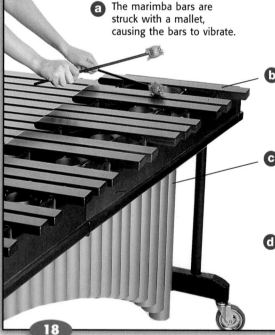

a The marimba bars are struck with a mallet, causing the bars to vibrate.

b The vibrating bars cause the air in the columns to vibrate.

Figure 23 *A marimba produces notes through the resonance of air columns.*

c The lengths of the columns have been adjusted so that the resonant frequency of the air column matches the frequency of the bar.

d The air column resonates with the bar, increasing the amplitude of the vibrations to produce a loud note.

IS THAT A FACT!

Earthquakes send out waves that cause Earth's surface to vibrate. In 1985, a severe earthquake occurred in Mexico City. The earthquake was especially destructive because the frequency of the waves matched the natural frequency of many buildings, causing them to vibrate and collapse.

The Tacoma Narrows Bridge Resonance was partially responsible for the destruction of the Tacoma Narrows Bridge, in Washington. The bridge opened in July 1940 and soon earned the nickname Galloping Gertie because of its wavelike motions. These motions were created by wind that blew across the bridge. The wind caused vibrations that were close to a resonant frequency of the bridge. Because the bridge was in resonance, it absorbed a large amount of energy from the wind, which caused it to vibrate with a large amplitude.

On November 7, 1940, a supporting cable slipped, and the bridge began to twist. The twisting of the bridge, combined with high winds, further increased the amplitude of the bridge's motion. Within hours, the amplitude became so great that the bridge collapsed, as shown in **Figure 24.** Luckily, all the people on the bridge that day were able to escape before it crashed into the river below.

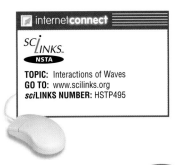

BRAIN FOOD

Resonance caused the collapse of a bridge near Manchester, England, in 1831. Cavalry troops marched across the bridge in rhythm with its resonant frequency. This caused the bridge to vibrate with a large amplitude and eventually to fall. Since that time, all troops are ordered to "break step" when they cross a bridge.

Figure 24 *The twisting motion that led to the destruction of the bridge was partially caused by resonance.*

SECTION REVIEW

1. Name two wave interactions that can occur when a wave encounters a barrier.

2. Describe what happens when a wave is refracted.

3. **Inferring Relationships** Sometimes when music is played loudly, you can feel your body shake. Explain what is happening in terms of resonance.

internetconnect

SciLINKS
NSTA

TOPIC: Interactions of Waves
GO TO: www.scilinks.org
*sci*LINKS NUMBER: HSTP495

19

Discovery Lab

Discovery Lab

USING SCIENTIFIC METHODS

Wave Energy and Speed

If you threw a small rock into a pond, waves would carry energy away from the point of origin. But if you threw a large rock into a pond, would the waves carry more energy away from the point of origin than waves created by a small rock? Would a large rock create waves that move faster than waves created by a small rock? In this lab, you'll answer these questions.

MATERIALS

👓 🦺

- shallow pan, approximately 20 cm × 30 cm
- newspaper
- plastic cup
- water
- 2 pencils
- stopwatch

20

Ask a Question

1. Do waves created by a large disturbance carry more energy than waves created by a small disturbance? Do waves created by a large disturbance travel faster than waves created by a small disturbance?

Form a Hypothesis

2. In your ScienceLog, write a few sentences that answer the questions above.

Test the Hypothesis

3. Place the pan on a few sheets of newspaper. Using the plastic cup, fill the pan with water.

4. Make sure that the water is still. Tap the surface of the water near one end of the pan with the eraser end of one pencil. This tap represents the small disturbance. In your ScienceLog, record your observations about the size of the waves that are created and the path that they take.

5. Repeat step 4. This time, use the stopwatch to measure the time it takes for one of the waves to reach the other side of the pan. Record your data in your ScienceLog. Perform this measurement two more times, and take the average of the three trials.

6. Repeat steps 4 and 5 using two pencils at once. The tap with the two pencils represents the large disturbance. (Try tapping the water using the same amount of force that you used with just one pencil.)

 Datasheets for LabBook

 Science Skills Worksheet "Interpreting Your Data"

Answer

2. Answers will vary but should address each question in step 1.

Analyze the Results

7 Compare the appearance of the waves created by one pencil with the appearance of the waves created by two pencils. Were there any differences in amplitude (wave height)?

8 Compare the amount of time required for the waves to reach the side of the pan. Did the waves travel faster when you used two pencils?

Draw Conclusions

9 Do waves created by a large disturbance carry more energy than waves created by a small disturbance? Communicate a valid conclusion, using your results. (Hint: Remember the relationship between amplitude and energy.)

10 Do waves created by a large disturbance travel faster than waves created by a small disturbance? Explain your answer.

Going Further

A tsunami is a giant ocean wave that can reach a height of 30 m. Tsunamis that reach land can cause injury and enormous property damage. Using what you just learned about wave energy and speed, explain why tsunamis are so dangerous. Make an inference about how scientists can predict when tsunamis will reach land.

Answers

7. The waves created by two pencils had a larger amplitude than the waves created by one pencil.

8. The amount of time it took for the waves to reach the side of the pan was the same for both trials. The waves appeared to travel at the same rate.

9. Yes; the large disturbance creates waves with a large amplitude. Because amplitude is related to energy, waves created by a large disturbance carry more energy.

10. No; all the waves appear to travel at the same speed because the times recorded for both trials were the same.

Going Further

Tsunamis have large amplitudes, so they carry a lot of energy that can cause injury and property damage. All waves in the ocean travel at the same speed. Therefore, scientists can determine when a tsunami will reach land.

Jennifer Ford
North Ridge Middle School
North Richland Hills, Texas

Chapter Highlights

Chapter Highlights

VOCABULARY DEFINITIONS

SECTION 1

wave a disturbance that transmits energy through matter or space

medium a substance through which a wave can travel

transverse wave a wave in which the particles of the wave's medium vibrate perpendicularly to the direction the wave is traveling

longitudinal wave a wave in which the particles of the medium vibrate back and forth along the path that the wave travels

SECTION 2

amplitude the maximum distance a wave vibrates from its rest position

wavelength the distance between one point on a wave and the corresponding point on an adjacent wave in a series of waves; for example, the distance between two adjacent crests or compressions

frequency the number of waves produced in a given amount of time

wave speed the speed at which a wave travels

SECTION 1

Vocabulary
- **wave** (p. 4)
- **medium** (p. 5)
- **transverse wave** (p. 7)
- **longitudinal wave** (p. 8)

Section Notes

- A wave is a disturbance that transmits energy.
- A medium is a substance through which a wave can travel. The particles of a medium do not travel with the wave.
- Waves that require a medium are called mechanical waves. Waves that do not require a medium are called electromagnetic waves.
- Particles in a transverse wave vibrate perpendicular to the direction the wave travels.
- Particles in a longitudinal wave vibrate back and forth in the same direction that the wave travels.
- Transverse and longitudinal waves can combine to form surface waves.

SECTION 2

Vocabulary
- **amplitude** (p. 10)
- **wavelength** (p. 11)
- **frequency** (p. 12)
- **wave speed** (p. 13)

Section Notes

- Amplitude is the maximum distance the particles in a wave vibrate from their rest position. Large-amplitude waves carry more energy than small-amplitude waves.
- Wavelength is the distance between two adjacent crests (or compressions) of a wave.
- Frequency is the number of waves that pass a given point in a given amount of time. High-frequency waves carry more energy than low-frequency waves.

☑ Skills Check

Math Concepts

WAVE-SPEED CALCULATIONS   The relationship between wave speed (v), wavelength (λ), and frequency (f) is expressed by the equation:

$$v = \lambda \times f$$

For example, if a wave has a wavelength of 1 m and a frequency of 6 Hz (6/s), the wave speed is calculated as follows:

$$v = 1 \text{ m} \times 6 \text{ Hz} = 1 \text{ m} \times 6/\text{s}$$
$$v = 6 \text{ m/s}$$

Visual Understanding

TRANSVERSE AND LONGITUDINAL WAVES
Two common types of waves are transverse waves (shown below) and longitudinal waves. Study Figure 5 on page 7 and Figure 6 on page 8 to review the differences between these two types of waves.

Lab and Activity Highlights

Wave Energy and Speed   PG 20

Wave Speed, Frequency, and Wavelength   PG 126

Datasheets for LabBook
(blackline masters for these labs)

SECTION 2

- Wave speed is the speed at which a wave travels. Wave speed can be calculated by multiplying the wavelength by the wave's frequency.

Labs

Wave Speed, Frequency, and Wavelength (p. 126)

SECTION 3

Vocabulary

reflection (p. 14)
refraction (p. 15)
diffraction (p. 15)
interference (p. 16)
standing wave (p. 18)
resonance (p. 18)

Section Notes

- Waves bounce back after striking a barrier during reflection.

- Refraction is the bending of a wave when it passes at an angle from one medium to another.

- Waves bend around barriers or through openings during diffraction. The amount of diffraction depends on the wavelength of the waves and the size of the barrier or opening.

- The result of two or more waves overlapping is called interference.

- Amplitude increases during constructive interference and decreases during destructive interference.

- Standing waves are waves in which portions of the wave do not move and other portions move with a large amplitude.

- Resonance occurs when a vibrating object causes another object to vibrate at one of its resonant frequencies.

SECTION 3

reflection the bouncing back of a wave after it strikes a barrier or an object

refraction the bending of a wave as it passes at an angle from one medium to another

diffraction the bending of waves around a barrier or through an opening

interference a wave interaction that occurs when two or more waves overlap

standing wave a wave that forms a stationary pattern in which portions of the wave do not move and other portions move with a large amplitude

resonance what occurs when an object vibrating at or near a resonant frequency of a second object causes the second object to vibrate

  Vocabulary Review Worksheet

Blackline masters of these Chapter Highlights can be found in the **Study Guide.**

---

internetconnect

GO TO: go.hrw.com

Visit the **HRW** Web site for a variety of learning tools related to this chapter. Just type in the keyword:

KEYWORD: HSTWAV

SCILINKS
NSTA

GO TO: www.scilinks.org

Visit the **National Science Teachers Association** on-line Web site for Internet resources related to this chapter. Just type in the *sci*LINKS number for more information about the topic:

TOPIC: The Nature of Waves   *sci*LINKS NUMBER: HSTP480
TOPIC: Properties of Waves   *sci*LINKS NUMBER: HSTP485
TOPIC: Types of Waves   *sci*LINKS NUMBER: HSTP490
TOPIC: Interactions of Waves   *sci*LINKS NUMBER: HSTP495

23

Lab and Activity Highlights

LabBank

Whiz-Bang Demonstrations, Pitch Forks

Calculator-Based Labs, In the Dog House

Long-Term Projects & Research Ideas,
It's a Whale of a Wave

Chapter Review

USING VOCABULARY

For each pair of terms, explain the difference in their meanings.

1. longitudinal wave/transverse wave
2. frequency/wave speed
3. wavelength/amplitude
4. reflection/refraction
5. constructive interference/destructive interference

UNDERSTANDING CONCEPTS

Multiple Choice

6. As the wavelength increases, the frequency
   a. decreases.
   b. increases.
   c. remains the same.
   d. increases, then decreases.

7. Which wave interaction explains why sound waves can be heard around corners?
   a. reflection   c. diffraction
   b. refraction   d. interference

8. Refraction occurs when a wave enters a new medium at an angle because
   a. the frequency changes.
   b. the amplitude changes.
   c. the wave speed changes.
   d. None of the above

9. The speed of a wave with a frequency of 2 Hz (2/s), an amplitude of 3 m, and a wavelength of 10 m is
   a. 0.2 m/s.   c. 12 m/s.
   b. 5 m/s.   d. 20 m/s.

10. Waves transfer
    a. matter.   c. particles.
    b. energy.   d. water.

11. A wave that is a combination of longitudinal and transverse waves is a
    a. sound wave.   c. rope wave.
    b. light wave.   d. surface wave.

12. The wave property that is related to the height of a wave is the
    a. wavelength.   c. frequency.
    b. amplitude.   d. wave speed.

13. During constructive interference,
    a. the amplitude increases.
    b. the frequency decreases.
    c. the wave speed increases.
    d. All of the above

14. Waves that don't require a medium are
    a. longitudinal waves.
    b. electromagnetic waves.
    c. surface waves.
    d. mechanical waves.

Short Answer

15. Draw a transverse and a longitudinal wave. Label a crest, a trough, a compression, a rarefaction, and wavelengths. Also label the amplitude on the transverse wave.

16. What is the relationship between frequency, wave speed, and wavelength?

17. Explain how two waves can cancel each other out.

Concept Mapping

18. Use the following terms to create a concept map: wave, refraction, transverse wave, longitudinal wave, wavelength, wave speed, diffraction.

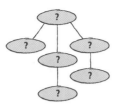

Concept Mapping

18. An answer to this exercise can be found at the front of this book.

CRITICAL THINKING AND PROBLEM SOLVING

19. After you set up stereo speakers in your school's music room, you notice that in certain areas of the room the sound from the speakers is very loud and in other areas the sound is very soft. Explain how interference causes this.

20. You have lost the paddles for the canoe you rented, and the canoe has drifted to the center of the pond. You need to get the canoe back to shore, but you do not want to get wet by swimming in the pond. Your friend on the shore wants to throw rocks behind the canoe to create waves that will push the canoe toward shore. Will this solution work? Why or why not?

21. Some opera singers have voices so powerful they can break crystal glasses! To do this, they sing one note very loudly and hold it for a long time. The walls of the glass move back and forth until the glass shatters. Explain how this happens in terms of resonance.

MATH IN SCIENCE

22. A fisherman in a rowboat notices that one wave crest passes his fishing line every 5 seconds. He estimates the distance between the crests to be 2 m and estimates the crests of the waves to be 0.4 m above the troughs. Using these data, determine the amplitude and wave speed of the waves. Remember that wave speed is calculated with the formula $v = \lambda \times f$.

INTERPRETING GRAPHICS

23. Rank the waves below from highest energy to lowest energy, and explain your reasoning.

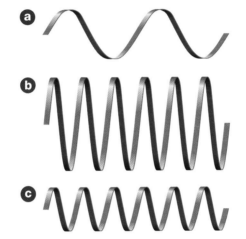

Reading Check-up

Take a minute to review your answers to the Pre-Reading Questions found at the bottom of page 2. Have your answers changed? If necessary, revise your answers based on what you have learned since you began this chapter.

 25

Concept Mapping Transparency 20

Blackline Masters of this Chapter Review can be found in the **Study Guide.**

CRITICAL THINKING AND PROBLEM SOLVING

19. With constructive interference, the crest of one wave overlaps with the crest of another wave, making a new wave with a higher crest and greater amplitude, or loudness. With destructive interference, the crest of one wave overlaps with the trough of another wave, decreasing the amplitude and making the sound softer.

20. Waves carry energy, not matter. So waves will make the canoe bob up and down in the pond but will not push the canoe closer to the shore.

21. The vibrations from the singer's voice cause the glass to vibrate at one of its resonant frequencies. It does not take much energy to make it vibrate with a large amplitude. But the glass is not very flexible, so it shatters.

MATH IN SCIENCE

22. wavelength is 2 m, frequency is 1 wave/5 s = 0.2 Hz, so $v = 2$ m × 0.2 Hz = 0.4 m/s

Amplitude is half the distance between the crests and troughs. The amplitude is 0.4 m/2 = 0.2 m.

INTERPRETING GRAPHICS

23. rank: *b, c, a*
Wave *b* has a high frequency and a large amplitude. Wave *c* has a high frequency and a small amplitude. Wave *a* has a low frequency and a small amplitude.

high frequency and large amplitude = more energy
low frequency and small amplitude = less energy

Background

A radio telescope collects radio waves, just as an optical telescope collects visible light. However, to bring radio waves into sharp focus, a radio telescope must be much larger than an optical telescope because radio waves have much longer wavelengths than wavelengths of visible light.

While some objects that give off relatively few radio waves are best observed by optical telescopes, objects that produce more radio waves are best observed by radio telescopes. However, objects that produce both visible light and radio waves are best observed with radio telescopes, which produce images with higher resolution than those produced by optical telescopes.

Radio telescopes do have one disadvantage. They create images from only one wavelength at a time. Using a radio telescope is like looking at an object through a lens that allows you to see only green light. If you want to see the object in another color, such as red or blue, you have to change the lens. This is exactly what astronomers have to do with radio telescopes.

Science, Technology, and Society

The Ultimate Telescope

The largest telescopes in the world don't depend on visible light, lenses, or mirrors. Instead, they collect radio waves from the far reaches of outer space. One radio telescope, called the Very Large Array (VLA), is located in a remote desert in New Mexico.

From Radio Waves to Computer Images

Objects in space give off radio waves that radio telescopes collect. A bowl-shaped dish called a reflector focuses the radio waves onto a small radio antenna hung over the center of the dish. The antenna converts the waves into electric signals. The signals are relayed to a radio receiver, where they are amplified and recorded on tape that can be read by a computer. The computer combines the signals to create an image of the source of the radio waves.

A Marvel at "Seeing"

Radio telescopes have some distinct advantages over optical telescopes. They can "see" objects that are as far as 13 billion light-years away. They can even detect objects that don't release any light at all. Radio telescopes can be used in any kind of weather, can receive signals through atmospheric pollution, and can even penetrate the cosmic dust and gas clouds that occupy vast areas of space. However, radio telescopes must be large in order to be accurate.

Telescope Teamwork

The VLA is an array of 27 separate radio telescopes mounted on railroad tracks and electronically linked by computers. Each of the

▲ *Only a few of the 27 radio telescopes of the VLA, near Datil, New Mexico, can be seen in this photograph.*

27 reflectors is 25 m in diameter. When they operate together, they work like a single telescope with a diameter of 47 km! Using the VLA, astronomers have been able to explore distant galaxies, pulsars, quasars, and possible black holes.

A system of telescopes even larger than the VLA has been used. In the Very Long Baseline Array (VLBA), radio telescopes in different parts of the world all work together. The result is a telescope that is almost as large as the Earth itself!

What Do They See?

▶ Find out about some of the objects "seen" by the VLA, such as pulsars, quasars, and possible black holes. Prepare a report or create a model of one of the objects, and make a presentation to your class. Use diagrams and photographs to make your presentation more interesting.

26

Information for What Do They See?
Provide students with some popular astronomy books and magazines. You may wish to contact NASA's Space Science Institute, which operates the Hubble Space Telescope. The telescope takes numerous photographs daily that are eventually released to the public.

ACROSS _{THE} SCIENCES

PHYSICAL SCIENCE • LIFE SCIENCE

Sounds of Silence

It's morning on the African savanna. Suddenly, without a sound, a family of elephants stops eating and begins to move off. At the same moment, about 6 km away, other members of the same family move off in a direction that will reunite them with the first group. How did the groups know when it was time to go?

Do You Hear What I Hear?

Elephants do much of their communicating by infrasound. This is sound energy with a frequency too low to be heard by humans. These infrasonic conversations take place through deep, soft rumblings produced by the animals. Though humans can't hear the sounds, elephants as far as 10 km away respond quickly to the messages.

Because scientists couldn't hear the elephant "conversations," they couldn't understand how the animals coordinated their activities. Of course, the elephants, which have superb low-frequency hearing, heard the messages clearly. It turns out that much elephant behavior is affected by infrasonic messages. For instance, one kind of rumble from a mother to her calf tells the calf it is all right to nurse. Another rumble, from the group's leader, is the "time to move on" message. Still another infrasonic message may be sent to other elephant groups in the area, warning them of danger.

Radio Collars

Once scientists learned about elephants' infrasonic abilities, they devised ways to study the sounds. Researchers developed radio collars for individual animals to wear. The collars are connected to a computer that helps researchers identify which elephant sent the message. The collars also record the messages. This information helps scientists understand both the messages and the social organization of the group.

Let's Talk

Elephants have developed several ways to "talk" to each other. For example, they greet each other by touching trunks and tusks. And elephants have as many as 25 vocal calls, including the familiar bellowing trumpet call (a sign of great excitement). In other situations, they use chemical signals.

▲ *Two elephants greeting each other*

Recently, researchers recording elephant communications found that when elephants vocalize their low-frequency sounds, they create seismic waves. Elephant messages sent by these underground energy waves may be felt more than 8 km away. Clearly, there is a lot more to elephant conversations than meets the ear!

On Your Own

▶ Elephants are very intelligent and highly sociable. Find out more about the complex social structure of elephant groups. Why is it important for scientists to understand how elephants communicate with each other? How can that understanding help elephants?

27

Background

Elephants are highly intelligent and very social animals. Each herd or family has a highly complex social arrangement. The family is usually led by the oldest female, the matriarch of the group. She is responsible for leading the family to the best feeding grounds and away from danger. The family group usually consists of the matriarch, her female relatives of all ages, and young males. When males reach sexual maturity (at about age 14), they leave (or are nudged out of) the family and go off on their own or join all-male bachelor herds.

Sample Answer to On Your Own

Elephant herds need large amounts of food and water and large areas in which to roam. Humans kill elephants for a variety of reasons, such as to obtain the ivory in the elephants' tusks or to protect farmland from being trampled by elephants. Humans are also occupying more and more of the natural habitat of elephants. If scientists learn to understand elephant communication and behavior, they can devise plans that use those natural behaviors to protect and preserve elephant herds and habitats from human destruction. For instance, scientists might broadcast sounds that elephants recognize as danger signals to warn the animals away from a particular location.

Chapter Organizer

CHAPTER ORGANIZATION	TIME MINUTES	OBJECTIVES	LABS, INVESTIGATIONS, AND DEMONSTRATIONS
Chapter Opener pp. 28–29	45	National Standards: UCP 2, SAI 1, HNS 1, 3	**Start-Up Activity,** A Homemade Guitar, p. 29
Section 1 What Is Sound?	90	▶ Describe how sound is caused by vibrations. ▶ Explain how sound is transmitted through a medium. ▶ Explain how the human ear works, and identify its parts. UCP 1, 2, SAI 1, ST 2, SPSP 1, 5, HNS 1, PS 3a	**QuickLab,** Good Vibrations, p. 30 **Demonstration,** p. 30 in ATE **Whiz-Bang Demonstrations,** Hear Ye, Hear Ye **Whiz-Bang Demonstrations,** Jingle Bells, Silent Bells
Section 2 Properties of Sound	90	▶ Compare the speed of sound in different media. ▶ Explain how frequency and pitch are related. ▶ Describe the Doppler effect, and give examples of it. ▶ Explain how amplitude and loudness are related. UCP 1, 3, SAI 1, ST 2, SPSP 5, HNS 1, 3, PS 3a; Labs UCP 2, SAI 1, 2	**Demonstration,** p. 38 in ATE **QuickLab,** Sounding Board, p. 39 **Discovery Lab,** Easy Listening, p. 128 **Datasheets for LabBook,** Easy Listening **Whiz-Bang Demonstrations,** The Sounds of Time
Section 3 Interactions of Sound Waves	90	▶ Explain how echoes are produced, and describe their use in locating objects. ▶ Give examples of constructive and destructive interference of sound waves. ▶ Identify three sound-wave interactions, and give examples of each. UCP 1–3, ST 2, SPSP 5; Labs UCP 2, 3, SAI 1, 2, PS 3a	**Demonstration,** p. 41 in ATE **Skill Builder,** Tuneful Tube, p. 131 **Design Your Own,** The Speed of Sound, p. 130 **Skill Builder,** The Energy of Sound, p. 52 **Datasheets for LabBook** **Whiz-Bang Demonstrations,** A Hot Tone
Section 4 Sound Quality	90	▶ Define sound quality. ▶ Describe how each family of musical instruments produces sound. ▶ Explain how noise is different from music. UCP 1, 2, 5, SPSP 1–3	**Demonstration,** pp. 48, 49 in ATE **Interactive Explorations CD-ROM,** Sound Bite! *A **Worksheet** is also available in the **Interactive Explorations Teacher's Edition.*** **EcoLabs & Field Activities,** An Earful of Sounds **Long-Term Projects & Research Ideas,** The Caped Ace Flies Again

*See page **T23** for a complete correlation of this book with the*

NATIONAL SCIENCE EDUCATION STANDARDS.

TECHNOLOGY RESOURCES

 Guided Reading Audio CD
English or Spanish, Chapter 2

 Science Discovery Videodiscs:
Image and Activity Bank with Lesson Plans: Making a Pitch
Science Sleuths: Noises in School

 CNN. **Science, Technology & Society,**
Salmon Sound Barriers, Segment 25
Learning from Frog Ears, Segment 26

 Interactive Explorations CD-ROM,
CD 3, Exploration 6, Sound Bite!

 One-Stop Planner CD-ROM
with Test Generator

Chapter 2 • The Nature of Sound

CLASSROOM WORKSHEETS, TRANSPARENCIES, AND RESOURCES	SCIENCE INTEGRATION AND CONNECTIONS	REVIEW AND ASSESSMENT
Directed Reading Worksheet **Science Puzzlers, Twisters & Teasers**		
Directed Reading Worksheet, Section 1 **Transparency 284,** Sounds from a Stereo Speaker **Transparency 285,** How the Human Ear Works	**Biology Connection,** p. 31 **Connect to Life Science,** p. 31 in ATE **Astronomy Connection,** p. 32 **Science, Technology, and Society:** Jurassic Bark, p. 58 **Holt Anthology of Science Fiction,** *Ear*	**Homework,** p. 32 in ATE **Section Review,** p. 34 **Quiz,** p. 34 in ATE **Alternative Assessment,** p. 34 in ATE
Directed Reading Worksheet, Section 2 **Transparency 286,** Pitch Depends on Frequency **Transparency 286,** Frequencies Heard by Different Animals **Transparency 287,** The Doppler Effect **Reinforcement Worksheet,** Doppler Dan's Dump Truck	**MathBreak,** Speed of Sound, p. 36 **Connect to Earth Science,** p. 36 in ATE **Math and More,** p. 36 in ATE **Biology Connection,** p. 37 **Connect to Life Science,** p. 38 in ATE **Multicultural Connection,** p. 40 in ATE	**Section Review,** p. 40 **Quiz,** p. 40 in ATE **Alternative Assessment,** p. 40 in ATE
Directed Reading Worksheet, Section 3 **Transparency 154,** How Sonar Works **Transparency 288,** Echolocation	**Cross-Disciplinary Focus,** p. 42 in ATE **Connect to Earth Science,** p. 42 in ATE **Apply,** p. 43 **Real-World Connection,** p. 43 in ATE **Cross-Disciplinary Focus,** p. 44 in ATE **Real-World Connection,** p. 44 in ATE **Real-World Connection,** p. 45 in ATE	**Section Review,** p. 43 **Self-Check,** p. 45 **Section Review,** p. 47 **Quiz,** p. 47 in ATE **Alternative Assessment,** p. 47 in ATE
Directed Reading Worksheet, Section 4 **Critical Thinking Worksheet,** The Noise Police	**Multicultural Connection,** p. 50 in ATE **Environment Connection,** p. 51	**Self-Check,** p. 49 **Homework,** p. 49 in ATE **Section Review,** p. 51 **Quiz,** p. 51 in ATE **Alternative Assessment,** p. 51 in ATE

END-OF-CHAPTER REVIEW AND ASSESSMENT

Chapter Review in Study Guide
Vocabulary and Notes in Study Guide
Chapter Tests with Performance-Based Assessment, Chapter 2 Test
Chapter Tests with Performance-Based Assessment, Performance-Based Assessment 2
Concept Mapping Transparency 21

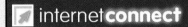

internet connect

 Holt, Rinehart and Winston On-line Resources
go.hrw.com

For worksheets and other teaching aids related to this chapter, visit the HRW Web site and type in the keyword: **HSTSND**

 National Science Teachers Association
www.scilinks.org

Encourage students to use the *sci*LINKS numbers listed in the internet connect boxes to access information and resources on the **NSTA** Web site.

Chapter Resources & Worksheets

Visual Resources

TEACHING TRANSPARENCIES

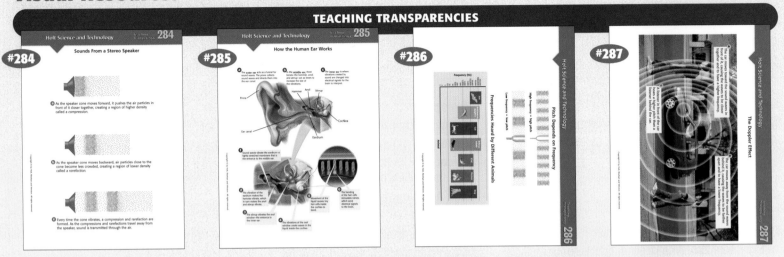

#284 — Sounds From a Stereo Speaker

#285 — How the Human Ear Works

#286 — Pitch Depends on Frequency / Frequencies Heard by Different Animals

#287 — The Doppler Effect

TEACHING TRANSPARENCIES

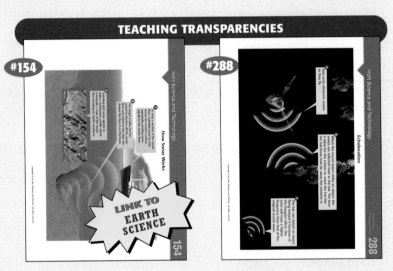

#154 — How Sonar Works — LINK TO EARTH SCIENCE

#288 — Echolocation

CONCEPT MAPPING TRANSPARENCY

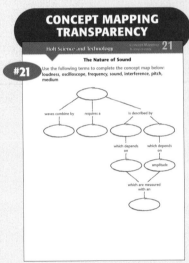

#21 — The Nature of Sound

Use the following terms to complete the concept map below:
loudness, oscilloscope, frequency, sound, interference, pitch, medium

Meeting Individual Needs

DIRECTED READING

#2 — The Nature of Sound

Chapter Introduction

As you begin this chapter, answer the following.

1. Read the title of the chapter. List three things that you already know about this subject.

2. Write two questions about this subject that you would like answered by the time you finish this chapter.

3. How does the title of the Start-Up Activity relate to the subject of the chapter?

Section 1: What Is Sound?

4. What are two sounds you hear indoors?

Sound Is Produced by Vibrations

5. The complete back-and-forth motion of an object is called a

REINFORCEMENT & VOCABULARY REVIEW

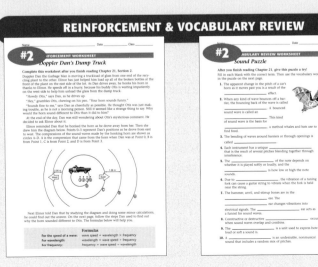

#2 — Doppler Dan's Dump Truck

#2 — Sound Puzzle

SCIENCE PUZZLERS, TWISTERS & TEASERS

#2 — The Nature of Sound

Wordy Numbers

1. Vanity phone numbers are numbers that can be spelled out in easy-to-remember words. For example, a car dealer might choose the number 289-2277, which can be spelled as BUY CARS. What word from the chapter could each of the numbers below represent?

a. 367-7537 (Hint: What an effect!)

b. 332-4235 (Hint: The louder the bigger!)

c. 942-7283 (Hint: Some pagers do.)

d. (737) 662-6231 (Hint: Be sympathetic!)

e. 848-6537 (Hint: Are you ready to rumble?)

Chapter 2 • The Nature of Sound

Review & Assessment

STUDY GUIDE

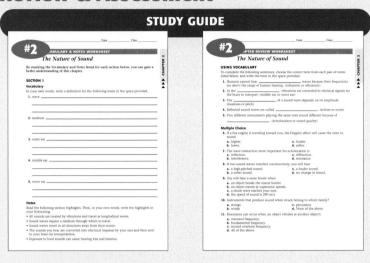

CHAPTER TESTS WITH PERFORMANCE-BASED ASSESSMENT

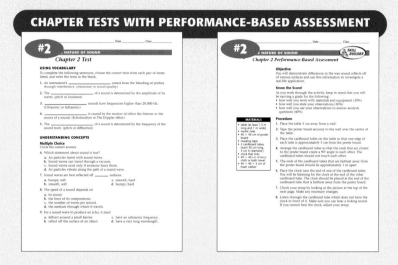

Lab Worksheets

WHIZ-BANG DEMONSTRATIONS

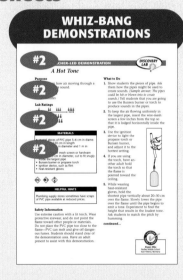

ECOLABS & FIELD ACTIVITIES

LONG-TERM PROJECTS & RESEARCH IDEAS

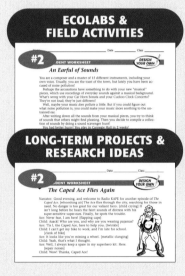

DATASHEETS FOR LABBOOK

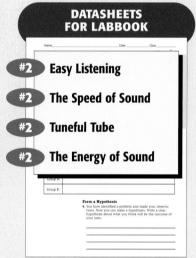

- #2 Easy Listening
- #2 The Speed of Sound
- #2 Tuneful Tube
- #2 The Energy of Sound

Applications & Extensions

CRITICAL THINKING & PROBLEM SOLVING

SCIENCE, TECHNOLOGY & SOCIETY

INTERACTIVE EXPLORATIONS

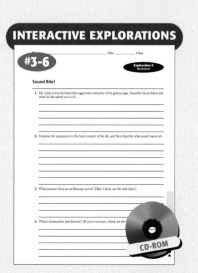

Chapter Background

SECTION 1

What Is Sound?

▶ **Doppler Effect**

In 1842, the Doppler effect was explained by the Austrian physicist Christian Doppler (1803–1853). He noted that there is a change in wavelength of both light and sound when either the source or the receiver (or both, if they move at different velocities) moves. If the wavelength becomes shorter and the frequency of the sound becomes higher, it is known as blue shift. If the wavelength increases and the frequency becomes lower, it is known as red shift.

- In acoustical Doppler effects, the frequency depends on the speed of the observer relative to the speed of the source.

IS THAT A FACT!

- ➥ Singing sand dunes can make two very different sounds: some dunes "whistle" or "squeak" in the 500–2500 Hz range, while others "boom" at frequencies of 50–300 Hz. Interestingly, the booming sands can be felt as well; the dune trembles noticeably as it booms.

- ➥ Only sand grains with certain sizes and shapes whistle or squeal. Sands in many locations, including beach sands in a variety of places, can be induced to whistle. Scientists are less certain what factors create "booming" dunes, although grains of a certain size and shape seem to be required.

SECTION 2

Properties of Sound

▶ **Loudness**

Loudness is expressed in decibels. An increase of 10 dB multiplies the intensity of a sound by 10 times. An increase of 20 dB is 10 × 10, or 100 times louder.

▶ **Robert Boyle (1627–1691)**

Robert Boyle, a British scientist who lived in Ireland, performed a famous experiment in 1660. When a bell was suspended in a vacuum, the clapper could be seen striking the bell, but no sound was heard. This demonstration proved that sound is dependent on a medium.

IS THAT A FACT!

- ➥ The longest distance traveled by any audible sound in air is about 4,600 km. The volcanic explosion on the Indonesian island of Krakatau, in 1883, propelled a column of smoke and ash more than 80 km into the air. The explosion sounded like distant cannon fire to people in Australia, Singapore, and Rodriguez Island—4,600 km away in the Indian Ocean. Waves reached the Pacific coastline of Colombia, 19 hours later, and tsunamis were recorded in other parts of South America. Remnants of the giant tsunamis were detected in the English Channel, halfway around the Earth from where the eruption took place.

- ➥ Sound travels 1.7 km in about 5 seconds in air that is 20°C. Sound travels the same distance (1.7 km) in just over 1 second underwater and in only three-tenths of a second in steel.

SECTION 3

Interactions of Sound Waves

▶ **Bat Sonar Beats Human Technology**
Experiments conducted at Brown University found that bat sonar can detect the difference between echoes just two- to three-millionths of a second apart. The best naval sonar could differentiate between echoes about 5 to 10 millionths of a second apart.

IS THAT A FACT!

• Nikola Tesla, a Croatian inventor, once created a man-made earthquake by making a steam-driven oscillator vibrate at the same frequency as the ground. Tesla had accurately determined the resonant frequency of the Earth! In a similar experiment, Tesla proved theories of seismic wave activity by sending waves of energy through the Earth. As these waves of energy returned, Tesla added electric current to them and thereby created a man-made bolt of lightning that measured 40 m. The accompanying thunder was heard for more than 35 km!

SECTION 4

Sound Quality

▶ **Recording Sound**
The two basic methods of recording sound are analog and digital recording. In analog recording, the recording medium varies continuously with the incoming signal. In digital recording, the signal is recorded as a rapid sequence of coded measurements.

• Both methods preserve the varying voltage of the sound signal, but digital recording eliminates the hiss or electrical noise. Analog recordings can be improved by a noise reduction system, such as the Dolby® system.

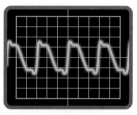

Piano   Violin

IS THAT A FACT!

◆ Notes on a musical scale are set by exact frequencies. Although humans can hear frequencies as low as 20 Hz, the lowest frequency heard as a note is about 30 Hz. The highest frequency audible to humans is about 20,000 Hz. Middle C on the piano has a frequency of 263 Hz.

◆ Little was known about the science of sound until the 1600s. The Greeks were more interested in music than in the scientific aspects of sound. However, the Greek philosopher and mathematician Pythagoras (c. 580–500 B.C.) discovered that doubling the frequency of a pitch produces a pitch one octave higher.

For background information about teaching strategies and issues, refer to the *Professional Reference for Teachers.*

Pre-Reading Questions

Students may not know the answers to these questions before reading the chapter, so accept any reasonable response.

Suggested Answers

1. Sound travels from one place to another by vibrating the particles in a medium.

2. The frequency of a sound wave determines the sound's pitch, and the amplitude of the sound wave determines the sound's loudness.

3. Sound waves can reflect off a barrier or can diffract around it. Sound waves can interfere with one another, and they sometimes form standing waves.

CHAPTER
2

The Nature of Sound

Sections

Pre-Reading Questions

1. How does sound travel from one place to another?

2. What determines a sound's pitch and loudness?

3. What can happen when sound waves interact with each other?

The Nature of Sound

SOUND UNDER THE SEA

Look at these dolphins swimming swiftly and silently through their watery world. Wait a minute—swiftly? Yes. Silently? No way! Dolphins use sound to communicate. In fact, each dolphin has a special whistle that it uses to identify itself. Dolphins also use sound to locate their food and find their way through murky water. In this chapter, you'll learn more about the properties and the interactions of sound waves. You'll also learn how sound is used to locate objects.

 internet**connect**

HRW On-line Resources

go.hrw.com
For worksheets and other teaching aids, visit the HRW Web site and type in the keyword: **HSTSND**

SCILINKS.
NSTA

www.scilinks.com
Use the *sci*LINKS numbers at the end of each chapter for additional resources on the **NSTA** Web site.

Smithsonian Institution

www.si.edu/hrw
Visit the Smithsonian Institution Web site for related on-line resources.

CNNfyi.com

www.cnnfyi.com
Visit the CNN Web site for current events coverage and classroom resources.

A HOMEMADE GUITAR

In this chapter, you will learn about sound. You can start by making your own guitar. It won't sound as good as a real guitar, but it will help you explore the nature of sound.

Procedure

1. Stretch a **rubber band** lengthwise around an empty **shoe box.** Gently pluck the rubber band. In your ScienceLog, describe what you hear.

2. Stretch **another rubber band of a different thickness** around the box. Pluck both rubber bands. Describe the difference in the sounds.

3. Put a **pencil** across the center of the box and under the rubber bands, and pluck again. Compare this sound with the sound you heard before the pencil was used.

4. Move the pencil closer to one end of the shoe box. Pluck on both sides of the pencil. Describe the differences in the sounds you hear.

Analysis

5. How did the thicknesses of the rubber bands affect the sound?

6. In steps 3 and 4, you changed the length of the rubber bands. What is the relationship between the length of the rubber band and the sound that you hear?

29

A HOMEMADE GUITAR

MATERIALS
FOR EACH GROUP: • thin rubber band • thick rubber band • shoe box • pencil

Safety Caution

Remind students to review all safety cautions and icons before beginning this lab activity.

Teacher's Notes

1. Students should hear a sound and see the rubber band vibrate.

2. Students should hear a higher pitch or note from the thinner rubber band. They might not use the words *pitch* or *note* at this point, but they should be able to notice and describe the differences between the two sounds.

3. When the pencil is used, the pitch of the sound is higher.

4. A high pitch is produced by the short part of the rubber band, and a low pitch is produced by the longer part of the rubber band.

Answers to START-UP Activity

5. The thicker the rubber band is, the lower the pitch.

6. The shorter the rubber band is, the higher the pitch.

Focus

What Is Sound?

This section introduces sound and how it is produced. Students learn how sound waves travel, and how the human ear works.

 **Bellringer**

If you've ever been near a large fireworks display, you may have *felt* the sound of the explosions. Think of other instances when you might feel sound and describe them in your ScienceLog.

1 Motivate

DEMONSTRATION

Set up a stereo system with speakers (these must have woofers that reproduce low-frequency sounds) in the classroom, and remove the outer cover of the speakers. Play music that has a strong bass beat or bass chords. Students will be able to see the woofers vibrating with the bass sounds. Challenge them to explain why the vibrations of the woofers can be seen but the vibrations of the tweeters are almost imperceptible.

QuickLab

MATERIALS

FOR EACH GROUP:
• tuning fork
• rubber eraser
• small plastic cup of water

Safety Caution: Remind students that the tuning forks should not touch their eyes or eyeglasses.

Terms to Learn

wave
medium
outer ear
middle ear
inner ear

What You'll Do

◆ Describe how sound is caused by vibrations.
◆ Explain how sound is transmitted through a medium.
◆ Explain how the human ear works, and identify its parts.

QuickLab

Good Vibrations

1. Gently strike a **tuning fork** on a **rubber eraser.** Watch the prongs, and listen for a sound. Describe what you see and hear.

2. Lightly touch the fork with your fingers. What do you feel?

3. Grasp the prongs of the fork firmly with your hand. What happens to the sound?

4. Strike the tuning fork on the stopper again, and dip the prongs in a **cup of water.** Describe what happens to the water.

5. Record your observations in your ScienceLog.

30

What Is Sound?

Think about all the sounds you hear every day. Indoors, you might hear people talking, the radio blaring, or dishes clattering in the kitchen sink. Outdoors, you might hear birds singing, cars driving by, or a mosquito buzzing in your ear. That's a lot of different sounds! In this section, you'll explore some common characteristics of the different sounds you hear.

Sound Is Produced by Vibrations

As different as they are, all sounds have some things in common. One characteristic of sound is that it is created by vibrations. A *vibration* is the complete back-and-forth motion of an object. **Figure 1** shows an example of how sound is created by vibrations.

Figure 1 Sounds from a Stereo Speaker

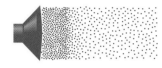

a As the speaker cone moves forward, it pushes the air particles in front of it closer together, creating a region of higher density and pressure called a *compression.*

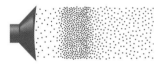

b As the speaker cone moves backward, air particles close to the cone become less crowded, creating a region of lower density and pressure called a *rarefaction.*

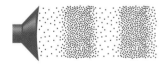

c Every time the cone vibrates, compression and rarefaction are formed. As the compressions and rarefactions travel away from the speaker, sound is transmitted through the air.

Answers to QuickLab

1. Students should hear a faint sound coming from the tuning fork. They may or may not see the prongs of the tuning fork vibrate—this will depend on how hard the fork was struck and on the size of the fork.

2. Students should feel that the prongs are vibrating.

3. After the students grasp the prongs, the sound will immediately stop.

4. The vibrations of the prongs will create waves in the water in the cup.

Sound Travels as Longitudinal Waves A **wave** is a disturbance that transmits energy through matter or space. In a longitudinal wave, particles vibrate back and forth along the path that the wave travels. Longitudinal (LAHN juh TOOD nuhl) waves consist of compressions and rarefactions. Sound is transmitted through the vibrations and collisions of particles of matter, such as air particles. Because the particles vibrate back and forth along the paths that sound travels, sound travels as longitudinal waves.

Sound waves travel in all directions away from their source as illustrated in **Figure 2**. However, air or other matter does not travel with the sound waves. The particles of air only vibrate back and forth in place. If air did travel with sound, wind gusts from music speakers would blow you over at a school dance!

Biology
C O N N E C T I O N

The vibrations that produce your voice are made inside your throat. When you speak, laugh, or sing, your lungs force air up your windpipe, causing your vocal cords to vibrate.

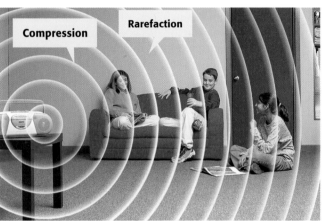

Figure 2 *You can't actually see sound waves, but they can be represented by spheres that spread out in all directions.*

Creating Sound Vs. Detecting Sound

> *Have you heard this riddle before? If a tree falls in the forest and no one is around to hear it, does the tree make a sound?*

Think about this situation for a minute. When a tree falls and hits the ground, the tree and the ground vibrate. These vibrations create compressions and rarefactions in the surrounding air. So, yes, there would be a sound!

Making sound is separate from detecting sound. The fact that no one heard the tree fall doesn't mean that there wasn't a sound. A sound was created—it just wasn't detected.

31

READING STRATEGY

Activity Have students write in their ScienceLog all the different sounds they hear during a typical day. Have students describe which sounds they enjoy and which are unpleasant to the ear and why.

CONNECT TO
LIFE SCIENCE

The vocal cords are located in an organ in the throat called the larynx. Besides producing sound, the larynx controls the flow of air during breathing. The vocal cords are located in the center of the larynx. They are made of thin strips of muscle. They form a V-shaped opening in the airway. Other small muscles stretch and loosen the vocal cords to produce different sounds as air moves across them.

 Teaching Transparency 284 "Sounds from a Stereo Speaker"

 Directed Reading Worksheet Section 1

internet**connect**

SC**LINKS** NSTA

TOPIC: What Is Sound?
GO TO: www.scilinks.org
*sci***LINKS NUMBER:** HSTP505

DISCUSSION

Some science fiction movies are full of scenes of roaring space-craft, drilling on asteroids, or deafening explosions during fictional space battles. Discuss with students why these movies are not scientifically accurate.

GROUP ACTIVITY

Have groups of students search the school and grounds to record a variety of sounds. If possible, use a tape recorder or video camera.

Instruct them to find the following sounds:

- high-pitched sound
- sound from above or overhead
- repeating sound
- sound that would startle
- irritating sound
- sound made by an animal
- sound made by wind
- sound made by something moving

Students should record what the sound is and where it was made. Compare and discuss what different groups found.

Figure 3 *You can still hear traffic sounds when you are in a car because sound waves can travel through the glass windows and metal body of the car.*

Astronomy
CONNECTION

The moon has no atmosphere, so there is no air through which sound can travel. The astronauts who walked on the moon had to use radios to talk to each other even when they were standing side by side. Radio waves could travel between the astronauts because they are electromagnetic waves, which don't require a medium. The radio speakers were inside the astronauts' helmets, which were filled with air for the astronauts to breathe.

Sound Waves Require a Medium

Another characteristic of sound is that all sound waves require a medium. A **medium** is a substance through which a wave can travel. In the example of a falling tree on the previous page, the medium is air. Most of the sounds that you hear travel through air at least part of the time. But sound waves can also travel through other materials, such as water, glass, and metal, as shown in **Figure 3.**

What would happen if a tree fell in a vacuum? No sound would be created because in a vacuum, there are no air particles to vibrate. Sound cannot travel in a vacuum. This helps to explain the effect described in **Figure 4.** Sound must travel through air or some other medium to reach your ears and be detected.

Figure 4 *Tubing is connected to a pump that is removing air from the jar. As the air is removed, the ringing alarm clock gets quieter and quieter.*

How You Detect Sound

Imagine you are watching a suspenseful movie. Just before a door is opened, the background music becomes louder. You know that there is something scary behind that door! Now imagine watching the same scene without the sound. It's hard to figure out what's going on without sound to help you understand what you see. Your ears play an important role in this understanding. On the next page, you will see how your ears convert sound waves into electrical signals, which are then sent to your brain for interpretation.

32

Homework

Because so many young people listen to very loud music through headphones, one of the next major industries may be the manufacturing of hearing aids. Have students research the different kinds of hearing aids available, how they work, and their costs.

 SCIENCE

A cricket hears through its front legs and produces a series of chirps, or trills, by rubbing its two front wings together. And the pistol shrimp makes a sound much like a gunshot by snapping shut its enlarged claw.

How the Human Ear Works

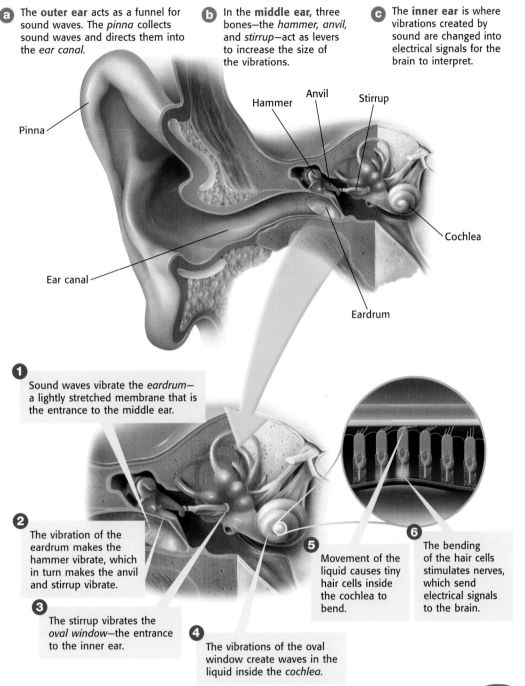

(a) The **outer ear** acts as a funnel for sound waves. The *pinna* collects sound waves and directs them into the *ear canal.*

(b) In the **middle ear,** three bones—the *hammer, anvil,* and *stirrup*—act as levers to increase the size of the vibrations.

(c) The **inner ear** is where vibrations created by sound are changed into electrical signals for the brain to interpret.

Pinna

Hammer

Anvil

Stirrup

Ear canal

Cochlea

Eardrum

1 Sound waves vibrate the *eardrum*—a lightly stretched membrane that is the entrance to the middle ear.

2 The vibration of the eardrum makes the hammer vibrate, which in turn makes the anvil and stirrup vibrate.

3 The stirrup vibrates the *oval window*—the entrance to the inner ear.

4 The vibrations of the oval window create waves in the liquid inside the *cochlea.*

5 Movement of the liquid causes tiny hair cells inside the cochlea to bend.

6 The bending of the hair cells stimulates nerves, which send electrical signals to the brain.

33

Teaching Transparency 285 "How the Human Ear Works"

BRAIN FOOD

The inner ear contains the organs that are responsible for maintaining balance. These organs are located in a hollow region called the vestibule. Therefore, the sense of balance is sometimes referred to as the *vestibular sense.*

GUIDED PRACTICE

Have students read the information with the pictures on this page and ask these questions:

What is the function of the outer ear? (to collect sound waves and direct them into the ear canal) the bones in the middle ear? (The three bones act as levers to increase the size of vibrations.) the inner ear? (to convert vibrations into electrical signals for the brain to interpret)

DISCUSSION

Discuss the following with students to help them realize how remarkable the ear is:

- One part of the ear is not labeled in this diagram: the semicircular canals. The canals are located in the inner ear, but they do not contribute to the hearing process. The canals help you keep your balance by allowing you to determine which way is up.

- The bones in the middle ear, which are the smallest bones in the body, act as levers to increase the amplitude of the vibrations.

MEETING INDIVIDUAL NEEDS

Learners Having Difficulty

Using colored pencils, have students draw and label the parts of the ear. They can trace the diagram in the book or draw it freehand. Have students write short descriptions of how the ear works. Be sure students understand how sound waves are collected, amplified, and converted into electrical signals.

Sheltered English

1. Name the three bones in the ear that act as levers. (hammer, stirrup, anvil)

2. Suppose you had hearing loss or tinnitus. How might it affect your daily life, and what changes would you make? (Accept all reasonable answers.)

3. What is necessary for sound to travel from its source to a listener? (a medium through which the sound waves can travel)

ALTERNATIVE ASSESSMENT

Have students write letters to a fictional boss explaining that they are having a hearing problem at work. They should explain the problem, what it is, and what corrections could be made in the workplace for the benefit of everyone who works there.

internet connect

SCi LINKS
NSTA

TOPIC: The Ear
GO TO: www.scilinks.org
*sci*LINKS NUMBER: HSTP510

Could a dinosaur have played a horn? Check it out on page 58.

Hearing Loss and Deafness The many parts of the ear must work together for you to hear sounds. If any part of the ear is damaged or does not work properly, hearing loss or deafness may result.

One of the most common types of hearing loss is called *tinnitus* (ti NIE tuhs), which results from long-term exposure to loud sounds. Loud sounds can cause damage to the hair cells and nerve endings in the cochlea. Damage to the cochlea or any part of the inner ear usually results in permanent hearing loss.

People who have tinnitus often complain about hearing a ringing in their ears. They also have difficulties understanding other people and hearing the difference between words that sound very similar. Tinnitus can affect people of any age. Fortunately, tinnitus can be prevented. **Figure 5** shows some ways that you can protect yourself from hearing loss.

Figure 5 *Reducing exposure to loud sounds will protect your ears.*

Wearing ear protection while working with machinery blocks out some of the sounds that can injure your ears.

Turning your radio down will prevent hearing loss, especially when you use headphones.

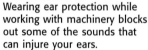

internet connect

SCi LINKS
NSTA

TOPIC: What Is Sound?, The Ear
GO TO: www.scilinks.org
*sci*LINKS NUMBER: HSTP505, HSTP510

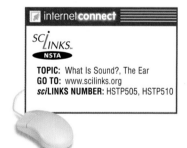

SECTION REVIEW

1. Describe how a bell produces sound.

2. Explain why a person at a rock concert will not feel gusts of wind coming out of the speakers.

3. Name the three main parts of the ear, and briefly explain the function of each part.

4. **Inferring Conclusions** If a meteorite crashed on the moon, would you be able to hear it on Earth? Why or why not?

34

▼ *Answers to Section Review*

1. When a bell swings back and forth, the clapper strikes the side of the bell and causes the bell to vibrate. The vibrations of the bell produce the sound.

2. A person will not feel gusts of wind coming from speakers at a rock concert because air and other matter does not travel with sound waves. The air particles only vibrate back and forth in place.

3. The outer ear directs sound into the middle ear, where the amplitude of the sound is increased. In the inner ear, vibrations created by the sound are changed into electrical signals for the brain to interpret.

4. From Earth, you would not be able to hear a meteor crash on the moon because there is no medium between the moon and Earth through which sound can travel.

Terms to Learn

pitch   Doppler effect
infrasonic   loudness
ultrasonic   decibel

What You'll Do

- Compare the speed of sound in different media.
- Explain how frequency and pitch are related.
- Describe the Doppler effect, and give examples of it.
- Explain how amplitude and loudness are related.

Properties of Sound

Imagine you are swimming in a neighborhood pool. You hear many different sounds as you float on the water. Some are high, like the laughter of small children, and some are low, like the voices of men. Some sounds are loud, like the *BOING* of the diving board, and some are soft, like the sound of water lapping on the sides of the pool. The differences between the sounds—how high or low and how loud or soft they are—depend on the properties of the sound waves. In this section, you will learn about properties of sound.

The Speed of Sound Depends on the Medium

If two people at the other end of the pool shout at you at the same time, will you hear one person's voice before the other? No—the sounds of their voices will reach you at the same time. The time it takes for the sounds to reach you does not depend on who shouted or how loudly the person shouted. The speed of sound depends only on the medium through which the sound is traveling. Assuming that your head is above water, the sounds of the voices traveled through air to your ears and therefore traveled at the same speed.

Speed Changes When the Medium Changes The speed of sound through any medium is constant if the properties of the medium do not change. The chart at left shows the speed of sound in different media. If the properties of a medium change, the speed of sound through that medium will change. On the next page, you will explore how a change in one property—temperature—affects the speed of sound through air.

Speed of Sound in Different Media at 20°C	
Medium	**Speed (m/s)**
Air	343
Helium	1,005
Water	1,482
Sea water	1,522
Wood (oak)	3,850
Glass	4,540
Steel	5,200

35

IS THAT A FACT!

In some western movies, a character would be shown putting an ear to the hard ground to find out if someone was coming. This technique actually works because sound travels faster and with less loss of energy through the ground than through air.

Directed Reading Worksheet Section 2

Focus

Properties of Sound

In this section, students learn about properties of sound, what affects the speed of sound, and how pitch and frequency are related. Students also learn about the Doppler effect and how volume and amplitude are related.

🔔 Bellringer

Ask students the following question:

You are the commander of a space station located about halfway between Earth and the moon. You are in the Command Center, and your chief of security tells you that sensors have just detected an explosion 61.054 km from the station. How long will it be before you hear the sound of the explosion? (You won't hear it. Sound waves will not travel in the vacuum of space.)

1 Motivate

ACTIVITY

MATERIALS
FOR EACH PAIR OF STUDENTS:
• 2 paper cups
• several types of string, 6 m each

Have students punch a hole in the bottom of each cup, insert one end of the string into each cup, and tie a knot in the string. Have one student from each pair talk quietly into the cup while the other listens through the second cup. Have each pair experiment with the types of string, the tension of the strings, and lengths of the strings to see which combination works best.

CONNECT TO
EARTH SCIENCE

Weather has been found to have an influence on the movement of sound waves. Wind and temperature gradients can refract sound waves. Turbulence in the atmosphere scatters sound waves and can change the amplitude of sound waves. Depending on the humidity, temperature, and atmospheric pressure, the atmosphere can even absorb some of the energy of sound waves.

Answers to MATHBREAK

air: 1,715 m; water: 7,410 m, steel: 26,000 m

MATH and MORE

The temperature is 20°C. You are standing next to a railing located in a national park. The railing is 7,700 m long. One-half of the railing is solid oak. The other half of the railing is made of steel. Your friend is at the other end of the railing, and she hits the railing with a hammer. How long will it take for the sound to get to you through the railing? Less than 1 second? Between 1 and 2 seconds? More than 2 seconds? Explain your answer. (between 1 and 2 seconds; Sound travels 3,850 m through oak and 5,200 m through steel in 1 second. Therefore, sound will take between 1 and 2 seconds to travel through the 7,700 m rail.)

How long will it take the sound to reach you through the air? (between 22 and 23 seconds)

MATHBREAK

Speed of Sound

The speed of sound depends on the medium through which sound is traveling and the medium's temperature. Sound travels at 343 m/s through air that has a temperature of 20°C. How far will sound travel in 3 seconds through air at 20°C?

distance = speed × time

distance = $343 \frac{m}{s} \times 3 \, s$

distance = 1,029 m

Now It's Your Turn

How far does sound travel in 5 seconds through air, water, and steel at 20°C? Use the speeds given in the chart on the previous page.

The Speed of Sound Depends on Temperature In 1947, American pilot Chuck Yeager became the first person to travel faster than the speed of sound. But he was flying at a speed of only 293 m/s! If the speed of sound in air is 343 m/s (as shown in the chart on the previous page), how did Yeager fly faster than the speed of sound? The answer has to do with the temperature of the air.

In general, the cooler the medium, the slower the speed of sound. This happens because particles in cool materials move slower than particles in warmer materials. When the particles move slower, they transmit energy more slowly. Therefore, sound travels more slowly in cold air than in hot air.

Chuck Yeager flew at 12,000 m above sea level. At that height the temperature of the air is so low that the speed of sound is only 290 m/s. So when he flew at 293 m/s, he was flying 3 m/s faster than the speed of sound.

Pitch Depends on Frequency

Think about the guitar you made at the beginning of this chapter. You used two rubber bands of different thicknesses as strings. You probably noticed that the thicker rubber band made a lower sound than the thinner rubber band made. How low or high you perceive a sound to be is the **pitch** of that sound.

The pitch of a sound is determined by the frequency of the sound wave, as shown in **Figure 6**. The *frequency* of a wave is the number of waves produced in a given time. Frequency is expressed in *hertz* (Hz), where 1 Hz = 1 wave per second.

Figure 6 *The thicker tuning fork vibrates at a lower frequency. Therefore, it creates a sound with a lower pitch.*

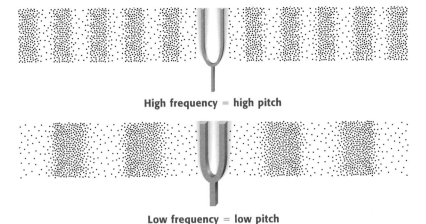

High frequency = high pitch

Low frequency = low pitch

LabBook PG 128
Easy Listening

Teaching Transparency 286
"Pitch Depends on Frequency"
"Frequencies Heard by Different Animals"

Science Bloopers

In 1742, the freezing point of water was set by the Swedish astronomer Anders Celsius (1701–1744) at 100°C and the boiling point was set at 0°C. Carolus Linnaeus (1707–1778) reversed the scale, but a textbook gave Celsius the credit and his name continues to be associated with this temperature scale.

Frequency and Hearing Some people use dog whistles to call their dog. But when you see someone blow a dog whistle, the whistle seems silent to you. That's because the frequency of the sound wave is out of the range of human hearing. But the dog hears a very high pitch from the whistle and comes running! The graph below compares the range of frequencies that humans and animals can hear.

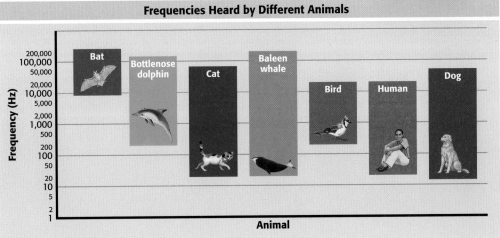

Frequencies Heard by Different Animals

Frequency (Hz) / Animal

Frequencies You Can Hear The average human ear can detect sounds that have frequencies between 20 Hz and 20,000 Hz. Examples of sounds within this range include the lowest sound a pipe organ can make (about 40 Hz) and the screech of a bat (10,000 Hz or higher). The range of hearing varies from person to person. Young children can often hear sounds with frequencies above this range, while many elderly people have difficulty hearing sounds higher than 8,000 Hz.

Frequencies You Can't Hear Sounds that are outside the range of human hearing have special names. Sounds with frequencies that are lower than 20 Hz are described as **infrasonic**. Sounds with frequencies that are higher than 20,000 Hz are described as **ultrasonic**. The sounds are given these names because *sonic* refers to sound, *infra* means "below," and *ultra* means "beyond."

Ultrasonic waves have a variety of applications. For example, ultrasonic waves are used to clean jewelry and to remove ice from metal. Scientists hope to use this technology to remove ice from airplane wings, car windshields, and freezers. You will learn about other uses of ultrasonic waves in the next section.

Biology CONNECTION

Kidney stones—deposits of calcium salts that form inside kidneys—can cause a great deal of pain. Sometimes they are so large that they have to be removed by a doctor. Surgery was once the primary way to remove kidney stones, but now ultrasonic waves can be used to break kidney stones into smaller pieces that can pass out of the body with urine.

37

IS THAT A FACT!

Studies now show that regions of hair cells within the inner ear are actually "tuned" to specific frequencies. Because of their differences in size and shape, hair cells have a specific resonance at which they vibrate. This means that certain frequencies will activate some hair cells but not others.

MEETING INDIVIDUAL NEEDS

Learners Having Difficulty
Have students use colored pencils to draw a diagram showing the Doppler effect. Have them include a listener, a vehicle, and lines depicting sound waves.

DEMONSTRATION

Find a noisemaker that produces a constant sound (a small buzzer or something similar). Attach the noisemaker to the end of a string or rope approximately 70–90 cm long. (It may be necessary to do this demonstration outside.)

Let students hear the noise from the noisemaker. Stand away from the students and away from any walls. Swing the noisemaker by the string in a wide circle over your head. Ask students to explain what they hear in terms of the Doppler effect. (When the noisemaker is coming toward them, they will hear a higher pitch because the sound waves are closer together. When it is moving away from them, they will hear a lower pitch because the sound waves are farther apart.)

CONNECT TO
LIFE SCIENCE

The loudest bird in North America is the whooping crane. Its call can be heard from about 5 km away.

Teaching Transparency 287
"The Doppler Effect"

The Doppler Effect Have you ever been passed by a car with its horn honking? If so, you probably noticed the sudden change in pitch—sort of an *EEEEEEOOooooowwn* sound—as the car sped past you. The pitch you heard was higher while the car was approaching than it was after the car passed. This is a result of the Doppler effect. For sound waves, the **Doppler effect** is the apparent change in the frequency of a sound caused by the motion of either the listener or the source of the sound. **Figure 7** explains the Doppler effect. Keep in mind that the frequency of the car horn does not really change; it only sounds like it does. The driver of the car always hears the same pitch because the driver is moving with the car.

Figure 7 *The Doppler effect occurs when the source of a sound is moving relative to the listener.*

a The car moves toward the sound waves in front of it, causing the waves to be closer together and to have a higher frequency.

b The car moves away from the sound waves behind it, causing the waves to be farther apart and to have a lower frequency.

c A listener in front of the car hears a higher pitch than a listener behind the car.

Loudness Is Related to Amplitude

If you gently tap a bass drum, you will hear a soft rumbling. But if you strike the drum with a large force, you will hear a loud *BOOM!* By changing the force you use to strike the drum, you change the loudness of the sound that is created. **Loudness** is how loud or soft a sound is perceived to be.

Energy and Vibration The harder you strike a drum, the louder the boom. As you strike the drum harder, you transfer more energy to the drum. The drum moves with a larger vibration and transfers more energy to the surrounding air. This increase in energy causes air particles to vibrate farther from their rest positions.

38

CROSS-DISCIPLINARY FOCUS

History The Doppler effect is named after the Austrian mathematician Christian Doppler (1803–1853), who first proposed it in 1842 in a paper describing the colored light of double stars. In 1845, Doppler applied his theory to sound waves and tested it with trumpet players on a train.

In 1929, astronomer Edwin Hubble (1889–1953) used Doppler's theory to interpret his measurements and show that the farther away from Earth a galaxy is, the faster it is moving away from Earth and the more the light from that galaxy is "shifted" toward the red end of the spectrum.

Increasing Amplitude When you strike a drum harder, you are increasing the amplitude of the sound waves being created. The *amplitude* of a wave is the maximum distance the particles in a wave vibrate from their rest positions. The larger the amplitude, the louder the sound, and the smaller the amplitude, the softer the sound. **Figure 8** shows one way to increase the loudness of a sound. Do the QuickLab on this page to investigate the loudness and pitch of sounds.

Figure 8 *An amplifier increases the amplitude of the sound generated by an electric guitar.*

Measuring Loudness The most common unit used to express loudness is the **decibel (dB).** The faintest sounds an average human ear can hear are at a level of 0 dB. The level of 120 dB is sometimes called the threshold of pain because sounds at that level and higher can cause your ears to hurt. Continued exposure to sounds above 85 dB causes gradual hearing loss by permanently damaging the hair cells in your inner ear. The chart below shows the decibel levels of some common sounds.

Some Common Decibel Levels

Sound	Decibel level
The softest sounds you can hear	0
Whisper	20
Purring cat	25
Normal conversation	60
Lawn mower, vacuum cleaner, truck traffic	80
Chain saw, snowmobile	100
Sandblaster, loud rock concert, automobile horn	115
Threshold of pain	120
Jet engine 30 m away	140
Rocket engine 50 m away	200

39

3) Extend

REAL-WORLD CONNECTION

Listening to loud music and attending loud concerts can be harmful to your hearing. Loudness is expressed in *decibels* (dB). Long-term exposure to sounds above 85 dB is considered hazardous to your hearing. Sounds louder than 85 dB take less time to cause hearing damage. Music concerts are often 110 dB or louder, so the potential for hearing damage is very real.

RESEARCH

 Have students select one of the topics they read about in this section (speed of sound, Doppler effect, or loudness) and find ways that the topic is relevant to their everyday lives. They may wish to research supersonic flight, Doppler radar, or hearing damage due to exposure to louds sounds. Students can share their findings in a variety of ways. **Sheltered English**

IS THAT A FACT!

The decibel is one-tenth of a Bel, which is a unit of measurement used to compare two levels of sound intensity. The Bel is named for Alexander Graham Bell (1847–1922), the inventor of the telephone.

 Reinforcement Worksheet
"Doppler Dan's Dump Truck"

internet connect

SCI LINKS
NSTA
TOPIC: Properties of Sound
GO TO: www.scilinks.org
*sci*LINKS NUMBER: HSTP515

Multicultural CONNECTION

An oscilloscope is a device that visually represents sound as an electric wave. The first oscilloscope, a modification of the cathode ray, was invented in 1897 by a German physicist named Karl Ferdinand Braun (1850–1918).

Quiz

1. Name three properties of sound. (The speed of sound depends on the medium; pitch depends on frequency; and loudness depends on amplitude.)

2. Explain how a person can observe the Doppler effect. (When a loud noise is moving toward or away from an observer, the sound appears to change pitch because the sound waves are moving closer together or farther apart.)

3. What is the difference between ultrasonic and infrasonic waves? (Ultrasonic waves are waves above 20,000 Hz, and infrasonic waves are those below 20 Hz.)

ALTERNATIVE ASSESSMENT

Concept Mapping Have students create a concept map showing the properties of sound. Concept maps should include the vocabulary terms from this section and examples illustrating the terms.

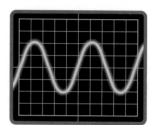

Figure 9 *An oscilloscope can be used to represent sounds.*

Figure 10 **"Seeing" Sounds**

The graph on the right has a **larger amplitude** than the graph on the left. Therefore, the sound represented on the right is **louder** than the one on the left.

The graph on the right has a **lower frequency** than the one on the left. So the sound represented on the right has a **lower pitch** than the one on the left.

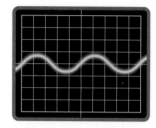

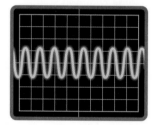

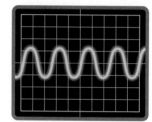

"Seeing" Sounds Because sound waves are invisible, their amplitude and frequency is impossible to measure directly. However, technology can provide a way to "see" sound waves. A device called an *oscilloscope* (uh SIL uh SKOHP), shown in **Figure 9,** is used to graph representations of sound waves.

A microphone first converts the sound wave into an electric current. The oscilloscope then converts the electric current into graphs such as the ones shown in **Figure 10.** Notice that the graphs look like transverse waves instead of longitudinal waves. The highest points (crests) of these waves represent compressions, and the lowest points (troughs) represent rarefactions. By looking at the displays on the oscilloscope, you can quickly see the difference in both amplitude and frequency of sound waves.

internet connect

SCiLINKS.
NSTA

TOPIC: Properties of Sound
GO TO: www.scilinks.org
*sci*LINKS NUMBER: HSTP515

SECTION REVIEW

1. In general, how does changing the temperature of a medium affect the speed of sound through that medium?

2. What properties of waves affect the pitch and loudness of sound?

3. **Inferring Conclusions** Will a listener notice the Doppler effect if he or she and the source of the sound are traveling toward each other? Explain your answer.

▼ **Answers to Section Review**

1. In general, increasing the temperature of a medium will increase the speed of sound through that medium. Likewise, decreasing the temperature will decrease the speed of sound.

2. The frequency of the sound wave affects the pitch of the sound, and the amplitude of the sound wave affects the loudness of the sound.

3. Yes; the sound waves in front of the source will become closer together as the source moves forward. Also, the listener will "meet" the sound waves more rapidly by moving toward the source. The movements of both the source and the listener will make the pitch of the sound higher.

Terms to Learn

reflection   sonic boom
echo   standing wave
echolocation   resonance
interference   diffraction

What You'll Do

- ◆ Explain how echoes are produced, and describe their use in locating objects.
- ◆ Give examples of constructive and destructive interference of sound waves.
- ◆ Identify three sound-wave interactions, and give examples of each.

Interactions of Sound Waves

Beluga whales, such as those shown in **Figure 11,** communicate by using a wide variety of sounds, including clicks, chirps, whistles, trills, screeches, and moos. The sounds they make can be heard above and below water. Because of the wide range of sounds they make, belugas have been nicknamed "sea canaries." But belugas use sound for more than just communication—they also use reflected sound waves to find fish, crabs, and shrimp to eat. In this section you'll learn about reflection and other interactions of sound waves.

Figure 11 *Beluga whales depend on sound interactions for survival.*

Reflection of Sound Waves

Reflection is the bouncing back of a wave after it strikes a barrier. You're probably already familiar with a reflected sound wave, otherwise known as an **echo.** The amount a sound wave will reflect depends on the reflecting surface. Sound waves reflect best off smooth, hard surfaces. That's why a shout in an empty gymnasium can produce an echo, but a shout in an empty auditorium usually does not, as shown in **Figure 12.**

Figure 12
Sound Reflection and Absorption

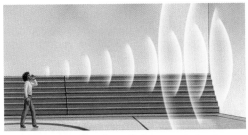

Sound waves easily reflect off the smooth, hard walls of a gymnasium. That's why you hear an echo.

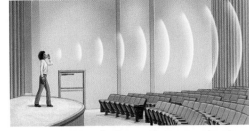

In well-designed auditoriums, echoes are reduced by soft materials that absorb sound waves and by irregular shapes that scatter sound waves.

41

**Directed Reading
Worksheet** Section 3

IS THAT A FACT!

According to Greek mythology, echoes originated when the angry goddess Hera placed a curse on the wood nymph Echo that caused her to repeat whatever was said to her.

Focus

Interactions of Sound Waves

In this section students learn about reflection and echolocation. They also learn about constructive and destructive wave interference, resonance, and diffraction.

🔔 Bellringer

Put these questions on the board:

- On an oscilloscope, does a wave with a larger amplitude (greater crests and troughs) indicate louder sound or higher pitch? (louder sound)
- As frequency increases, does pitch get higher or lower? (higher)
- What is the speed of sound dependent on? (Sample answer: the medium)
- What do you think happens when two sound waves interact with each other? (Answers will vary.)

1) Motivate

DEMONSTRATION

Fill a shallow 9 × 12 in. pan with water. Let it sit until the surface of the water becomes still. Tap a tuning fork, and touch the fork to the surface of the water. Ask students to explain in their ScienceLog why the water moves.

Language Arts The power of sound is so strong that stories have been written about it. In Homer's epic poem *The Odyssey* the war hero Odysseus makes his journey home after the Trojan War. Odysseus and his crew sail near an island where beautiful women sing so sweetly that men are lured to their death. While his men put wax in their ears, Odysseus chooses to be lashed to the mast so that he can hear the beautiful music but not be lured onto the rocks. Have students write a story in which the plot depends on a sound. Students must include science concepts learned in this chapter.

BRAIN FOOD

Can people learn echolocation? Many blind people know how to locate items by clicking their fingers or listening to their own footsteps.

CONNECT TO
EARTH SCIENCE

Use Teaching Transparency 154 to show students how scientists use sound waves to map the ocean floor.

Teaching Transparency 154 "How Sonar Works" LINK TO EARTH SCIENCE

Teaching Transparency 288 "Echolocation"

Echolocation Beluga whales use echoes to find food. The process of using reflected sound waves to find objects is called **echolocation.** Other animals—such as dolphins, bats, and some species of birds—also use echolocation to hunt food and detect objects in their paths. **Figure 13** shows how echolocation works.

Figure 13 *Bats use echolocation to navigate around barriers and to find insects to eat.*

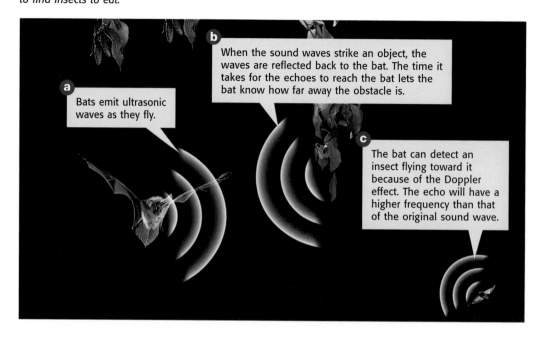

a Bats emit ultrasonic waves as they fly.

b When the sound waves strike an object, the waves are reflected back to the bat. The time it takes for the echoes to reach the bat lets the bat know how far away the obstacle is.

c The bat can detect an insect flying toward it because of the Doppler effect. The echo will have a higher frequency than that of the original sound wave.

Echolocation Technology Humans use echoes to locate objects underwater and underground by using sonar (**so**und **na**viga-tion **a**nd **r**anging). *Sonar* is a type of electronic echolocation. **Figure 14** shows how sonar works. Ultrasonic waves are used because their short wavelengths provide more details about the objects they reflect off. Sonar can also help navigators on ships detect icebergs and can help oceanographers map the ocean floor.

Figure 14 *A depth finder sends ultrasonic waves down into the water. The time it takes for the echo to return helps the fishermen determine the location of the fish.*

IS THAT A FACT!

Dolphins use echolocation by emitting rapid, high-pitched clicks and listening for the returning echo. The closer a dolphin gets to an object, the faster the clicks return. As a dolphin moves its head side to side to scan, it detects both distance and shape. Dolphins can detect an object that is 2 cm in diameter more than 70 m away in open water.

Insightful Technology

Many people who are blind use a cane to help them detect obstacles while they are walking. Now engineers have developed a sonar cane, shown at right, to help blind people even more. The cane emits and detects sound waves. Based on your knowledge of echolocation, explain how you think this cane works.

Ultrasonography Another type of electronic echolocation is used in a medical procedure called *ultrasonography*. Ultrasonography uses echoes to "see" inside a patient's body without performing surgery. A device called a transducer produces ultrasonic waves, which reflect off the patient's internal organs. These echoes are then converted into images that can be seen on a television monitor, as shown in **Figure 15**. Ultrasonography is used to examine kidneys, gallbladders, and other abdominal organs and to check the development of an unborn baby in a mother's body. Ultrasonic waves are safer than X rays because sound waves are less harmful to human tissue.

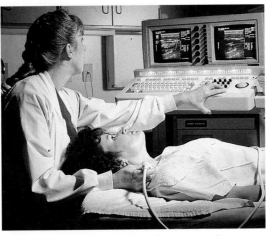

Figure 15 *Images created by ultrasonography are fuzzy, but they are a safe way to see inside a patient's body.*

SECTION REVIEW

1. Describe a place in which you would expect to hear echoes.
2. How do bats use echoes to find insects to eat?
3. **Comparing Concepts** Explain how sonar and ultrasonography are similar when used to locate objects.

43

REAL-WORLD CONNECTION

As mentioned on page 37, patients who have kidney stones can have them removed painlessly with an ultrasonic procedure called lithotripsy. Kidneys are not the only part of the body where ultrasound is used for diagnosis or treatment. Ultrasonography is used to examine the liver, spleen, pancreas, stomach, esophagus, large intestine, small intestine, colon, heart, cranial arteries, and eyes. Dentists use ultrasonic devices to remove plaque from the patients' teeth. Veterinarians can also use ultrasound to examine and treat their animal patients.

Answer to APPLY

The sonar cane is an application of electronic echolocation. Like a bat, the cane sends out sound waves. When the cane detects an echo, it calculates how far away the obstacle is. It then gives warning to its visually impaired user if the user is in danger of running into something.

MEETING INDIVIDUAL NEEDS

Advanced Learners Explain to students that highway departments often construct irregularly shaped concrete walls that divide residential areas from major roads. This is to ensure that traffic sounds coming from the roads are minimized in the residential areas. Have students explain how such walls could reduce sound, and have them design or draw other barriers that would accomplish the same thing.

▼ Answers to Section Review

1. Accept all reasonable answers. Students should name places that have hard, smooth surfaces (the school gym, a mountain valley, an open space near a building, a large school courtyard, and so on).

2. A bat sends out a sound and listens for the echo. The time it takes the echo to return tells the bat how far away the object is. A bat can tell if an object is a moving insect because of the Doppler effect. The echo from the moving insect tells the bat in which direction the insect is moving.

3. Both ultrasonography and sonar use sound waves and echoes. The time it takes for the echo to return is used to determine the distance to an object.

Advanced Learners Destructive interference can make it hard to hear in some parts of a theater or auditorium. To reduce the effects of destructive interference, sounds are usually amplified electronically and speakers are located in different places. But sound waves from the many speakers can also produce destructive interference. Also, sound waves reflected from the walls and other surfaces can interfere with waves from the speakers. Have students find out how theaters, concert halls, and recording studios are designed and built to reduce destructive interference. Encourage them to use models or posters to show their results.

CROSS-DISCIPLINARY FOCUS

Music In 1962, New York City's Avery Fisher Hall opened, but there were problems with the hall's acoustics. There were too many echoes and dead spots caused by sound waves interfering with one another. In 1976, the hall's interior was removed and was replaced with an interior that produced better acoustics.

REAL-WORLD CONNECTION

Some livestock ranchers use machines that are similar to medical ultrasound devices to measure the fat layers in their cattle and pigs. These devices use frequencies of sound that are far above the range of human hearing to determine the amount of body fat in the animals.

Interference of Sound Waves

Another interaction of sound waves is interference. **Interference** is the result of two or more waves overlapping. **Figure 16** shows how two sound waves can combine by both constructive and destructive interference.

Figure 16 *Sound waves from two speakers producing sound of the same frequency combine by both constructive and destructive interference.*

Constructive Interference
As the compressions of one wave overlap the compressions of another wave, the sound will be louder because the amplitude is increased.

Destructive Interference
As the compressions of one wave overlap the rarefactions of another wave, the sound will be softer because the amplitude is decreased.

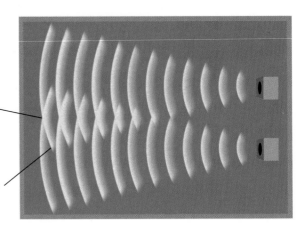

Orchestras and bands take advantage of constructive interference when several instruments play the same notes. The sound waves from the instruments combine by constructive interference to produce a louder sound. But destructive interference may keep you from hearing the concert. "Dead spots" are areas in an auditorium where sound waves reflecting off the walls interfere destructively with the sound waves from the stage. If you are at a concert and you can't hear the orchestra very well, try changing seats before you decide to get your ears checked!

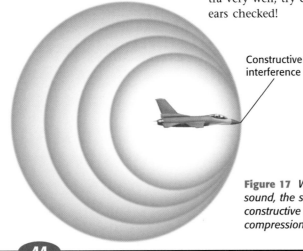

Constructive interference

The Sound Barrier As the source of a sound—such as a jet plane—accelerates to the speed of sound, the sound waves in front of the jet plane compress closer and closer together. **Figure 17** shows what happens as a jet plane reaches the speed of sound.

Figure 17 *When a jet plane reaches the speed of sound, the sound waves in front of the jet combine by constructive interference. The result is a high-density compression that is called the sound barrier.*

44

IS THAT A FACT!

Mach number is not a speed. It is the ratio between the speed of an object, usually an airplane, and the speed of sound in the medium in which the object is traveling. A plane traveling at Mach 3.0 is traveling at three times whatever the speed of sound is at the plane's altitude.

WEIRD SCIENCE

The speed of sound is about 343 m/s at sea level at 20°C and is known as Mach 1. As a plane passes through the sound barrier created at this speed, the resulting shock wave increases the drag on the plane. The plane has to be equipped to control this change in airflow.

Shock Waves and Sonic Booms For the jet in Figure 17 to travel faster than the speed of sound, it must overcome the pressure of the compressed sound waves. **Figure 18** shows what happens as soon as the jet achieves supersonic speeds—speeds faster than the speed of sound. At these speeds, the sound waves trail off behind the jet and combine at their outer edges to form a shock wave.

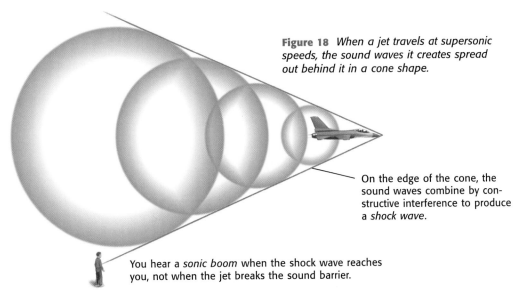

Figure 18 *When a jet travels at supersonic speeds, the sound waves it creates spread out behind it in a cone shape.*

On the edge of the cone, the sound waves combine by constructive interference to produce a *shock wave*.

You hear a *sonic boom* when the shock wave reaches you, not when the jet breaks the sound barrier.

A **sonic boom** is the explosive sound heard when a shock wave reaches your ears. Sonic booms can be so loud that they can hurt your ears and break windows. They can even make the ground shake as it does during an earthquake.

Self-Check

Explain why two people will not hear a sonic boom at the same time if they are standing a block or two apart. *(See page 152 to check your answer.)*

Standing Waves When you play a guitar, you can make some pleasing sounds and maybe even play a tune. But have you ever watched a guitar string after you've plucked it? You may have noticed that the string vibrates as a standing wave. A **standing wave** is a result of interference in which portions of the wave are at the rest position and other portions have a large amplitude.

The cracking sound made by a whip is actually a miniature sonic boom caused by the shock wave formed as the tip of the whip travels faster than the speed of sound!

45

REAL-WORLD CONNECTION

The sound transmission class (STC) rating tells how well building materials insulate sound. The higher the number, the more the material blocks sound.

STC #	What can be heard
25	Normal speech can be heard.
30	Loud speech can be heard.
35	Loud speech is audible but not intelligible.
42	Loud speech is audible as a murmur.
45	A person must strain to hear loud speech.
48	Some loud speech is barely audible.
50	Loud speech is inaudible.

Have students research what sort of building materials have the STC ratings given above. Then, have students design a house and use this rating system to determine what building materials to use. Ask them to explain why they put the materials where they did.

Answer to Self-Check

A person hears a sonic boom when a shock wave reaches his or her ears. If two people are standing a block or two apart, the shock wave will reach them at different times, so they will hear a sonic boom at different times.

IS THAT A FACT!

A double sonic boom occurs when the space shuttle enters the atmosphere. Whenever a craft exceeds Mach 1, one shock wave is formed at the nose and another shock wave is formed at the tail. If the shock waves are more than 0.10 s apart, you hear two sonic booms.

3) Extend

RESEARCH

For more than a century, people have been recording and playing sound. Have students research the history and development of sound recording, including the latest stereo systems used in theaters. Encourage them to find creative ways, such as recordings, to present their findings.

MEETING INDIVIDUAL NEEDS

Advanced Learners Have students research active noise control (ANC), which reduces or eliminates low-frequency sounds through destructive interference. The system broadcasts sound waves through speakers that are 180° out of phase with the noise. Encourage students to create models or posters to demonstrate their findings.

When overtones are exact multiples of the fundamental, they are often called "harmonics." However, confusion sometimes results because harmonics are numbered to include the fundamental, but overtones are not. As a result, the first overtone is the second harmonic, the second overtone is the third harmonic, and so on.

Tuneful Tube

TOPIC: Interactions of Sound Waves
GO TO: www.scilinks.org
sciLINKS NUMBER: HSTP520

Resonant Frequencies Although you can see only one standing wave, the guitar string actually creates several standing waves of different frequencies at the same time. The frequencies at which standing waves are made are called *resonant frequencies*. Resonant frequencies are sometimes called by special names, as shown in **Figure 19.**

Figure 19 *A plucked string vibrates at several resonant frequencies.*

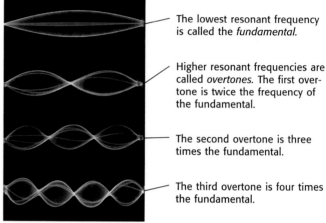

The lowest resonant frequency is called the *fundamental.*

Higher resonant frequencies are called *overtones.* The first overtone is twice the frequency of the fundamental.

The second overtone is three times the fundamental.

The third overtone is four times the fundamental.

A tuning fork and a plastic tube make beautiful music together on page 131 of the LabBook.

Resonance Would you believe that you can make a guitar string make a sound without touching it? You can do this if you have a tuning fork, shown in **Figure 20,** that vibrates at one of the resonant frequencies of the guitar string. Strike the tuning fork, and hold it close to the string. The string will start to vibrate and produce a sound. The effect is the greatest when the resonant frequency of the tuning fork matches the fundamental frequency of the string.

Using the vibrations of the tuning fork to make the string vibrate is an example of resonance. **Resonance** occurs when an object vibrating at or near a resonant frequency of a second object causes the second object to vibrate.

Figure 20 *When struck, a tuning fork can make certain objects vibrate.*

46

Diffraction of Sound Waves

Have you ever noticed the different sounds of thunder? From a distance, thunder sounds like a low rumbling. From nearby, thunder sounds like a loud *CRACK*! A type of wave interaction called diffraction causes this difference. **Diffraction** is the bending of waves around barriers or through openings. It is how sound waves travel around the corners of buildings and through doorways. The amount of diffraction is greatest when the size of the barrier or the opening is the same size or smaller than the wavelength of the sound waves, as shown in **Figure 21**.

Figure 21   Determining the Amount of Diffraction

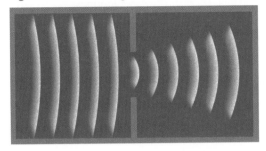 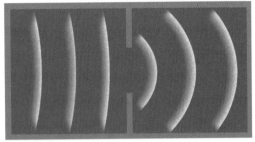

High-frequency sound waves have short wavelengths and do not diffract very much when they travel through a doorway. Therefore, high pitches can be hard to hear when you are in the next room.

Low-frequency sound waves have longer wavelengths, so they diffract more through doorways. Therefore, you can hear lower pitches better when you are in the next room.

So what about thunder? Thunder consists of both high- and low-frequency sound waves. When lightning strikes nearby, you hear all the sound waves together as a loud cracking noise. But when the lightning strikes far away, buildings, trees, hills, and other barriers stop most of the high-frequency waves. Only the low-frequency waves can diffract around these large objects, and thus you hear only a low rumbling.

SECTION REVIEW

1. How is a sound barrier formed?

2. When you are in a classroom, why can you hear voices from the hallway even when you cannot see who is talking?

3. **Inferring Conclusions**   Your friend is playing a song on a piano. Whenever your friend hits a certain key, the lamp on top of the piano rattles. Explain why this happens.

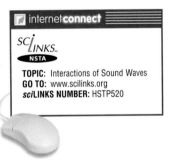

internet connect

SCI LINKS
NSTA

TOPIC: Interactions of Sound Waves
GO TO: www.scilinks.org
sciLINKS NUMBER: HSTP520

47

LabBook   **PG 130**
The Speed of Sound

Focus

Sound Quality

This section defines *sound quality* and explains how the three main musical-instrument families (wind, percussion, and string) produce sound. Students learn the difference between music and noise.

Bellringer

Ask the following questions:

- Which strings on a piano have lower pitch? (the longer and thicker strings)

- Why does a tuba have a lower pitch than a trumpet? (Sample answer: A tuba has a longer and larger air column.)

- Why are some sounds pleasing to hear and some sounds not? Explain your answer. (Accept all reasonable answers.)

1 Motivate

DEMONSTRATION

This should be a brief demonstration just to show students the variety of ways that musical instruments can make sounds. Ask two or three different volunteers who play musical instruments to demonstrate them for the class. Without discussing the different families of instruments, have students compare the sound quality of instruments within a family and from different families. Tell the band or orchestra members that they will have a chance to perform later in the lesson. A more extensive demonstration is found on page 49.

 Directed Reading Worksheet Section 4

Terms to Learn

sound quality
noise

What You'll Do

◆ Define sound quality.
◆ Describe how each family of musical instruments produces sound.
◆ Explain how noise is different from music.

Sound Quality

Have you ever been told that some music you really like is just a lot of noise? If you have, you know that people sometimes disagree about the difference between noise and music. You probably think of noise as sounds you don't like and think of music as sounds that are interesting and pleasant to hear. But there is actually a difference between music and noise, and the difference has to do with sound quality.

What Is Sound Quality?

If the same note is played with the same loudness on a piano and on a violin, could you tell the instruments apart without looking? Although the notes played are identical, you probably could tell them apart because the sounds the instruments produce are not the same. The notes sound different because each instrument actually produces several different pitches: the fundamental and several overtones. These pitches are modeled in **Figure 22**. The result of several pitches blending together through interference is **sound quality**. Each instrument has a unique sound quality. **Figure 23** shows how the sound quality differs when two instruments play the same note.

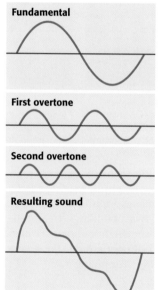

Fundamental

First overtone

Second overtone

Resulting sound

Figure 22 The top three diagrams represent three different pitches played at the same time. The bottom diagram shows the result when the pitches blend through interference.

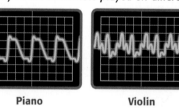

Figure 23 An oscilloscope shows the difference in sound quality of the same note played on different instruments.

Piano   **Violin**

48

IS THAT A FACT!

Many cultures write and play music on a basic eight-tone scale, although the notes or tones may vary greatly from scale to scale. Other cultures use a five-tone, or *pentatonic,* scale. Whichever scale is used, each note has a characteristic frequency and the notes span a frequency range called an octave.

Sound Quality of Instruments

When you listen to an orchestra play you can hear many different kinds of instruments. The difference in sound quality among the instruments comes from the structural differences of the instruments. All instruments produce sound with vibrations. But the part of the instrument that vibrates and how the vibrations are made vary from instrument to instrument. Even so, all instruments fall within three main families: string instruments, wind instruments, and percussion instruments.

String Instruments Violins, guitars, and banjos are examples of string instruments. They produce sound when their strings vibrate after being plucked or bowed. **Figure 24** shows how two different string instruments produce sounds.

✓ **Self-Check**

Which wave interaction is most important in determining sound quality? *(See page 152 to check your answer.)*

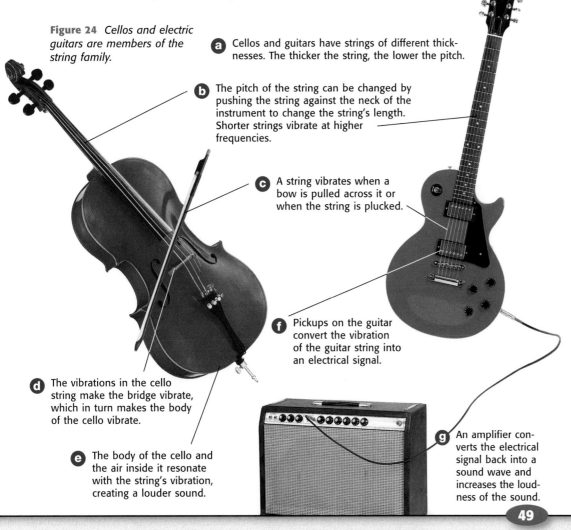

Figure 24 *Cellos and electric guitars are members of the string family.*

a Cellos and guitars have strings of different thicknesses. The thicker the string, the lower the pitch.

b The pitch of the string can be changed by pushing the string against the neck of the instrument to change the string's length. Shorter strings vibrate at higher frequencies.

c A string vibrates when a bow is pulled across it or when the string is plucked.

f Pickups on the guitar convert the vibration of the guitar string into an electrical signal.

d The vibrations in the cello string make the bridge vibrate, which in turn makes the body of the cello vibrate.

e The body of the cello and the air inside it resonate with the string's vibration, creating a louder sound.

g An amplifier converts the electrical signal back into a sound wave and increases the loudness of the sound.

49

2 Teach

READING 📖 STRATEGY

Prediction Guide Before reading these two pages, ask students to name the three major families of musical instruments and to give as many examples of each family as they can.

DEMONSTRATION

Some of your students may be in the school orchestra or band. Ask them to bring in their musical instruments. Let them explain and demonstrate how their instrument works. Have students identify which family of instruments theirs is from and the range of frequency and pitch their instrument can make. Then let the band or orchestra members play for the class!

Homework

Have students write in their ScienceLog about a sound or some music that is important to them. The sound or music may have changed their perspective about something, or maybe it changed their attitude or mood. Maybe it is just a favorite song. Ask them to explain why they think music can produce a change in a person's mood.

Answer to Self-Check

Interference is the most important wave interaction for determining sound quality.

IS THAT A FACT!

The pickup on an electric guitar is a set of magnets wrapped by thousands of turns of wire. The vibrations of the guitar strings create disturbances in the magnetic fields. These disturbances produce electrical impulses in the coils of wire, and these impulses are transmitted to an amplifier, where they are converted into sounds.

ACTIVITY

Making Models Have pairs of students design and make a model of a simple musical instrument. They may use rubber bands, boxes, cans, yarn, paper, scissors, tacks, and wire. Have them present their instrument and explain the type of instrument they have made and the portion that produces the sound.

DEBATE

Noise Pollution at Airports: Who Has the Right? Should people in a neighborhood have a say in whether airplanes can fly over their homes? Should taxpayers pay to have an airport moved to a less populated location? Students can check the regulations at their local airport to find out what the restrictions are. Have students research and debate advantages to adding runways to crowded airports versus maintaining quiet neighborhoods.

internetconnect

SCiLINKS   **TOPIC:** Sound Quality
NSTA   **GO TO:** www.scilinks.org
           *sci*LINKS NUMBER: HSTP525

Wind Instruments A wind instrument produces sound when a vibration is created at one end of its air column. The vibration creates standing waves in the air column. Wind instruments are sometimes divided into two groups—woodwinds and brass. Examples of woodwinds are saxophones, oboes, and recorders. Brass instruments include French horns, trombones, and tubas. A woodwind instrument and a brass instrument are shown in **Figure 25.**

Figure 25 *Clarinets are woodwind instruments, and trumpets are brass instruments.*

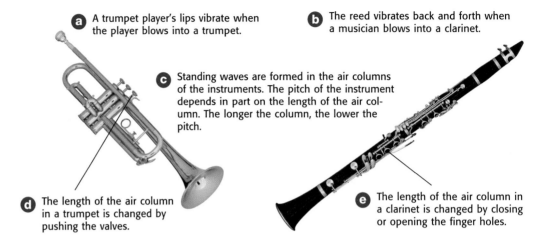

a A trumpet player's lips vibrate when the player blows into a trumpet.

b The reed vibrates back and forth when a musician blows into a clarinet.

c Standing waves are formed in the air columns of the instruments. The pitch of the instrument depends in part on the length of the air column. The longer the column, the lower the pitch.

d The length of the air column in a trumpet is changed by pushing the valves.

e The length of the air column in a clarinet is changed by closing or opening the finger holes.

Percussion Instruments Drums, bells, and cymbals are examples of percussion instruments. They produce sound when struck. Different-sized instruments are used to get different pitches. Usually, the larger the instrument, the lower the pitch. **Figure 26** shows examples of percussion instruments.

Figure 26 *Drums and cymbals in a trap set are examples of percussion instruments.*

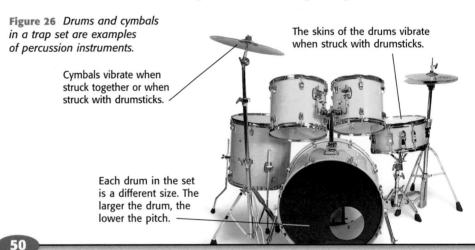

The skins of the drums vibrate when struck with drumsticks.

Cymbals vibrate when struck together or when struck with drumsticks.

Each drum in the set is a different size. The larger the drum, the lower the pitch.

50

🌐 Multicultural CONNECTION

Drums, the most common percussion instruments, have been around since at least 6000 B.C. Drums are found in almost every culture and have been used for a number of purposes, including music. In some African cultures, drums were used to transmit messages over many miles. In Europe, infantry regiments once used snare drums to transmit coded orders to soldiers.

Music or Noise?

Most of the sounds we hear are noises. The sound of a truck roaring down the highway, the slamming of a door, and the jingle of keys falling to the floor are all noises. **Noise** can be described as any undesired sound, especially a nonmusical sound, that includes a random mix of pitches. **Figure 27** shows the difference between a musical sound and noise on an oscilloscope.

Figure 27 *A note from a French horn produces a sound wave with a repeating pattern, but noise from a clap produces complex sound waves with no pattern.*

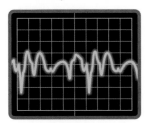
French horn

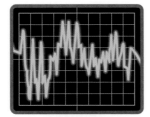
A sharp clap

Noise Pollution The amount of noise around you can become so great that it is not only bothersome but can cause health problems. When noise reaches a level that causes pain or damages the body, it is considered *noise pollution*.

Noise pollution can damage the inner ear, causing permanent hearing loss. Noise pollution can also contribute to sleeplessness, high blood pressure, and stress. Because of these health concerns, the federal government has set noise exposure limits for people who work in areas with loud noises. Noise pollution also makes the environment less livable for humans as well as wildlife.

SECTION REVIEW

1. What is the role of interference in determining sound quality?

2. Name the three families of musical instruments, and describe how vibrations are created in each family.

3. **Interpreting Graphics** Look at the oscilloscope screen at right. Do you think the sound represented by the wave on the screen was noise or music? Explain your answer.

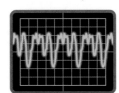

Environment CONNECTION

The Los Angeles International Airport was built next to the main habitat of an endangered butterfly species called the El Segundo blue. The noise pollution from the airport has driven people and other animals from the area, but the butterflies are not affected because they have no ears!

internet**connect**

SCI LINKS
NSTA

TOPIC: Sound Quality
GO TO: www.scilinks.org
*sci*LINKS NUMBER: HSTP525

51

Skill Builder Lab

The Energy of Sound
Teacher's Notes

Time Required

One or two 45-minute class periods

Lab Ratings

EASY ——————▶ HARD

TEACHER PREP ♦♦
STUDENT SET-UP ♦
CONCEPT LEVEL ♦♦♦♦
CLEAN UP ♦

Safety Caution

Make sure students are at a safe distance before you perform the Part D exercise. You might wish to take the class outside.

Answers

2. The water begins to move. Vibrations from the tuning fork caused the water's movement.

6. The vibrating tuning fork causes the air to vibrate at a certain frequency. The energy of the vibrations is transferred through the air to the second tuning fork, which starts to resonate (vibrate at the same frequency).

7. Hitting the first tuning fork harder causes a larger amount of energy to be transferred from the tuning fork to the air. However, the vibration of the air particles is not at the same frequency as the second tuning fork and will therefore not cause the second tuning fork to make a sound.

The Energy of Sound

In this chapter, you learned about properties and interactions of sound. In this lab, you will perform several activities that will show that the properties and interactions of sound all depend on one thing—the energy carried by sound waves.

MATERIALS

• 2 tuning forks of the same frequency and 1 of a different frequency
• pink rubber eraser
• small plastic cup filled with water
• rubber band
• piece of string, 50 cm long

Part A: Sound Vibrations
Procedure

1 Lightly strike a tuning fork with the eraser. Slowly place the prongs of the tuning fork in the plastic cup of water. Record your observations in your ScienceLog.

Analysis

2 How do your observations show that sound waves are carried through vibrations?

Part B: Resonance
Procedure

3 Strike a tuning fork with the eraser. Quickly pick up a second tuning fork in your other hand, and hold it about 30 cm from the first tuning fork.

4 Place the first tuning fork against your leg to stop its vibration. Listen closely to the second tuning fork. Record your observations, as well as the frequencies of the two tuning forks.

5 Repeat steps 3 and 4, using the remaining tuning fork as the second tuning fork.

Analysis

6 Explain why you can hear a sound from the second tuning fork when the frequencies of the tuning forks used are the same.

52

Datasheets for LabBook

CLASSROOM
TESTED & APPROVED

Kevin McCurdy
Elmwood Junior High
Rogers, Arkansas

7. When using tuning forks of different frequencies, predict whether you would hear a sound from the second tuning fork if you strike the first tuning fork harder. Explain your reasoning.

Part C: Interference

Procedure

8. Using the two tuning forks with the same frequency, place a rubber band tightly over the prongs near the base of one tuning fork. Strike both tuning forks at the same time against the eraser. Hold a tuning fork 3 to 5 cm from each ear. If you cannot hear any differences, move the rubber band farther down on the prongs. Strike again. Record your observations in your ScienceLog.

Analysis

9. Did you notice the sound changing back and forth between loud and soft? A steady pattern like this is called a beat frequency. Infer how this changing pattern of loudness and softness is related to interference (both constructive and destructive).

Part D: The Doppler Effect

Procedure

10. Your teacher will tie the piece of string securely to the base of one tuning fork. Your teacher will then strike the tuning fork and will carefully swing the tuning fork in a circle overhead. Record your observations in your ScienceLog.

Analysis

11. Did the tuning fork make a different sound when your teacher was swinging it than when he or she was holding it? If yes, explain why.

12. Is the actual frequency of the tuning fork changing? Explain.

Draw Conclusions, Parts A–D

13. Explain how your observations from each part of this lab show that sound waves carry energy from one point to another through a vibrating medium.

Going Further
Particularly loud thunder can cause the windows of your room to rattle. How is this evidence that sound waves carry energy?

Going Further

It takes energy to move the windows to cause them to rattle. Therefore, energy from the thunder's sound waves must be transferred through the air to the windows.

Answers

9. The loudness corresponds to constructive interference (when the crests of the sound waves overlap, increasing the amplitude), and the softness corresponds to destructive interference (when the crests and troughs of sound waves overlap, decreasing the amplitude).

11. Yes. As the tuning fork swings toward the listeners, the pitch is higher because the sound waves in front of it are closer together and therefore have a higher frequency. As the tuning fork swings away from the listeners, the pitch is lower because the sound waves are farther apart and therefore have a lower frequency.

12. No. The pitch you hear changes because of the Doppler effect, but the actual frequency of the tuning fork does not change.

13. Part A shows that the vibrations of the tuning fork have energy that does work on the water. Part B shows that the energy from one vibrating tuning fork can be passed by vibrations through the air to cause another tuning fork to vibrate. Part C shows that the energy from each vibrating tuning fork can travel through the air as waves that can interfere with each other. Part D shows that the vibrations from a tuning fork travel through the air to your ears, and the amount of energy being carried by the vibration determines what is heard (higher pitch = higher frequency = higher energy).

53

Chapter Highlights

Chapter Highlights

VOCABULARY DEFINITIONS

SECTION 1

wave a disturbance that transmits energy through matter or space

medium a substance through which a wave can travel

outer ear the part of the ear that acts as a funnel to direct sound waves into the middle ear

middle ear the part of the ear where the amplitude of sound vibrations is increased

inner ear the part of the ear where vibrations created by sound are changed into electrical signals for the brain to interpret

SECTION 2

pitch how high or low a sound is perceived to be

infrasonic the term describing sounds with frequencies lower than 20 Hz

ultrasonic the term describing sounds with frequencies higher than 20,000 Hz

Doppler effect the apparent change in the frequency of a sound caused by the motion of either the listener or the source of the sound (refers to sound only)

loudness how loud or soft a sound is perceived to be

decibel the most common unit used to express loudness

SECTION 1

Vocabulary
- **wave** *(p. 31)*
- **medium** *(p. 32)*
- **outer ear** *(p. 33)*
- **middle ear** *(p. 33)*
- **inner ear** *(p. 33)*

Section Notes
- All sounds are created by vibrations and travel as longitudinal waves.
- Sound waves require a medium through which to travel.
- Sound waves travel in all directions away from their source.
- The sounds you hear are converted into electrical impulses by your ears and then sent to your brain for interpretation.
- Exposure to loud sounds can cause hearing loss and tinnitus.

SECTION 2

Vocabulary
- **pitch** *(p. 36)*
- **infrasonic** *(p. 37)*
- **ultrasonic** *(p. 37)*
- **Doppler effect** *(p. 38)*
- **loudness** *(p. 38)*
- **decibel** *(p. 39)*

Section Notes
- The speed of sound depends on the medium through which the sound is traveling. Changes in temperature of the medium can affect the speed of sound.
- The pitch of a sound depends on frequency. High-frequency sounds are high-pitched, and low-frequency sounds are low-pitched.
- Humans can hear sounds with frequencies between 20 Hz and 20,000 Hz.

- The Doppler effect is the apparent change in frequency of a sound caused by the motion of either the listener or the source of the sound.
- The loudness of a sound increases as the amplitude increases. Loudness is expressed in decibels.
- An oscilloscope can be used to "see" sounds.

Labs
Easy Listening *(p. 128)*

☑ Skills Check

Math Concepts

THE SPEED OF SOUND The speed of sound depends on the medium through which the sound waves are traveling. The speed of sound through wood at 20°C is 3,850 m/s. The distance sound will travel through wood in 5 seconds can be calculated as follows:

$$\text{distance} = \text{speed} \times \text{time}$$
$$= 3{,}850 \; \tfrac{m}{\cancel{s}} \times 5 \; \cancel{s}$$
$$= 19{,}250 \text{ m}$$

Visual Understanding

HOW THE HUMAN EAR WORKS The human ear has several parts that are divided into three regions—the outer ear, the middle ear, and the inner ear. Study the diagram on page 33 to review how the ear works.

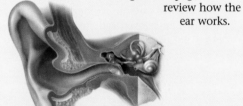

Lab and Activity Highlights

The Energy of Sound **PG 52**

Easy Listening **PG 128**

The Speed of Sound **PG 130**

Tuneful Tube **PG 131**

Data Sheets for LabBook
(blackline masters for these labs)

VOCABULARY DEFINITIONS, *continued*

SECTION 3

SECTION 3

Vocabulary

reflection *(p. 41)*

echo *(p. 41)*

echolocation *(p. 42)*

interference *(p. 44)*

sonic boom *(p. 45)*

standing wave *(p. 45)*

resonance *(p. 46)*

diffraction *(p. 47)*

Section Notes

- Echoes are reflected sound waves.

- Some animals use echolocation to find food or navigate around objects. Sonar and ultrasonography are types of echolocation.

- Sound barriers and shock waves are created by interference. You hear a sonic boom when a shock wave reaches your ears.

- Standing waves form at an object's resonant frequencies.

- Resonance occurs when a vibrating object causes a second object to vibrate at one of its resonant frequencies.

- The bending of sound waves around barriers or through openings is called diffraction. The amount of diffraction depends on the wavelength of the waves as well as the size of the opening.

Labs

The Speed of Sound *(p. 130)*

Tuneful Tube *(p. 131)*

SECTION 4

Vocabulary

sound quality *(p. 48)*

noise *(p. 51)*

Section Notes

- Different instruments have different sound qualities.

- The three families of instruments are strings, winds, and percussion.

- The sound quality of noise is not pleasing because it is a random mix of frequencies.

SECTION 3

reflection the bouncing back of a wave after it strikes a barrier or an object

echo a reflected sound wave

echolocation the process of using reflected sound waves to find objects

interference a wave interaction that occurs when two or more waves overlap and combine

sonic boom the explosive sound heard when a shock wave from an object traveling faster than the speed of sound reaches a person's ears

standing wave a wave that forms a pattern in which portions of the wave do not move and other portions move with a large amplitude

resonance what occurs when an object vibrating at or near a resonant frequency of a second object causes the second object to vibrate

diffraction the bending of waves around barriers or through openings

SECTION 4

sound quality the result of several pitches blending together through interference

noise any undesired sound, especially a nonmusical sound, that includes a random mix of pitches

 internet **connect**

GO TO: go.hrw.com

Visit the **HRW** Web site for a variety of learning tools related to this chapter. Just type in the keyword:

KEYWORD: HSTSND

 SC**i**LINKS**SM**
N S T A

GO TO: www.scilinks.org

Visit the **National Science Teachers Association** on-line Web site for Internet resources related to this chapter. Just type in the *sci*LINKS number for more information about the topic:

TOPIC: What Is Sound?   *sci*LINKS NUMBER: HSTP505
TOPIC: The Ear   *sci*LINKS NUMBER: HSTP510
TOPIC: Properties of Sound   *sci*LINKS NUMBER: HSTP515
TOPIC: Interactions of Sound Waves   *sci*LINKS NUMBER: HSTP520
TOPIC: Sound Quality   *sci*LINKS NUMBER: HSTP525

55

 Vocabulary Review Worksheet

 Blackline masters of these Chapter Highlights can be found in the **Study Guide.**

Lab and Activity Highlights

LabBank

 EcoLabs & Field Activities, An Earful of Sounds

Whiz-Bang Demonstrations,
- A Hot Tone
- Jingle Bells, Silent Bells
- Hear Ye, Hear Ye
- The Sounds of Time

 Long-Term Projects & Research Ideas, The Caped Ace Flies Again

Interactive Explorations CD-ROM

 CD 3, Exploration 6, "Sound Bite!"

USING VOCABULARY

1. ultrasonic
2. inner ear
3. loudness
4. echoes
5. sound quality

UNDERSTANDING CONCEPTS

Multiple Choice

6. a
7. a
8. c
9. c
10. c
11. d
12. d
13. a

Short Answer

14. If a fish is moving away from the whale, the echo off the fish that the whale hears will have a lower pitch than the original sound. If the fish is moving toward the whale, the echo off the fish heard by the whale will have a higher pitch than the original sound.

15. When a jet is traveling at super-sonic speeds, the sound waves trail behind it in a cone shape. On the edge of the cone, the sound waves combine by constructive interference and form a shock wave.

16. The outer ear acts like a funnel and directs sound waves into the middle ear. In the middle ear, the hammer, the anvil, and the stirrup work as levers to increase the amplitude of the vibrations. In the inner ear, the vibrations are translated into electrical signals for the brain to interpret.

Chapter Review

USING VOCABULARY

To complete the following sentences, choose the correct term from each pair of terms listed below:

1. Humans cannot hear __?__ waves because their frequencies are above the range of human hearing. (*infrasonic* or *ultrasonic*)

2. In the __?__, vibrations are converted to electrical signals for the brain to interpret. (*middle ear* or *inner ear*)

3. The __?__ of a sound wave depends on its amplitude. (*loudness* or *pitch*)

4. Reflected sound waves are called __?__. (*echoes* or *noise*)

5. Two different instruments playing the same note sound different because of __?__. (*echolocation* or *sound quality*)

UNDERSTANDING CONCEPTS

Multiple Choice

6. If a fire engine is traveling toward you, the Doppler effect will cause the siren to sound
   a. higher.　　　　　c. louder.
   b. lower.　　　　　d. softer.

7. The wave interaction most important for echolocation is
   a. reflection.　　　c. diffraction.
   b. interference.　　d. resonance.

8. If two sound waves interfere constructively, you will hear
   a. a high-pitched sound.
   b. a softer sound.
   c. a louder sound.
   d. no change in sound.

9. You will hear a sonic boom when
   a. an object breaks the sound barrier.
   b. an object travels at supersonic speeds.
   c. a shock wave reaches your ears.
   d. the speed of sound is 290 m/s.

10. Instruments that produce sound when struck belong to which family?
    a. strings　　　　c. percussion
    b. winds　　　　d. none of the above

11. Resonance can occur when an object vibrates at another object's
    a. resonant frequency.
    b. fundamental frequency.
    c. second overtone frequency.
    d. All of the above

12. The amount of diffraction that a sound wave undergoes depends on
    a. the frequency of the wave.
    b. the amplitude of the wave.
    c. the size of the barrier.
    d. Both (a) and (c)

13. A technological device that can be used to "see" sound waves is a(n)
    a. oscilloscope.　　c. transducer.
    b. sonar.　　　　d. amplifier.

Short Answer

14. Describe how the Doppler effect helps a beluga whale determine whether a fish is moving away from it or toward it.

15. How is interference involved in forming a shock wave?

16. Briefly describe how the three parts of the ear work.

56

Concept Mapping
Transparency 21

Concept Mapping

17. Use the following terms to create a concept map: sound, sound wave, pitch, loudness, decibel, hertz, frequency, amplitude.

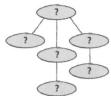

18. An anechoic chamber is a room where there is almost no reflection of sound waves. Anechoic chambers are often used to test sound equipment, such as stereos. The walls of such chambers are usually covered with foam triangles. Explain why this design eliminates echoes in the room.

19. Suppose you are sitting in the passenger seat of a parked car. You hear sounds coming from the stereo of another car parked on the opposite side of the street. You can easily hear the low-pitched bass sounds but cannot hear any high-pitched sounds coming from the parked car. Explain why you think this happens.

20. After working in a factory for a month, a man you know complains about a ringing in his ears. What might be wrong with him? What do you think may have caused his problem? What can you suggest to prevent further hearing loss?

MATH IN SCIENCE

21. How far does sound travel in 4 seconds through water at 20°C and glass at 20°C? Refer to the chart on page 35 for the speed of sound in different media.

INTERPRETING GRAPHICS

Use the oscilloscope screens below to answer the following questions:

22. Which sound is probably noise?

23. Which represents the softest sound?

24. Which represents the sound with the lowest pitch?

25. Which two sounds were produced by the same instrument?

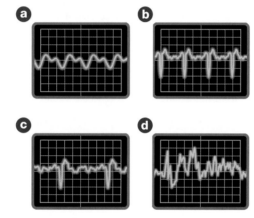

Reading Check-up

Take a minute to review your answers to the Pre-Reading Questions found at the bottom of page 28. Have your answers changed? If necessary, revise your answers based on what you have learned since you began this chapter.

57

Concept Mapping

17. An answer to this exercise can be found at the front of this book.

CRITICAL THINKING AND PROBLEM SOLVING

18. The foam triangles reduce echoes in two ways. The soft foam absorbs the sound waves, and the irregular shapes of the triangles sticking out from the walls scatter the sound waves.

19. Sample answer: Low frequency sounds diffract more than high frequency sounds. Therefore, low frequency bass sounds coming from the car are more likely to reach your ears than high frequency sounds.

20. The man is probably suffering from tinnitus. His condition was probably caused by exposure to loud sounds in the factory where he works. To prevent further hearing loss, you could tell him to wear earplugs or earmuffs while at work.

MATH IN SCIENCE

21. water: 5,928 m; glass: 18,160 m

INTERPRETING GRAPHICS

22. d
23. a
24. c
25. b and c

Blackline masters of this Chapter Review can be found in the **Study Guide**.

Background

Computed axial tomography (CAT scanning), which has been used for many years in medicine, is now being used by paleontologists to study the internal structure of fossils. CAT scanning can provide interior views of a fossil without even touching the fossil's surface.

To understand how CAT scanning works, imagine moving an object through the center of a circle. The CAT scan looks at the object and takes an X-ray picture of it from every point around the circle. A computer then recreates a two-dimensional picture, using each of the X-ray points around the circle. In this way, the CAT scan shows what you would see if you had taken a slice out of the object and were looking at the cross section.

If a paleontologist needs to reconstruct an entire skull, a series of two-dimensional "slice" shots are taken and combined through computer imaging to produce a three-dimensional image of the skull—inside and out!

Science, Technology, and Society

Jurassic Bark

Imagine you suddenly hear an incredibly loud honking sound, like a trombone or a tuba. "Must be band tryouts," you think. You turn to find the noise and find yourself face to face with a 10 m long, 2,800 kg dinosaur with a huge tubular crest extending back more than 2 m from its snout. Do you run? No—your musical friend, *Parasaurolophus,* is a vegetarian.

Now there's no way you'll bump into this extinct hadrosaur, a duck-billed dinosaur that existed about 75 million years ago in the late Cretaceous period. But through recent advances in computer technology, you can hear how *Parasaurolophus* might have sounded.

▶ *Aside from a role in the* Jurassic Park *movies, the* Parasaurolophus *dinosaur's biggest claim to fame is the enormous crest that extends back from its snout.*

A Snorkel or a Trombone?

Parasaurolophus's crest contained a network of tubes connected to the animal's breathing passages. Some scientists believe the dinosaurs used the distinctive crest to make sounds. Other scientists theorize that the crest allowed *Parasaurolophus* to stay underwater and feed, that it was used to regulate body temperature, or that it allowed the animals to communicate with each other by exhaling strongly through the crest.

The study of the *Parasaurolophus*'s potential sound-making ability really began after a 1995 expedition in northwestern New Mexico uncovered an almost-complete fossil skull of an adult. With this nearly complete skull and some modern technology, scientists tested the noise-making qualities of the crest.

Dino Scan

In Albuquerque, New Mexico, Dr. Carl Diegert of Sandia National Laboratories and Dr. Tom Williamson of the New Mexico Museum of Natural History and Science teamed up to use CT (Computed Tomography). With this scanning system, they created three-dimensional images of the crest's internal structure. The results showed that the crest had more tubes than previously thought as well as additional chambers.

Sound That Funky Horn

Once the crest's internal structure was determined, Diegert used powerful computers and special software to produce a sound that *Parasaurolophus* might have made. Since it is not known whether *Parasaurolophus* had vocal cords, Diegert made different versions of the sound by simulating the movement of air through the crest in several ways. Intrigued by Diegert's results, other researchers are trying to reproduce the sounds of other dinosaurs. In time, *Parasaurolophus* might be just one of a band of musical dinosaurs.

On Your Own

▶ *Parasaurolophus* is just one type of hadrosaur recognized for the peculiar bony crest on top of its head. On your own, research other hadrosaurs that had a bony crest similar to that of the *Parasaurolophus*. What are the names of these dinosaurs?

58

Answer to On Your Own

Parasaurolophus is only one of a number of crested hadrosaurs, also referred to as lambeosaurs. Other lambeosaurs include *Corythosaurus* and *Lambeosaurus*.

Science Fiction

"Ear"

by Jane Yolen

"Jily put on her Ear and sighed. The world went from awful silence to the pounding rhythms she loved. Without the Ear she was locked into her own thoughts and the few colors her eyes could pick out. But with the Ear she felt truly connected to the world."

Jily and her friends, Sanya and Feeny, live in a time not too far in the future. It is a time when everyone's hearing is damaged. People communicate using sign language—unless they put on their Ear. Then the whole world is filled with sounds. Of course, there are rules. No Ears allowed in school. Ears are only to be worn on the street, at night. Life is so much richer with an Ear, a person would have to be crazy to go without one.

The Low Down, the first club Jily and her friends visit, is too quiet for Jily's tastes. She wants to leave and tries to find Sanya and Feeny. But Sanya is dancing by herself, even though there is no music. When Jily finds Feeny, they notice some Earless kids their own age. Earless people never go to clubs, and Jily finds their presence offensive. But Feeny is intrigued.

Everyone is given an Ear at the age of 12 but has to give it up at the age of 30. Why would these kids want to go out without their Ears before the age of 30? Jily thinks the idea is ridiculous and doesn't stick around to find out the answer to such a question. But, it is an answer that will change her life by the end of the next day.

Read the rest of Jily's story, "Ear" by Jane Yolen, in the *Holt Anthology of Science Fiction.*

59

Further Reading If you liked this story, you can read more by Jane Yolen. Some of her other works include:

- *The Devil's Arithmetic,* Viking, 1988
- *Dragon's Blood: A Fantasy,* Delacorte, 1982
- *The Emperor and the Kite,* Philomel, 1997

Chapter Organizer

CHAPTER ORGANIZATION	TIME MINUTES	OBJECTIVES	LABS, INVESTIGATIONS, AND DEMONSTRATIONS
Chapter Opener pp. 60–61	45	National Standards: UCP 2, SAI 1, 2, ST 2, SPSP 5, HNS 1, PS 3c	**Start-Up Activity,** Colors of Light, p. 61
Section 1 **What Is Light?**	90	▶ Explain why electromagnetic waves are transverse waves. ▶ Describe how electromagnetic waves are produced. ▶ Calculate distances traveled by light using the value for speed of light. UCP 1, 2, SPSP 5, PS 3a	**Demonstration,** p. 62 in ATE
Section 2 **The Electromagnetic Spectrum**	90	▶ Identify how EM waves differ from each other. ▶ Describe some uses for radio waves and microwaves. ▶ Give examples of how infrared waves and visible light are important in your life. ▶ Explain how ultraviolet light, X rays, and gamma rays can be both helpful and harmful. UCP 2, SAI 1, 2, SPSP 1, 3–5, HNS 1, PS 3a, 3f	
Section 3 **Interactions of Light Waves**	90	▶ Compare regular reflection with diffuse reflection. ▶ Describe absorption and scattering of light. ▶ Explain how refraction can create optical illusions and separate white light into colors. ▶ Describe diffraction and interference of light. UCP 2, PS 3c	**QuickLab,** Scattering Milk, p. 75 **Demonstration,** p. 77 in ATE
Section 4 **Light and Color**	135	▶ Name and describe the three ways light interacts with matter. ▶ Explain how the color of an object is determined. ▶ Compare the primary colors of light and the primary pigments. PS 3c; Labs UCP 2, 3, SAI 1, 2, PS 3a–3c	**Demonstration,** pp. 79, 82 in ATE **Discovery Lab,** What Color of Light Is Best for Green Plants? p. 132 **Discovery Lab,** Which Color Is Hottest? p. 133 **QuickLab,** Rose-Colored Glasses? p. 82 **Skill Builder,** Mixing Colors, p. 84 **Long-Term Projects & Research Ideas,** The Image of the Future

See page **T23** *for a complete correlation of this book with the*

NATIONAL SCIENCE EDUCATION STANDARDS.

TECHNOLOGY RESOURCES

 Guided Reading Audio CD English or Spanish, Chapter 3

 One-Stop Planner CD-ROM with Test Generator

 CNN. Scientists in Action, Slow Light Scientist, Segment 28

 Interactive Explorations CD-ROM, CD 3, Exploration 7, In the Spotlight

CLASSROOM WORKSHEETS, TRANSPARENCIES, AND RESOURCES	SCIENCE INTEGRATION AND CONNECTIONS	REVIEW AND ASSESSMENT
Directed Reading Worksheet **Science Puzzlers, Twisters & Teasers**		
Transparency 289, Electromagnetic Waves **Directed Reading Worksheet,** Section 1 **Transparency 290,** The Production of Light	**Multicultural Connection,** p. 63 in ATE **MathBreak,** p. 64 **Science, Technology, and Society:** Fireflies Light the Way, p. 90	**Section Review,** p. 64 **Quiz,** p. 64 in ATE **Alternative Assessment,** p. 64 in ATE
Transparency 291, The Electromagnetic Spectrum **Directed Reading Worksheet,** Section 2 **Transparency 196,** The H-R Diagram: A **Transparency 197,** The H-R Diagram: B	**Astronomy Connection,** p. 65 **Cross-Disciplinary Focus,** p. 66 in ATE **Connect to Earth Science,** p. 69 in ATE **Connect to Life Science,** p. 69 in ATE **Biology Connection,** p. 70 **Apply,** p. 71 **Eureka!** It's a Heat Wave! p. 91	**Homework,** p. 66 in ATE **Section Review,** p. 69 **Section Review,** p. 72 **Quiz,** p. 72 in ATE **Alternative Assessment,** p. 72 in ATE
Transparency 292, Reflection **Directed Reading Worksheet,** Section 3 **Transparency 293,** White Light Is Separated by a Prism **Reinforcement Worksheet** **Transparency 294,** Constructive and Destructive Interference **Critical Thinking Worksheet,** Now You See It, Now You Don't	**Multicultural Connection,** p. 73 in ATE **Multicultural Connection,** p. 74 in ATE **Connect to Life Science,** p. 76 in ATE **Cross-Disciplinary Focus,** p. 76 in ATE **Real-World Connection,** p. 76 in ATE **Real-World Connection,** p. 77 in ATE **Connect to Life Science,** p. 77 in ATE	**Homework,** p. 74 in ATE **Section Review,** p. 78 **Quiz,** p. 78 in ATE **Alternative Assessment,** p. 78 in ATE
Directed Reading Worksheet, Section 4	**Connect to Life Science,** p. 80 in ATE **Connect to Earth Science,** p. 81 in ATE **Multicultural Connection,** p. 81 in ATE **Geology Connection,** p. 83 **Cross-Disciplinary Focus,** p. 83 in ATE	**Homework,** pp. 79, 80 in ATE **Self-Check,** p. 81 **Section Review,** p. 83 **Quiz,** p. 83 in ATE **Alternative Assessment,** p. 83 in ATE

END-OF-CHAPTER REVIEW AND ASSESSMENT

Chapter Review in Study Guide
Vocabulary and Notes in Study Guide
Chapter Tests with Performance-Based Assessment, Chapter 3 Test, Performance-Based Assessment 3
Concept Mapping Transparency 22

 internet **connect**

 go. hrw .com **Holt, Rinehart and Winston On-line Resources**

go.hrw.com

For worksheets and other teaching aids related to this chapter, visit the HRW Web site and type in the keyword: **HSTLGT**

 SCI*LINKS* NSTA **National Science Teachers Association**

www.scilinks.org

Encourage students to use the *sci*LINKS numbers listed in the internet connect boxes to access information and resources on the **NSTA** Web site.

Chapter Resources & Worksheets

Visual Resources

TEACHING TRANSPARENCIES

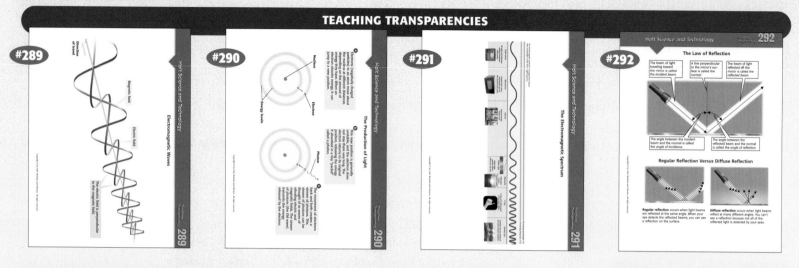

#289 Electromagnetic Waves

#290 The Production of Light

#291 The Electromagnetic Spectrum

#292 The Law of Reflection

TEACHING TRANSPARENCIES

CONCEPT MAPPING TRANSPARENCY

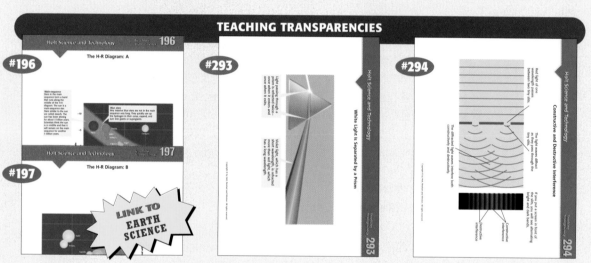

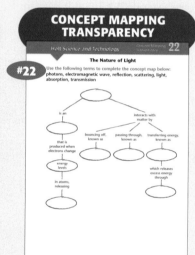

#196 The H-R Diagram: A

#197 The H-R Diagram: B

LINK TO EARTH SCIENCE

#293 White Light Is Separated by a Prism

#294 Constructive and Destructive Interference

#22 The Nature of Light

Meeting Individual Needs

DIRECTED READING

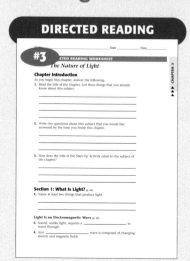

#3 DIRECTED READING WORKSHEET
The Nature of Light

REINFORCEMENT & VOCABULARY REVIEW

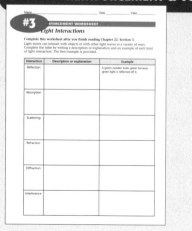

#3 REINFORCEMENT WORKSHEET
Light Interactions

VOCABULARY REVIEW WORKSHEET

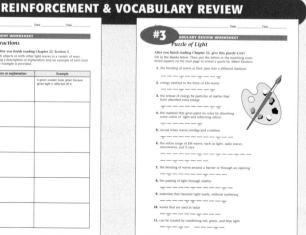

#3 VOCABULARY REVIEW WORKSHEET
Puzzle of Light

SCIENCE PUZZLERS, TWISTERS & TEASERS

#3 SCIENCE PUZZLERS, TWISTERS & TEASERS
The Nature of Light

Review & Assessment

STUDY GUIDE

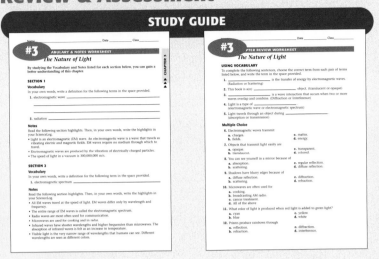

CHAPTER TESTS WITH PERFORMANCE-BASED ASSESSMENT

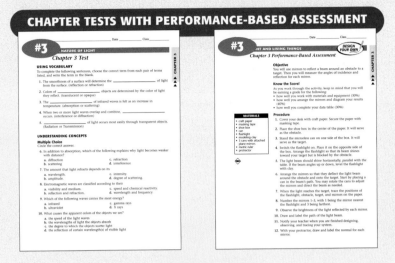

Lab Worksheets

LONG-TERM PROJECTS & RESEARCH IDEAS

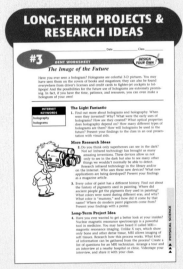

DATASHEETS FOR LABBOOK

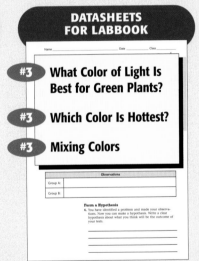

Applications & Extensions

CRITICAL THINKING & PROBLEM SOLVING

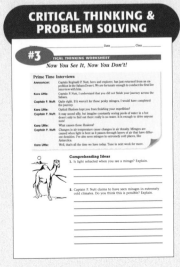

SCIENTISTS IN ACTION

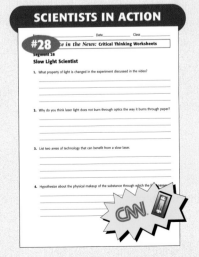

INTERACTIVE EXPLORATIONS

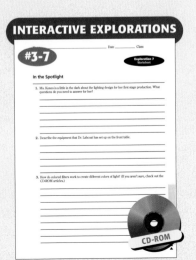

Chapter Background

SECTION 1

▶ What Is Light?

The nature of light has been debated for thousands of years. The argument about how light travels—as a wave or as a particle—began with the Greek mathematician and philosopher Pythagoras (c. 580–500 B.C.). Pythagoras and his followers believed that light is emitted from a source in the form of tiny particles.

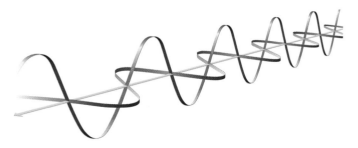

- However, Empedocles (c. 490–430 B.C.), another Greek philosopher, taught that light travels from its source as waves.

- In the fifth century B.C., the Greek philosophers Socrates (c. 470–399 B.C.) and Plato (c. 428–348 B.C.) thought that the eyes emitted streamers, or filaments, and that sight occurred when these streamers made contact with objects.

- Even as late as the 1600s, René Descartes (1596–1650), the great French mathematician and philosopher, held beliefs similar to those of Socrates and Plato.

IS THAT A FACT!

- ➴ Galileo Galilei (1564–1642) once tried to measure the speed of light from a lantern from one hilltop to another. He soon realized that light traveled very fast.

SECTION 2

▶ The Electromagnetic Spectrum

- In 1865, James Clerk Maxwell (1831–1879), a Scottish physicist, developed a theory stating that certain waves are propagated through space at the speed of light. In fact, his equations predicted that energy of the waves was equally divided between an electric field and a magnetic field. He called the waves electromagnetic waves.

- In 1886, Heinrich Hertz (1859–1894) was trying to prove Maxwell's equations experimentally. His experimentation was very fruitful: Not only did he prove Maxwell correct, but he also discovered radio waves. The unit for frequency was named in his honor.

IS THAT A FACT!

- ➴ The infrared portion of the spectrum was discovered by William Herschel (1738–1822), a famous British astronomer. In 1800, he was investigating the heat produced by certain waves located just below the red part of the visible spectrum. He named the waves *infrared. Infra* is a Latin word meaning "below."

- ➴ In 1895, Wilhelm Roentgen (1845–1923) serendipitously discovered X rays. While working with a barium ore, he discovered that the ore glowed when placed near a tube in which an electric current was passing. He experimented and found that the ore would glow even if placed behind substances that would block ordinary light.

- ➴ Roentgen didn't know the source of the radiation that caused the barium to glow, so he called the source X rays. He received the first Nobel Prize in physics for his discovery of X rays.

SECTION 3

▶ Interactions of Light Waves

Thomas Young (1773–1829) was a medical doctor born in Milverton, England. But Young had a variety of interests and wrote important papers in Egyptology and physics.

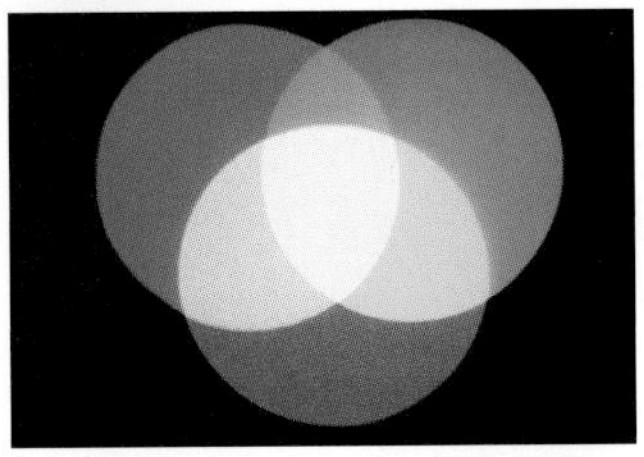

- Young aided in the translation of the Rosetta stone (1812–1813).
- In physics and the study of solid materials, the Young modulus (a measure of the strength and elasticity of a solid) is named after him for his work with solids.
- Young was the first to propose the three-primary-color model for vision.
- Young discovered the phenomenon of interference of light using an apparatus with a double slit. From his experiments, Young was able to measure the wavelengths of red and blue light. However, it was his revival of the wave theory of light that aided others in their search for the nature of light.

IS THAT A FACT!

- In the 1960s, earthquake lights were photographed in Japan. Earthquake lights are beams, columns, or fireballs of light seen just before the Earth begins to shake. This phenomenon has not been explained; however, one theory states that the cause may be the piezoelectric effect. This effect refers to the generation of an electrostatic voltage that occurs when great pressure is placed on quartz or other types of crystals.

SECTION 4

▶ Light and Color

In humans, light rays pass through the lens onto the retina. This back part of the eye contains two types of nerve cells, *rods* and *cones,* that respond to light energy.

- The visual system can be divided into two categories: *photopic vision* and *scotopic vision.* Photopic vision primarily utilizes cones, which detect light under high illumination. Scotopic vision involves rods, which detect light under low illumination.
- Rods are most sensitive to movement and to changes in light and dark. Rods do not respond to different frequencies of light, so they do not perceive color.
- Cones, on the other hand, come in three types and are sensitive to different frequencies and intensities of light. One type is triggered by light energy at the blue end of the spectrum, the second responds to the red end of the spectrum, and the third type is stimulated by the middle of the spectrum, or the greens.

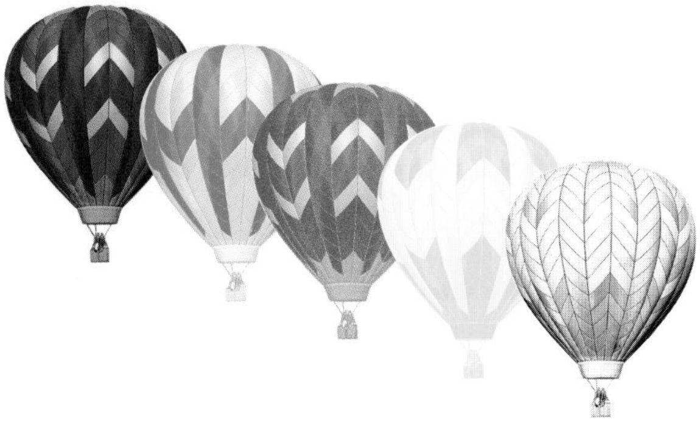

- When light energy stimulates the cones, they send signals to the brain. The brain interprets these signals as colors, depending on how many of each type of cone has been stimulated.

IS THAT A FACT!

- Experiments have shown that the human eye can *detect* a single photon of light. However, neural filters will only trigger a conscious response when between five and ten photons arrive within a certain period of time. This is so we won't see visual "noise" in low light!
- In 1932, John Logie Baird developed the first commercially viable electromechanical television system and sold over 10,000 sets!

For background information about teaching strategies and issues, refer to the *Professional Reference for Teachers.*

The Nature of Light

 Pre-Reading Questions

Students may not know the answers to these questions before reading the chapter, so accept any reasonable response.

Suggested Answers

1. Light can be thought of as a stream of photons that are produced by the movement of electrons between energy levels.

2. Light waves can interact through reflection, refraction, diffraction, interference, absorption, and scattering.

3. Colors of light are determined by the wavelength of a light wave. The different colors we see are determined by the wavelengths of light that reach our eyes.

The Nature of Light

 Pre-Reading Questions

1. What is light?

2. How do light waves interact?

3. Why are you able to see different colors?

60

WHAT ON EARTH...?

What kind of alien life lives on *this* planet? Actually, this isn't a planet at all. It's a photograph of something much, much smaller. Have you guessed yet? It's an ordinary soap bubble! The brightly colored swirls on the surface of this bubble are reflections of light. In this chapter, you will learn more about light, including how waves interact and why you can see different colors like the ones on the surface of this soap bubble.

---

internet connect

go.hrw.com	**www.scilinks.com**	**www.si.edu/hrw**	**www.cnnfyi.com**
HRW On-line Resources	SCiLINKS NSTA	Smithsonian Institution	CNNfyi.com
For worksheets and other teaching aids, visit the HRW Web site and type in the keyword: **HSTLGT**	Use the *sci*LINKS numbers at the end of each chapter for additional resources on the **NSTA** Web site.	Visit the Smithsonian Institution Web site for related on-line resources.	Visit the CNN Web site for current events coverage and classroom resources.

COLORS OF LIGHT

Is white light really white? In this activity, you will use a spectroscope to answer that question.

Procedure

1. Your teacher will give you a **spectroscope** or instructions for making one.

2. Turn on an **incandescent light bulb.** Look at the light bulb through your spectroscope. In your ScienceLog, write a description of what you see.

3. Repeat step 2 looking at a **fluorescent light.** Again, in your ScienceLog, describe what you see.

Analysis

4. Compare what you saw in step 2 with what you saw in step 3.

5. Both kinds of bulbs produce white light. What did you learn about white light using the spectroscope?

6. Light from the sun is white light. Make inferences about what you would see if you looked at sunlight using a spectroscope.
   Caution: Do NOT use your spectroscope to look at the sun. It does not give enough protection against bright sunlight.

61

COLORS OF LIGHT

MATERIALS

FOR EACH GROUP:
- clear incandescent light bulb
- fluorescent light bulb
- diffraction grating
- tape
- black construction paper
- paper-towel tube

Safety Caution

Students should avoid handling the hot bulbs.

Teacher's Notes

You can have the students make their own spectroscopes, or you can make a few ahead of time for the class.

Instructions for Making a Spectroscope

1. Cut a narrow slit in the center of a piece of black construction paper. Tape the paper to one end of a paper-towel tube. The paper should cover the opening of the tube.

2. Look through the open end of the tube at an incandescent light bulb. If no light passes through the slit in the paper, make the slit a little wider.

3. Hold a diffraction grating against the open end of the tube. Look at the light bulb through the grating. Make sure the slit in the paper is vertical.

4. Rotate the diffraction grating until you see colors inside the tube to the left and right sides of the slit. Tape the diffraction grating to the tube in this position.

Answers to START-UP Activity

2. Students should see a solid, continuous spectrum of colors on both sides of the tube. All colors should have the same brightness.

3. Students should see a spectrum of colors again. However, there will be bright bands and faint bands within the spectrum.

4. Accept all reasonable answers.

5. White light is made up of different colors of light.

6. Students should expect to see a solid, continuous spectrum of colors that resembles the spectrum of the light bulb.

Focus

What Is Light?

Students will learn what EM waves are, how they are produced, and how they differ from other waves. Students will also learn about the speed of light.

Bellringer

Draw a transverse wave with a wavelength of 1 m on the board. Label each part of the wave, such as the wavelength, crest, and trough. Have students copy the wave in their ScienceLog and label their drawing carefully. Ask them to explain in their own words what wavelength and frequency are and how the two are related. (Remind them that these are concepts they studied in Chapter 1.)

1 Motivate

DEMONSTRATION

Using tongs to hold one end of a small piece of copper wire, place the other end into the flame of a Bunsen burner. (Any source of thermal energy, such as a lighter, will work.) A green, luminous glow will be produced. Ask students to explain the source of the green glow. Guide the discussion to help students realize that atoms in the copper wire emit a green light when thermal energy is added.

Teaching Transparency 289
"Electromagnetic Waves"

Directed Reading Worksheet Section 1

Terms to Learn

electromagnetic wave
radiation

What You'll Do

- Explain why electromagnetic waves are transverse waves.
- Describe how electromagnetic waves are produced.
- Calculate distances traveled by light using the value for speed of light.

What Is Light?

We rely on light from the sun and from electric bulbs to help us see. But what exactly is light? Scientists are still studying light to learn more about its makeup and characteristics. Fortunately, much has already been discovered about light, as you will soon find out. You may even become enlightened!

Light Is an Electromagnetic Wave

Like sound, light is a type of energy that travels as a wave. But unlike sound, light does not require a medium through which to travel. Light is an **electromagnetic wave** (EM wave). An EM wave is a wave that can travel through space or matter and consists of changing electric and magnetic fields. A *field* is a region around an object that can exert a force, a push or pull, on another object without actually touching that object. For example, a magnet is surrounded by a magnetic field that can pull a paper clip toward it. But keep in mind that this field, like all fields, is not made of matter.

Figure 1 shows a diagram of an electromagnetic wave. Notice that the electric and magnetic fields are at right angles—or *perpendicular*—to each other. These fields are also perpendicular to the direction of the wave motion. Because of this arrangement, electromagnetic waves are transverse waves.

Figure 1 *Electromagnetic waves are transverse waves.*

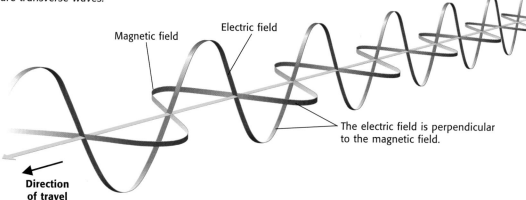

Magnetic field

Electric field

The electric field is perpendicular to the magnetic field.

Direction of travel

SCIENTISTS AT ODDS

Sir Isaac Newton (1642–1727) thought that a particle model best described the properties of light that he observed. Christian Huygens (1629–1695), a Dutch mathematician and scientist, disagreed with Newton's theory because Newton's particle model could not explain the diffraction of light. This argument was continued by other scientists for nearly 200 years, until the early 1900s. It was finally settled when Albert Einstein (1879–1955) and Maurice de Broglie (1875–1960) each arrived at the conclusion that EM waves are best described by a particle-wave model.

How Light Is Produced

An EM wave is produced by the vibration of an electrically charged particle. A particle with an electric charge is surrounded by an electric field. When the particle vibrates, or moves back and forth, the electric field around it vibrates too. When the electric field starts vibrating, a vibrating magnetic field is created. The vibration of an electric field and a magnetic field together produces an EM wave that carries energy released by the original vibration of the particle. The emission of energy in the form of EM waves is called **radiation.**

Sounds complicated, right? To better understand how light is produced, think about the following example. When you turn on a lamp, the electrical energy supplied to the filament in the bulb causes the atoms in the filament to vibrate. Charged particles inside the atoms then vibrate, and light is produced, as shown in **Figure 2.**

Extra! Extra! Read all about how light-producing fireflies save people's lives! Turn to page 90.

Figure 2 The Production of Light

a Electrons (negatively charged particles) in an atom move about the nucleus at different distances depending on the amount of energy they have. When an electron absorbs energy, it can jump to a new position.

b This new position is generally unstable, and the electron may not stay there very long. The electron returns to its original position, releasing the energy it absorbed in a tiny "packet" called a *photon.*

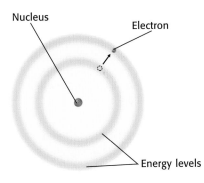

Nucleus

Electron

Energy levels

Photon

c The movement of electrons back and forth creates a stream of photons. This stream of photons can be thought of as waves of vibrating electric and magnetic fields. The stream of photons (the EM wave) carries the energy released by the electrons.

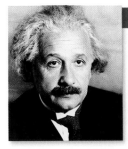

The Split Personality of Light

The fact that light is a wave explains certain behaviors of light, but not others. These puzzling behaviors of light are easier to explain if light is thought to consist of particles instead of waves. Scientists think that light has the properties of both a particle and a wave. Albert Einstein was one of many scientists who researched the dual nature of light. The idea that light can act as either particles or waves is known as the *particle-wave theory of light.*

63

IS THAT A FACT!

Galileo was perhaps the first scientist to suggest a method for measuring the speed of light. In 1675, the Danish astronomer Ole Roemer (1644–1710) was the first to demonstrate that the speed of light is finite by observing the eclipses of Jupiter's satellites.

Multicultural CONNECTION

Indian physicist Satyendra Nath Bose (1894–1974) published a paper in 1924 dealing with quantum mechanics. Albert Einstein read Bose's paper and praised it. Einstein then generalized Bose's theory into quantum statistics and described certain subatomic particles. When later experiments found the particles, they were named *bosons* in honor of Bose.

2 Teach

USING THE FIGURE

Using **Figure 2,** discuss with students the difficult concept that there are two different transverse waves vibrating perpendicular to one another. One wave is a vibrating electric field; the other is a vibrating magnetic field. Remind students that a vibrating electric field generates a magnetic field and a vibrating magnetic field generates an electric field. Together they form a single EM wave traveling in a particular direction. Sheltered English

DISCUSSION

Writing Physicist Paul Hewitt has stated that all that we see, even our own reflection, is from the past. Have students write about whether they think that this statement is true, and why or why not. Have students discuss what they have written.

3 Extend

RESEARCH

Have students research either Isaac Newton's, Christiaan Huygens's, or Albert Einstein's theories on the nature of light. Encourage students to hold a class debate about the positions of the scientists they research. As an alternative, have interested students research the history of how the speed of light was determined. Sheltered English

Teaching Transparency 290 "The Production of Light"

Section 1 • What Is Light? **63**

Quiz

1. If the circumference of Earth is 40,100 km, how many times can light travel around Earth in 1 second? (about 7 times)

2. Tiny packets of energy are called photons. (true)

3. EM radiation is produced by the vibrations of charged particles. (true)

4. In your own words, explain what light is and how it is produced. (Answers will vary but should discuss EM waves, transverse waves, electric and magnetic fields vibrating perpendicularly to each other, electrons, photons, and the particle-wave nature of light.)

ALTERNATIVE ASSESSMENT

Concept Mapping Have students prepare a concept map showing the properties of light. Their concept map should in some way illustrate which property or properties are described by the wave model of light and which are described by the particle model.

Answer to MATHBREAK

$$time = \frac{distance}{speed}$$

$$time = \frac{150{,}000{,}000{,}000 \text{ m}}{300{,}000{,}000 \text{ m/s}}$$

$$time = 500 \text{ seconds}$$

internet connect

SCi LINKS
NSTA

TOPIC: Using Light
GO TO: www.scilinks.org
*sci*LINKS NUMBER: HSTP528

TOPIC: Light Energy
GO TO: www.scilinks.org
*sci*LINKS NUMBER: HSTP529

MATH BREAK

Just How Fast Is Light?

To give you an idea of how fast light travels, calculate the time it takes for light to travel from Earth to the moon. The distance from Earth to the moon is 382,000,000 m.

$$speed = \frac{distance}{time}$$

This equation can be rearranged to solve for time:

$$time = \frac{distance}{speed}$$

$$time = \frac{382{,}000{,}000 \text{ m}}{300{,}000{,}000 \text{ m/s}}$$

$$time = 1.27 \text{ seconds}$$

Now It's Your Turn

The distance from the sun to Earth is 150,000,000,000 m. Calculate the time it takes for light to travel that distance.

internet connect

SCi LINKS
NSTA

TOPIC: Light Energy
GO TO: www.scilinks.org
*sci*LINKS NUMBER: HSTP529

The Speed of Light

Scientists have yet to discover anything in the universe that travels faster than light. In the near-vacuum of space, the speed of light is about 300,000,000 m/s. Light travels slightly slower in air, glass, and other types of matter. (Keep in mind that even though EM waves do not require a medium, they can travel through many substances.) Believe it or not, light can travel more than 880,000 times faster than sound! This explains the phenomenon described in **Figure 3.** And if you could run at the speed of light, you could travel around Earth 7.5 times in 1 second.

Figure 3 *Although thunder and lightning are produced at the same time, you usually see lightning before you hear thunder. That's because light travels much faster than sound.*

SECTION REVIEW

1. Why are electromagnetic waves transverse waves?

2. How is a sound wave different from an EM wave?

3. How does a charged particle produce an EM wave?

4. Making Inferences Explain why EM waves do not require a medium through which to travel.

5. Doing Calculations The distance from the sun to Jupiter is 778,000,000,000,000 m. How long does it take for light from the sun to reach Jupiter?

Answers to Section Review

1. EM waves are transverse waves because the electric and magnetic fields vibrate perpendicularly to the direction the wave is traveling.

2. A sound wave requires a medium through which to travel and an EM wave does not.

3. A vibrating charged particle produces a vibrating electric field that, in turn, produces a vibrating magnetic field. The two vibrating fields make up an electromagnetic wave.

4. EM waves travel through the vibrations of electric and magnetic fields. These fields are not made of matter. Therefore, EM waves can travel without passing through a medium.

5. time = 2,593 seconds (or 43.2 minutes)

The Electromagnetic Spectrum

When you look around, you can see objects because light reflects off them. But if a bee looked at the same objects, it would see them differently, as shown in **Figure 4.** This is because bees can see a kind of light that you can't see. This type of light is called ultraviolet light.

It might seem strange to you to call something you can't see *light,* because the light you are most familiar with is visible light. But ultraviolet light is very similar to visible light. Both visible light and ultraviolet light are types of EM waves. In this section you will learn about many other types of EM waves, including X rays, radio waves, and microwaves.

Figure 4 *The petals of the flower on the right look solid yellow to you. But a bee may see dark ultraviolet markings that make the same flower appear quite different to the bee.*

Astronomy
C O N N E C T I O N

Scientists know that all electromagnetic waves in empty space travel at the same speed. If EM waves traveled at different speeds, planets, stars, and galaxies would appear to be in different places depending upon which EM wave was used to view them. For example, using X rays to view a star might make the star appear to be in a different place than if radio waves were used.

Characteristics of EM Waves

Even though there are many types of EM waves, each type of wave travels at the same speed in a vacuum—300,000,000 m/s. How is this possible? Well, the speed of a wave is determined by multiplying its wavelength by its frequency. So EM waves having different wavelengths can travel at the same speed as long as their frequencies are also different. The entire range of EM waves is called the **electromagnetic spectrum.** Categories of waves in the EM spectrum include radio waves, microwaves, and visible light.

65

Learners Having Difficulty
Have students create in their ScienceLog an electromagnetic spectrum chart similar to the one found across the bottom of pages 66 and 67. As they read about each category of electromagnetic wave, have students write one or two facts about the category on their chart.
Sheltered English

CROSS-DISCIPLINARY FOCUS

History Have students find out about the lives and accomplishments of these pioneers in the study of EM waves.

• James Clerk Maxwell
• Heinrich Hertz
• Guglielmo Marconi
• Nikolai Tesla

(Maxwell introduced the theory of electromagnetic waves in 1865; Hertz created electromagnetic waves with a spark generator and reported that they could be transmitted over a distance; Marconi made the first wireless transmission across the Atlantic Ocean; Tesla developed the alternating current electrical system and some of the first electric motors.)

internetconnect

SCiLINKS.
NSTA

TOPIC: The Electromagnetic Spectrum
GO TO: www.scilinks.org
sciLINKS NUMBER: HSTP530

Radio Waves

Radio waves cover a wide range of waves in the EM spectrum. Radio waves have some of the longest wavelengths and the lowest frequencies of all EM waves. Therefore, radio waves are low energy waves. They carry enough energy, however, to be used for broadcasting radio signals. **Figure 5** shows how this process works.

Radio stations encode sound information into radio waves by varying either the waves' amplitude or their frequency. Changing amplitude or frequency is called modulation. You probably know that there are AM radio stations and FM radio stations. The abbreviation AM stands for amplitude modulation, and the abbreviation FM stands for frequency modulation. AM radio waves have longer wavelengths than FM radio waves.

Figure 5 *Radio waves cannot be heard, but they carry energy that can be converted into sound.*

1 A radio station converts sound into an electric current. The current produces radio waves that are sent out in all directions by the antenna.

2 A radio receives radio waves and then converts them into an electric current, which is then converted to sound.

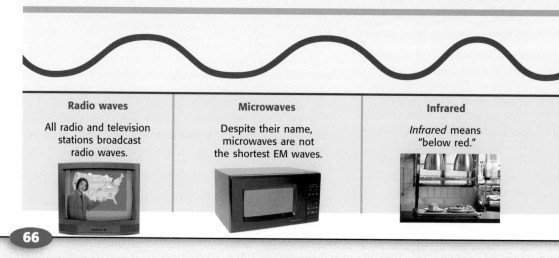

Electromagnetic Spectrum

The electromagnetic spectrum is arranged from long to short wavelength or from low to high frequency.

Radio waves	Microwaves	Infrared
All radio and television stations broadcast radio waves.	Despite their name, microwaves are not the shortest EM waves.	*Infrared* means "below red."

66

Homework

Concept Mapping Have students use the diagram of the EM spectrum on this page and page 67 to make a concept map of the different parts of the spectrum. Students should include one or more examples of how we use each part of the spectrum. Encourage them to be creative and to illustrate their concept map with drawings, photos, or images from magazines or newspapers.

AM and FM Radio Waves Although AM radio waves can travel farther than FM waves, as shown in **Figure 6,** many stations—especially those that broadcast mostly music—use FM waves. That's because more information can be encoded by using frequency modulation than by using amplitude modulation. Because FM waves carry more information, music broadcast from FM stations sounds better.

Figure 6 *The difference in the wavelengths of AM and FM radio waves affects how the waves interact with a layer of the atmosphere called the ionosphere.*

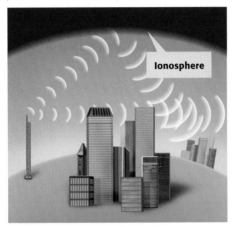

AM radio waves can reflect off the ionosphere. This helps AM waves travel long distances.

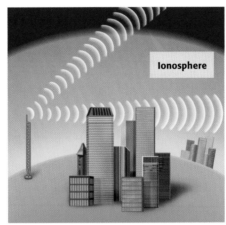

FM radio waves pass through the ionosphere. Therefore, FM waves cannot travel as far as AM waves.

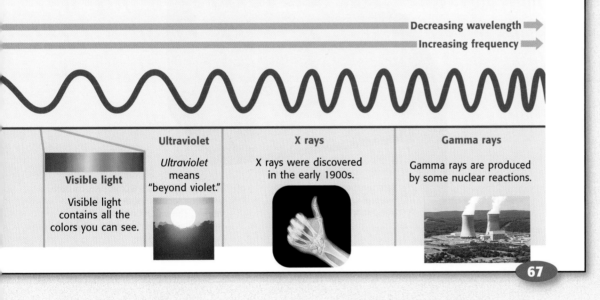

Decreasing wavelength ➡️

Increasing frequency ➡️

Visible light

Visible light contains all the colors you can see.

Ultraviolet

Ultraviolet means "beyond violet."

X rays

X rays were discovered in the early 1900s.

Gamma rays

Gamma rays are produced by some nuclear reactions.

67

WEIRD SCIENCE

Scientists recently conducted experiments that slowed down a beam of laser light to 17 m/s (38 mph)! This incredible phenomena was achieved by firing a laser beam through a gas cloud of sodium atoms cooled to only a fraction of a degree above absolute zero.

SCIENCE HUMOR

Q: How many actors does it take to change a light bulb?

A: Only one. They don't like to share the spotlight!

Prediction Guide Before students read this page, ask them:

If you were going to buy a radio station that would play mostly music, would you apply for an AM station license or an FM station license? Why? What if your station broadcast mostly news and sports? Which license would you apply for, and why?

Have students record their answers in their ScienceLog and have them evaluate their answers after reading this page.

RESEARCH

No one person is credited with the invention of television. Some pioneers of television technology include the German scientist Paul Nipkow (1860–1940), the American scientist and inventor Charles F. Jenkins (1867–1934), the Scottish inventor John Logie Baird (1888–1946), the Russian-born Vladymir Zworykin (1889–1982), the Japanese engineer Kenjiro Takayanagi (1899–1990), and American Philo T. Farnsworth (1906–1971). Have students research one or more of these developers of television technology. Encourage them to be creative with their presentations. Some students may want to build models of early television devices.

BRAIN FOOD

The frequencies at which radio and television stations broadcast in the United States are assigned by the Federal Communications Commission (FCC). In fact, the FCC has assigned frequencies for all devices that use radio waves. Such devices include garage door openers, baby monitors, radio controlled toys, and wildlife tracking collars.

Television and Radio Waves Television signals are also carried by radio waves. Most television stations broadcast radio waves that have shorter wavelengths and higher frequencies than those broadcast by radio stations. However, television signals are still broadcast using amplitude modulation and frequency modulation. Television stations use frequency-modulated waves to carry sound and amplitude-modulated waves to carry pictures.

Some waves carrying television signals are transmitted to satellites around the Earth. The waves are amplified and relayed back to ground antennae and then travel through cables to televisions in homes. This is how cable television works.

Microwaves

Microwaves have shorter wavelengths and higher frequencies than radio waves. Therefore, microwaves carry more energy than radio waves. You are probably familiar with microwaves—they are created in a microwave oven, like the model illustrated in **Figure 7.**

Figure 7 How a Microwave Oven Works

a A device called a magnetron produces microwaves by accelerating charged particles.

b The microwaves reflect off a metal fan and are directed into the cooking chamber.

c Microwaves can penetrate several centimeters into the food.

d The energy of the microwaves causes water molecules inside the food to vibrate. The vibration of the water molecules causes the temperature of the food to increase.

68

IS THAT A FACT!

One of the first public radio broadcasts in the United States occurred in 1910—a live concert of an opera featuring the great tenor Enrico Caruso.

WEIRD SCIENCE

When food is cooked in a microwave oven, the dish holding the food may get warm. But the microwave is not heating the dish. The dish is warmed by heat dissipating from the cooking food.

Radar Microwaves are also used in radar. Radar (**ra**dio **d**etection **a**nd **r**anging) is used to detect the speed and location of objects. **Figure 8** shows a police officer using radar to determine the speed of a car. The officer points the radar device at a car and presses a button. The device emits short pulses of microwaves that reflect off the car and return to the device. The rate at which the waves are reflected is used to calculate the speed of the car. Radar is also used to monitor the movement of airplanes and to help ship captains navigate at night or in foggy weather.

Figure 8 *Police officers use radar to detect cars going faster than the speed limit.*

Infrared Waves

Infrared waves have shorter wavelengths and higher frequencies than microwaves. So infrared waves can carry more energy than microwaves and radio waves carry.

When you sit outside on a sunny summer day, you feel warm because of *infrared waves* emitted by the sun. Infrared waves are absorbed by your skin when they strike your body. The energy of the waves causes the particles in your skin to vibrate faster, and you feel the increased vibration as an increase in temperature.

The sun is not the only source of infrared waves. Objects that emit infrared waves include stars, planets, buildings, trees, and you! The amount of infrared radiation emitted by an object varies depending on the object's temperature. Warmer objects give off more infrared radiation than cooler objects.

Your eyes can't see infrared waves, but there are devices that can detect infrared radiation. For example, infrared binoculars convert infrared radiation into light you can see. Such binoculars can be used to observe animals at night. **Figure 9** shows how certain photographic films are sensitive to infrared radiation.

Figure 9 *In this photograph, brighter colors indicate higher temperatures.*

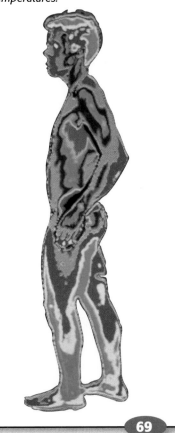

SECTION REVIEW

1. How do infrared waves differ from radio waves in terms of frequency and wavelength?

2. Describe two ways that radio waves are used for transmitting information.

3. **Inferring Relationships** Why do the frequencies of EM waves increase as the wavelengths decrease?

69

▼ *Answers to Section Review*

1. Infrared waves have shorter wavelengths and higher frequencies than radio waves, and they can carry more energy than radio waves.

2. Radio waves can transmit information by either AM (amplitude modulation) or FM (frequency modulation). Students may also say that radio waves can be used to transmit television and radio signals.

3. All electromagnetic waves that travel through the same medium travel at the same speed. Wave speed is frequency times wavelength. Because wave speed is constant, the frequencies of EM waves must increase as the wavelengths decrease.

2) Teach, *continued*

MISCONCEPTION ALERT

The range of the electromagnetic spectrum that humans can see is called the visible spectrum. However, other animals are able to see electromagnetic radiation with wavelengths outside of the visible spectrum. For example, bees and other insects use ultraviolet light (see page 71), and pit vipers can detect infrared radiation.

MEETING INDIVIDUAL NEEDS

Advanced Learners Ask students, "What is a rainbow?" Basically, a rainbow is sunlight spread out into its spectrum of colors. The colors are directed toward the viewer by raindrops or other water droplets in the air. But rainbows are more complex than this. Challenge students to research how rainbows are formed and why we see them as we do. Encourage students to be creative; presentations might include models of rainbows, photographs of rainbows, or creating a rainbow in the school parking lot.

REAL-WORLD CONNECTION

Therapy involving exposure to certain kinds of light has become an accepted treatment of a mood disorder known as *seasonal affective disorder*. Seasonal affective disorder, or SAD, is characterized by feelings of depression that typically occur during the fall and winter months. Researchers believe that the reduction in the amount of light that passes through the eyes during these months affects the release of important brain chemicals. The treatment, known as phototherapy, involves a 20–30 minute daily exposure to a specific kind of light.

Biology CONNECTION

Visible light provides the energy necessary for photosynthesis—the process by which plants make their own food. Photosynthesis is important to you for two reasons. First, during photosynthesis, plants produce oxygen for you to breathe. Second, the food produced by plants provides your body with energy. When you eat plants, or eat meat from animals that ate plants, you get energy to live from the food produced through photosynthesis.

Visible Light

Visible light is the very narrow range of wavelengths and frequencies in the electromagnetic spectrum that humans can see. Humans see the different wavelengths as different colors, as shown in **Figure 10.** The longest wavelengths are seen as red light, and the shortest wavelengths are seen as violet light. Because violet light has the shortest wavelength, it carries the most energy of the visible light waves.

Figure 10 *White light, such as light from the sun, is actually visible light of all wavelengths combined. You see all the colors of visible light in a rainbow.*

Colors of Light The range of colors is called the *visible spectrum*. When you list the colors, you might use the imaginary name "Roy G. Biv" to help you remember their order. The letters in Roy's name represent the first letter of each color of visible light: **r**ed, **o**range, **y**ellow, **g**reen, **b**lue, **i**ndigo, and **v**iolet. When all the colors of visible light are combined, you see the light as white light. Sunlight and light from incandescent light bulbs and fluorescent light bulbs are examples of white light. You can see the visible spectrum in **Figure 11.**

Figure 11 *The visible spectrum contains all colors of light.*

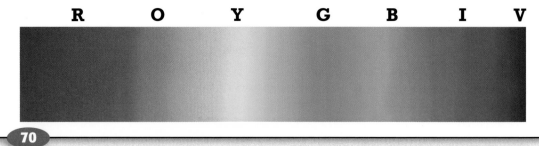

R   O   Y   G   B   I   V

IS THAT A FACT!

John Dalton (1766–1844), an English chemist and researcher of matter, suffered from colorblindness. Because he suffered from this malady, he was the first to study it and perform preliminary tests. In 1794, Dalton presented a paper on colorblindness before the Manchester Literary and Philosophical Society. Dalton's paper was the first known description of this vision phenomenon, and for many years colorblindness was called Daltonism.

Ultraviolet Light

Ultraviolet light is another type of electromagnetic wave produced by the sun. Ultraviolet waves have shorter wavelengths and higher frequencies than visible light. Therefore, ultraviolet waves carry more energy than visible light carries. This greater amount of energy affects us in both positive and negative ways.

Positive Effects On the positive side, ultraviolet waves produced artificially by ultraviolet lamps are used to kill bacteria on food and surgical instruments. In addition, limited exposure to ultraviolet light is beneficial to your body. When exposed to ultraviolet light, skin cells produce vitamin D, a substance necessary for the absorption of calcium by the intestines. Without calcium, your teeth and bones would be very weak.

Negative Effects On the negative side, overexposure to ultraviolet light can cause sunburn, skin cancer, damage to the eyes, wrinkles, and premature aging of the skin. Fortunately, much of the ultraviolet light from the sun does not reach the surface of the Earth. But you should still protect yourself against the ultraviolet light that does reach you. To do so, you should use sunscreen with a high SPF (**S**un **P**rotection **F**actor) and wear sunglasses that block out ultraviolet light, like the person on the left in **Figure 12.** You need this protection even on overcast days because ultraviolet light can travel through clouds.

Figure 12 *Sunscreen offers protection against a painful sunburn.*

Blocking the Sun

Sunscreens contain a chemical that prevents ultraviolet light from penetrating your skin. When you look at a bottle of sunscreen, you will see the abbreviation SPF followed by a number. The number is a guide to how long you can stay in the sun

without getting a sunburn. For example, if you use a sunscreen with SPF 15 and you normally burn after being in the sun for 10 minutes, you will be able to stay in the sun for 150 minutes without getting burned. Why do you think people who burn easily need a higher SPF?

IS THAT A FACT!

Ordinary window glass, which is made of silicon, is opaque to ultraviolet light. Suntanning lamps are made of quartz glass. Quartz glass transmits the ultraviolet rays needed for tanning.

SCIENCE HUMOR

Q: Why did the beam of light look sad after meeting with the prism?

A: It was all broken up inside!

Quiz

1. Why are X-ray machines used in some manufacturing processes? (X rays can detect flaws, cracks, or other defects inside an object that cannot be seen from the outside.)

2. Why are infrared sensors more useful at night? (Infrared sensors detect thermal energy given off by an object. During the daytime, temperature differences may not be as noticeable as they are at night.)

3. True or false: FM radio waves can travel greater distances than AM radio waves. (false)

ALTERNATIVE ASSESSMENT

Writing Have students write a short story in which the characters use or are affected by each of the different types of EM radiation.

SCIENTISTS AT ODDS

Some scientists consider cosmic photons to be EM waves. These photons have greater frequencies and shorter wavelengths than gamma rays. The incredible energy required to create these cosmic photons may come from supernovas or other astrophysical phenomena. Refer to Teaching Transparencies 196 and 197 to help students understand supernovas.

Teaching Transparencies 196, 197
"The H-R Diagram: A and B"

LINK TO EARTH SCIENCE

X Rays and Gamma Rays

X rays and gamma rays have some of the shortest wavelengths and highest frequencies of all EM waves. X rays carry a great deal of energy and easily penetrate a variety of materials. This characteristic makes X rays useful in the medical field, as shown in **Figure 13**. However, too much exposure to X rays can damage or kill living cells. Patients receiving X-ray examinations often wear a lead-lined apron to protect the parts of the body that do not need X-ray exposure.

Figure 13 *If you fall and hurt your arm, a doctor might use an X-ray machine to check for broken bones.*

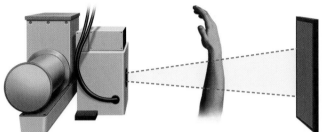
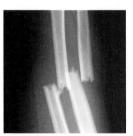

X rays travel easily through skin and muscle but are absorbed by bones.

The X rays that are not absorbed strike the film.

Bright areas appear on the film where X rays are absorbed by the bones.

Gamma rays carry large amounts of energy and can penetrate materials very easily. Every day you are exposed to small amounts of gamma rays that do not harm you. Because of their high energy, gamma rays are used to treat some forms of cancer. Radiologists focus the rays on tumors inside the body to kill the cancer cells. While this treatment can have positive effects, it often has negative side effects because some healthy cells are also killed.

internet connect

SCI LINKS
NSTA

TOPIC: The Electromagnetic Spectrum
GO TO: www.scilinks.org
*sci*LINKS NUMBER: HSTP530

SECTION REVIEW

1. Explain why ultraviolet light, X rays, and gamma rays can be both helpful and harmful.

2. Describe how three different types of electromagnetic waves have been useful to you today.

3. Comparing Concepts Compare the wavelengths and frequencies of infrared, ultraviolet, and visible light. How does the energy carried by each type of wave compare with the others?

▼ *Answers to Section Review*

1. Ultraviolet light is useful because it can kill bacteria and help the human body produce vitamin D. But overexposure to ultraviolet waves can cause sunburn, wrinkles, and skin cancer. X rays and gamma rays are used in medicine to check for broken bones and to treat cancer. Because X rays and gamma rays carry so much energy, they can kill healthy, living cells.

Therefore, exposure to both X rays and gamma rays should be limited.

2. Accept all reasonable answers.

3. wavelengths (longest to shortest): IR, visible light, UV light; frequencies (lowest to highest): IR, visible light, UV; energy (lowest to highest): IR, visible, UV. Light waves with shorter wavelengths and higher frequencies will carry greater amounts of energy.

Terms to Learn

reflection   refraction
law of reflection   diffraction
absorption   interference
scattering

What You'll Do

◆ Compare regular reflection with diffuse reflection.

◆ Describe absorption and scattering of light.

◆ Explain how refraction can create optical illusions and separate white light into colors.

◆ Describe diffraction and interference of light.

Interactions of Light Waves

Have you ever seen a cat's eyes glow in the dark when light shines on them? Cats have a special layer of cells in the back of their eyes that reflects light. This layer helps the cat see better by giving the eyes another chance to detect the light. Reflection is just one way light waves interact. All types of EM waves interact in several ways. Because we can see visible light, it is easier to explain interactions involving visible light.

Reflection

Reflection occurs when light or any other wave bounces off an object. When you see yourself in a mirror, you are actually seeing light that has been reflected twice—first from you and then from the mirror. Reflection allows you to see objects that don't produce their own light. When light strikes an object, some of the light reflects off of it and is detected by your eyes.

But if light is reflecting off you and off the objects around you, why can't you see your reflection on a wall? To answer this question, you must first learn about the law of reflection.

The Law of Reflection Light reflects off surfaces the same way that a ball bounces off the ground. If you throw the ball straight down against a smooth surface, it will bounce straight up. If you bounce it at an angle, it will bounce away at an angle. The **law of reflection** states that the angle of incidence is equal to the angle of reflection. *Incidence* is the falling of a beam of light on a surface. **Figure 14** illustrates this law.

Figure 14 **The Law of Reflection**

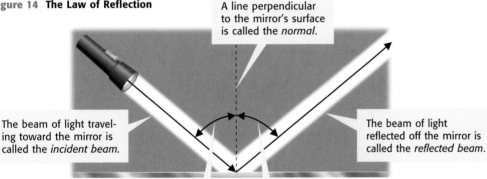

A line perpendicular to the mirror's surface is called the *normal.*

The beam of light traveling toward the mirror is called the *incident beam.*

The beam of light reflected off the mirror is called the *reflected beam.*

The angle between the incident beam and the normal is called the *angle of incidence.*

The angle between the reflected beam and the normal is called the *angle of reflection.*

73

Multicultural CONNECTION

Greek philosophers Hero and Ptolemy believed that eyes emitted rays that were reflected back by objects. However, an Iraqi scientist named Abu 'Ali al-Hasan ibn al-Haytham (c. 965–1039) believed differently. His theory of vision was very similar to today's: Objects are seen because of the light they reflect or emit.

Teaching Transparency 292 "The Law of Reflection"

Directed Reading Worksheet Section 3

SECTION **3**

Focus

Interactions of Light Waves

This section discusses reflection, refraction, diffraction, and interference of light waves. Students learn how light is absorbed and scattered and how white light can be separated into colors.

🔔 Bellringer

Have students do the following exercise:

Mirrors are common objects that most people use every day. From your experience, explain how mirrors work and describe what they do to light waves.

1 Motivate

ACTIVITY

Making a Periscope Place students in groups. Give each group a shoe box, two small hand mirrors, some modeling clay, and a pair of scissors. The mirrors must be small enough to stand upright inside the shoe box. Have students cut a 3 cm hole on the left side of each end of the box (so the holes will not be directly opposite each other). Then tell students that their job is to arrange the mirrors inside of the box with the modeling clay. The mirrors must be arranged in such a way that someone can look straight into one hole and see out of the other hole. Ask students to explain what property light must have that allows this experiment to work.

2 Teach

READING 📖 STRATEGY

Predicting Students have already studied mechanical waves, so ask them to predict some of the ways in which light waves might interact with each other. (Students should predict that light waves can be reflected, refracted, or diffracted and that they may interfere with each other.)

MEETING INDIVIDUAL NEEDS

Learners Having Difficulty
Provide each pair of students with a flashlight, a comb, a protractor, and a mirror. Have them stand the mirror on one edge with the reflecting side facing them. Have students place a sheet of paper on the table in front of the mirror and lay the protractor on top of the paper with the straight edge of the protractor against the mirror. Next, have them place the flashlight pointed toward the mirror at an angle and turn it on. The comb should be placed in front of the light. Have students trace the path of one of the beams and note the angle at which the beam strikes the mirror. Have students compare that angle with the angle of reflection.

Sheltered English

Teaching Transparency 292
"Regular and Diffuse Reflection"

Types of Reflection So back to the question, "Why can you see your reflection in a mirror but not in a wall?" The answer has to do with the differences between the two surfaces. If the reflecting surface is very smooth, like a mirror or polished metal, light beams reflect off all points of the surface at the same angle. This is called *regular reflection*. If the reflecting surface is slightly rough, like a wall, light beams will hit the surface and reflect at many different angles. This is called *diffuse reflection*. **Figure 15** illustrates the difference between the two types of reflection.

Figure 15 Regular Reflection Vs. Diffuse Reflection

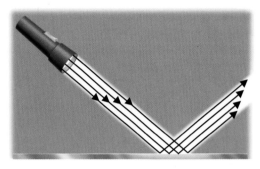 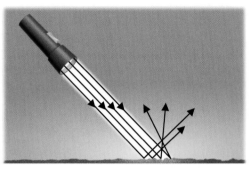

Regular reflection occurs when light beams are reflected at the same angle. When your eye detects the reflected beams, you can see a reflection on the surface.

Diffuse reflection occurs when light beams reflect at many different angles. You can't see a reflection because not all of the reflected light is directed toward your eyes.

Absorption and Scattering

You have probably noticed that when you use a flashlight, objects that are closer to you appear brighter than objects that are farther away. The light appears to weaken the farther it travels from the flashlight. This happens partially because the beam spreads out and partially because of absorption and scattering.

Absorption of Light The transfer of energy carried by light waves to particles of matter is called **absorption.** When you shine a flashlight in the air, the air particles absorb some of the energy from the light. This causes the light to become dim, as shown in **Figure 16.** The farther the light travels from the flashlight, the more it is absorbed by air particles.

Figure 16 *A beam of light becomes dimmer partially because of absorption and scattering.*

🌍 Multicultural CONNECTION

The French scientist Hippolyte-Louis Fizeau was the first person to measure the speed of light using a laboratory experiment. Fizeau used mirrors and a rotating toothed-wheel to break a beam of light into a series of pulses and then measure the speed of those pulses.

Homework

Have students determine the length and the placement of the shortest possible flat mirror in which a 2 m tall person could see his/her entire body. (1 m long; the top of the mirror should be placed slightly above eye level—one half the distance between the eyes and the top of the head)

Scattering of Light The release of light energy by particles of matter that have absorbed energy is called **scattering**. When the light is released, it scatters in all directions. Light from a flashlight is scattered out of the beam by air particles. This scattered light allows you to see objects outside of the beam, as shown in Figure 16 on the previous page. However, because light is scattered out of the beam, the beam becomes dimmer.

Scattering makes the sky blue. Light with shorter wavelengths is scattered more than light with longer wavelengths. Sunlight is made up of many different colors of light, but blue light (which has a very short wavelength) is scattered more than any other color. So when you look at the sky, you see a background of blue light. You can learn more about the scattering of light by doing the QuickLab at right.

Refraction

Imagine that you and a friend are at a lake. Your friend wades into the water. You look at her and are startled to see that her feet look like they are separated from her legs! You know her feet did not come off, so how can you explain what you see? The answer has to do with refraction.

Refraction is the bending of a wave as it passes at an angle from one medium to another. Refraction of light waves occurs because the speed of light varies depending on the material through which the waves are traveling. In a vacuum, light travels at 300,000,000 m/s, but it travels more slowly through matter. When a wave enters a new medium at an angle, the part of the wave that enters first begins traveling at a different speed from the rest of the wave. **Figure 17** shows how a light beam is bent by refraction.

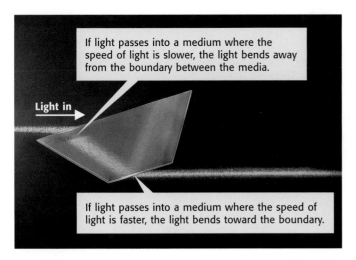

If light passes into a medium where the speed of light is slower, the light bends away from the boundary between the media.

Light in

If light passes into a medium where the speed of light is faster, the light bends toward the boundary.

Figure 17 *Light travels more slowly through glass than it does through air. Therefore, light refracts as it passes at an angle from air to glass or from glass to air.*

75

IS THAT A FACT!

A blue jay's feathers are not really blue. The air molecules on the surface barbs of the feathers scatter the red-and-green light of the visible spectrum, leaving blue light to reflect to our eyes.

BRAIN FOOD

The earliest mirrors date back to 6000 B.C. and were discovered in areas around Turkey and Egypt. These mirrors were about 90 mm in diameter and were made from flat pieces of polished igneous rock called obsidian.

Natural rainbows are visible only when the sun is lower than 42° above the horizon. This is because of the way water refracts through raindrops. It is unlikely that you will see a rainbow at noon!

CROSS-DISCIPLINARY FOCUS

Mathematics The first person to explain how rainbows form was René Descartes (1596–1650), a famous French mathematician and scientist. His explanation was published in 1637 in his book *Discours de la Methode*. Descartes reasoned that because rainbows also appear in waterfalls and water fountains, as well as in the sky, rainbows must be a result of drops of water affecting light waves.

REAL-WORLD CONNECTION

In recent decades, fiber optic technology has become a standard for the telecommunication industry. This technology utilizes information encoded into light beams that travel through small, pliable glass cables. These glass, or fiberoptic, cables are composed of two different types of optically conducting materials. The center, or *core,* is the glass through which the light travels. The *clad,* which surrounds the core, has a lower index of refraction and totally reflects light, thereby containing the light within the core regions.

Figure 18 *Refraction can create the illusion that the feet of the person in the water are separated from her legs. Try this for yourself!*

Optical Illusions Normally when you look at an object, the light reflecting off the object travels in a straight line from the object to your eye. Your brain always interprets light as traveling in straight lines. However, when you look at an object that is underwater, the light reflecting off the object does *not* travel in a straight line. Instead, it refracts. **Figure 18** shows how refraction creates an optical illusion.

Refraction and Color Separation You have already learned that white light is actually composed of all the colors of visible light. You also know that the different colors correspond to different wavelengths. When white light is refracted, the amount that the light bends depends on its wavelength. Light waves with short wavelengths bend more than light waves with long wavelengths. Because of this, white light can be separated into different colors during refraction, as shown in **Figure 19.** Color separation during refraction is responsible for the formation of rainbows. Rainbows are created when sunlight is refracted by water droplets.

Figure 19 *A prism is a piece of glass that separates white light into the colors of visible light by refraction.*

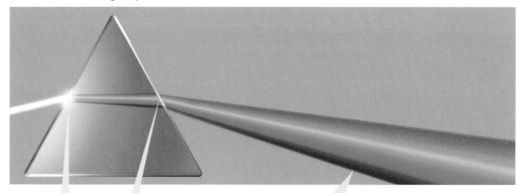

Light passing through a prism is refracted twice—once when it enters and once when it exits.

Violet light, which has a short wavelength, is refracted more than red light, which has a long wavelength.

Teaching Transparency 293
"White Light is Separated by a Prism"

IS THAT A FACT!

Some light bulbs and mirrors are frosted or etched to reduce glare or to create interesting visual effects. This process involves applying hydrofluoric acid, a powerful and toxic acid, directly to the glass. This acid reacts with silicon atoms in the glass to produce this effect.

Diffraction

Refraction isn't the only way light waves are bent. **Diffraction** is the bending of waves around barriers or through openings. The diffraction of light waves is not always easy to see. The diffraction of water waves, shown in **Figure 20,** is easier to see. The amount a wave diffracts depends on its wavelength and the size of the barrier or the opening. The greatest amount of diffraction occurs when the barrier or opening is the same size or smaller than the wavelength.

The wavelength of light is very small—about 100 times smaller than the thickness of a human hair! So in order for light to diffract very much, light has to be passing through a slit or some other opening that is very narrow.

Light waves cannot diffract very much around large obstacles, such as buildings. That's why you can't see around corners. But light waves always diffract a small amount. You can observe light waves diffracting if you examine the edges of a shadow. Diffraction causes the edges of shadows to be blurry.

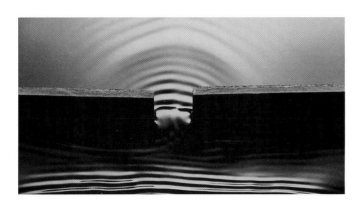

Figure 20 *Water waves are often used to model the behavior of light waves.*

Interference

Interference is a wave interaction that occurs when two or more waves overlap. Overlapping waves can combine by constructive or destructive interference.

Constructive Interference When waves combine by *constructive interference,* the resulting wave has a greater amplitude than the individual waves had. Constructive interference of light waves can be observed when light of one wavelength shines through two small slits onto a screen. The light on the screen will appear as a series of alternating bright and dark bands. The bright bands result from light waves combining through constructive interference to create a light wave with a greater amplitude.

Two lamps are brighter than one, but it's not because of constructive interference. It's because two lamps produce more energy in the form of photons than one lamp. As a result, the light has a greater intensity, which makes the room brighter.

CONNECT TO
LIFE SCIENCE

Archerfish *(Toxotes jaculator)* have the ability to correct for the refraction of light between air and water, and they have the ability to judge the distance to their prey. There are six species of archerfish that live in estuaries, wetlands, and fresh water in Southeast Asia, the western Pacific, and Australia. Archerfish can grow to 23 cm in length. Archerfish knock insects and other small prey from overhanging vegetation by spitting jets of water at them. Archerfish have a groove in the roof of their mouth. When the tongue is pressed against the groove and the gills are squeezed shut, a jet of water is produced. These fish can hit prey more than 1.5 m away!

3 Extend

DEMONSTRATION

Obtain a piece of diffraction grating and a laser. Darken the room, and point the laser at a wall. Ask the students to describe what they see on the wall. (a single red dot)

Place the diffraction grating in front of the laser light, and aim the beam at the same wall. Ask students what they see on the wall. (a series of small red dots)

Have students look at the dots carefully and describe what they see. (The dots aren't really round like the single dot.)

Pass out small pieces of diffraction grating and magnifying lenses. Encourage students to look carefully at the grating and to describe what they see. (lines)

Discuss diffraction with students and how diffracted laser light causes the series of flattened circles of light instead of a single dot.

REAL-WORLD CONNECTION

A common use of light interference is using laser light to create a hologram. Students will learn more about how holograms are produced in Chapter 4, "Light and Our World."

Reinforcement Worksheet
"Fiona, Private Eye"

Reinforcement Worksheet
"Light Interactions"

1. The moon does not produce light of its own. So where does moonlight come from? (Moonlight is sunlight that is reflected off of the moon to the Earth.)

2. Archerfish shoot jets of water at insects sitting on vegetation above the water, so they must adjust for refraction. Where is the ideal place for an archerfish to be in relation to its prey? Why? (The archerfish should be directly below its prey. Light entering the water perpendicular to the surface is not refracted.)

3. Explain how colors are separated in a rainbow. (Rainbows form when water droplets refract sunlight. Light of shorter wavelengths, such as violet, is refracted more than light of longer wavelengths, such as red.)

ALTERNATIVE ASSESSMENT

Concept Mapping Have students make a concept map that shows the following properties of light:

reflection, refraction, scattering, diffraction, and interference

Concept maps should include examples.

Teaching Transparency 294 "Constructive and Destructive Interference"

Critical Thinking Worksheet "Now You See It, Now You Don't"

Destructive Interference When waves combine by *destructive interference,* the resulting wave has a smaller amplitude than the individual waves had. Therefore, when light waves interfere destructively, the result will be dimmer light.

You do not see constructive or destructive interference of white light. To understand why, remember that white light is composed of waves with many different wavelengths. The waves rarely line up to combine in total destructive interference. However, if light of only one wavelength is used, both constructive and destructive interference are easily observed, as illustrated in **Figure 21**.

Figure 21 Constructive and Destructive Interference

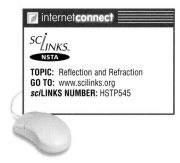

Red light of one wavelength passes between two tiny slits.

The light waves diffract as they pass through the tiny slits.

If you put a screen in front of the slits, you will see alternating bright and dark bands.

Constructive interference

Destructive interference

The diffracted light waves interfere both constructively and destructively.

internet**connect**

SCI*LINKS*
NSTA

TOPIC: Reflection and Refraction
GO TO: www.scilinks.org
*sci***LINKS NUMBER:** HSTP545

SECTION REVIEW

1. Explain the difference between absorption and scattering.

2. Why does a straw look bent in a glass of water?

3. Why do the edges of shadows seem blurry? Explain your answer.

4. Applying Concepts Explain why you can see your reflection on a spoon but not on a piece of cloth.

▼ *Answers to Section Review*

1. Absorbtion is the transfer of energy carried by light waves to particles of matter. Scattering is the release of light energy by particles that have absorbed energy.

2. A straw looks bent in a glass of water because of the refraction of light waves.

3. The edge of shadows seem blurry because light waves diffract around objects.

4. Light reflects off of a spoon by regular reflection, so you can see your image in the spoon. But light reflects off of a piece of cloth by diffuse reflection. Thus, you can see the cloth, but not your image.

Light and Color

Terms to Learn

transmission   opaque
transparent   pigment
translucent

What You'll Do

◆ Name and describe the three ways light interacts with matter.
◆ Explain how the color of an object is determined.
◆ Compare the primary colors of light and the primary pigments.

Have you ever wondered what gives an object its color? You already know that white light is made of all the colors of light. But when you see fruit in white light, you see color. For example, strawberries are red and bananas are yellow. Why aren't they all white? And how can a soda bottle be green and let you see through it at the same time? To answer these questions, you must first learn how light interacts with matter. Then you will understand why objects have different colors.

Light and Matter

When light strikes any form of matter, it can interact with the matter in three different ways—it can be reflected, absorbed, or transmitted. You learned about reflection and absorption in the previous section. **Transmission** is the passing of light through matter. You see the transmission of light all the time. All of the light that reaches your eyes is transmitted through air. Light can interact with matter in several ways at the same time, as shown in **Figure 22.**

Figure 22 *Light is transmitted, reflected, and absorbed when it strikes the glass in a window.*

You can see the glass and your reflection in it because light is **reflected** off the glass.

You can see objects outside because light is **transmitted** through the glass.

The glass feels warm when you touch it because some light is **absorbed** by the glass.

Light and Color

Students will learn how light interacts with matter. Students will also learn what determines the color of an object and will learn about the primary colors of light and the primary pigments. Students will explore what happens when colors of light or pigments are mixed.

🔔 Bellringer

Ask students the following:

What is your favorite color? It is a simple question, but have you ever thought about why you like a particular color more than others? In a short paragraph, explain why you like your favorite color. Also explain how certain colors affect your mood.

1) Motivate

DEMONSTRATION

Cover one lens of a high-intensity flashlight with a green filter and a second flashlight lens with a red filter. In a darkened room, turn the "green" light on, and shine it on a white sheet, white wall, or overhead screen. Turn the "red" light on, and shine it on a different area of the screen. Ask the students what colors they see. Ask students to predict what color they will see if you overlap the green and red light. The students will probably answer "brown." Slowly overlap the two colors. (Yellow will appear.)

SCIENCE HUMOR

Q: How many magicians does it take to change a light bulb?

A: Depends on what you want to change it into!

Homework

Challenge students to write a short explanation of why it is fortunate that some materials and objects transmit light. Why is it fortunate that some things are translucent or opaque? Accept all reasonable answers.

Directed Reading Worksheet Section 4

CONNECT TO
LIFE SCIENCE

Although the lens of the human eye is usually transparent, some conditions, such as cataracts, and injuries can make the lens translucent or even opaque. Most cataracts are the result of aging or long-term exposure to ultraviolet light. While you cannot stop the aging process, you can minimize exposure to UV light by wearing a hat and sunglasses.

GROUP ACTIVITY

Up to 1 in 12 men are reported to be colorblind. This does not mean that they see only in black and white. In fact, most color-blind people can't distinguish between red and green. Some people who are colorblind can't distinguish between red and yellow colors. With this in mind, consider the color of traffic lights. Have students design a traffic light or a flashing caution light that would be better suited for people who are colorblind.

Types of Matter Matter through which visible light is easily transmitted is said to be **transparent**. Air, glass, and water are examples of transparent matter. You can see objects clearly when you view them through transparent matter.

Sometimes windows in bathrooms are made of frosted glass. If you try to look through one of these types of windows, you will see only blurry shapes. You can't see clearly through a frosted window because it is translucent. **Translucent** matter transmits light but also scatters the light as it passes through the matter. Wax paper is an example of translucent matter.

Matter that does not transmit any light is said to be **opaque**. You cannot see through opaque objects. Metal, wood, and this book are examples of opaque objects. You can compare transparent, translucent, and opaque matter in **Figure 23.**

Figure 23 **What's for Lunch?**

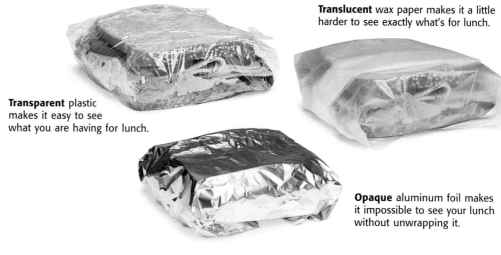

Translucent wax paper makes it a little harder to see exactly what's for lunch.

Transparent plastic makes it easy to see what you are having for lunch.

Opaque aluminum foil makes it impossible to see your lunch without unwrapping it.

Colors of Objects

How does the interaction of light with matter determine an object's color? You already know that the color of light is determined by the wavelength of the light wave. Red has the longest wavelength, violet has the shortest wavelength, and other colors have wavelengths in between.

The color that an object appears to be is determined by the wavelengths of light that reach your eyes. Light reaches your eyes after being reflected off an object or after being transmitted through an object. After reaching your eyes, light is converted into electrical impulses and interpreted by your brain as colors.

LabBook

What's a bean's favorite color? It's not a riddle, it's an experiment on page 132 of the LabBook.

80

Homework

Cone cells in our eyes react to wavelengths of light that we call red, green, and blue. Humans can detect a tremendous range of colors, hues, tints, and shades. Have students look around at home and make a table or chart of all the different colors they see. The title of the table is "colors," and the four main headings are "red," "green," "blue," and "others." Have students describe as many different colors, shades, and tints as they can.

Colors of Opaque Objects When white light strikes a colored opaque object, some colors of light are absorbed and some are reflected. Only the light that is reflected reaches your eyes and is detected. Therefore, the colors of light that are reflected by an opaque object determine the color you see. For example, if your sweater reflects blue light and absorbs all other colors, you will see that the sweater is blue. Another example is shown in **Figure 24.**

Self-Check

If blue light shines on a white sheet of paper, what color does the paper appear to be?

(Turn to page 152 to check your answer.)

Figure 24 *When white light shines on a strawberry, only red light is reflected. All other colors of light are absorbed. Therefore, the strawberry looks red to you.*

If green objects reflect green light and red objects reflect red light, what colors of light are reflected by the cow shown at right? Remember that white light includes all colors of light. So white objects—such as the white hair in the cow's hide—appear white because all the colors of light are reflected. On the other hand, black is the absence of color. When light strikes a black object, all the colors are absorbed.

Colors of Transparent and Translucent Objects
The color of transparent and translucent objects is determined differently from the color of opaque objects. Ordinary window glass is colorless in white light because it transmits all the colors that strike it. However, some transparent objects are colored. When you look through colored transparent or translucent objects, you see the color of light that was transmitted through the material. All the other colors were absorbed, as shown in **Figure 25.**

Figure 25 *This bottle is green because the plastic transmits only green light.*

CONNECT TO EARTH SCIENCE

Astronomers use starlight to calculate the temperature of stars. Because of its size and temperature, our sun is listed as a yellow dwarf. Interested students can do some research to find out more about how scientists use light to study stars and other objects in space.

LabBook PG 132
What Color of Light Is Best for Green Plants?

LabBook PG 133
Which Color Is Hottest?

READING STRATEGY

Prediction Guide Before students read the section about colors of opaque objects, ask them whether they would rather sit on a black bench or a white bench if both benches have been exposed to direct sunlight on a hot day. Ask students to explain their answer. Have students read the section and discuss it with them to make sure they understand why the black bench would be warmer. Ask them whether they would make the same choice if the same two benches were made of transparent or translucent plastic.
Sheltered English

Answer to Self-Check

The paper will appear blue because only blue light is reflected from the paper.

Multicultural CONNECTION

Colors are used as symbols in many human cultures. For example, red often represents warning or danger, while green can represent safety or safe passage. In the Ukraine, there is a long tradition of egg art—the coloring and decorating of eggs—to express emotions and to send messages. Choosing the right color is important. Egg decorators know, for instance, that red stands for love, green for growth, pink for success, and black for remembrance.

Interactive Explorations CD-ROM In the Spotlight

internetconnect

SCiLINKS
NSTA
TOPIC: Colors
GO TO: www.scilinks.org
*sci*LINKS **NUMBER:** HSTP550

3) Extend

DEMONSTRATION

Take three small, high-intensity flashlights or slide projectors, and cover one light with a red filter (or colored cellophane), one with a green filter, and one with a blue filter. Darken the room as much as possible. Shine the lights on a white screen without mixing any colors. Then, mix two or more colors from the lights. Before each combination, ask students to predict what color will be produced.

GOING FURTHER

Divide the class into small groups. Distribute a page from the Sunday comics to each group and ask students to list the colors they see on the page. Then give each group one or more magnifying lenses, and instruct students to look very carefully at the different colors. Ask them to list the colors they see under the magnifying lens. Have them list the colors of dots necessary to make a colored image. For instance, "What colors of dots produce a true green in a cartoon image?" (yellow and cyan)

MATERIALS

FOR EACH STUDENT:
• 4 plastic filters

Teacher Notes: Used but still functioning filters can be obtained from your school's theater department.

The colors you see on a color television are produced by color addition of the primary colors of light. A television screen is made up of groups of tiny red, green, and blue dots. These dots are made of chemicals called phosphors. Each phosphor dot will glow red, green, or blue—depending on the type of phosphor it is—when the dot is hit by an electron beam. The colors emitted by the glowing phosphor dots add together to produce all the different colors you see on the screen.

QuickLab

Rose-Colored Glasses?

1. Obtain **four plastic filters**— red, blue, yellow, and green.
2. Look through one filter at an object across the room. Describe the object's color.
3. Repeat step 2 with each of the filters.
4. Repeat step 2 with two or three filters together.
5. Why do you think the colors change when you use more than one filter?
6. Write your observations and answers in your ScienceLog.

82

Mixing Colors of Light

In order to get white light, you need to combine all colors of light, right? Well, that's one way of doing it. You can also get white light by adding just three colors of light together—red, blue, and green—as shown in **Figure 26**. In fact, these three colors can be combined in different ratios to produce all colors of visible light. Red, blue, and green are therefore called the *primary colors of light.*

Color Addition   When colors of light combine, more wavelengths of light are present. Therefore, combining colors of light is called color addition. When two primary colors are added together, a *secondary color* is produced. The secondary colors are cyan (blue plus green), magenta (blue plus red), and yellow (red plus green).

Figure 26 *Primary colors—written in white—combine to produce white light. Secondary colors—written in black—are the result of two primary colors added together.*

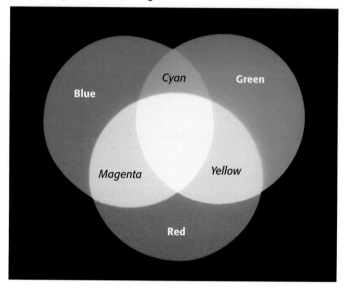

Mixing Colors of Pigment

If you have ever tried mixing paints in art class, you know that you can't make white paint by mixing red, blue, and green paint. The difference between mixing paint and mixing light is due to the fact that paint contains pigments. A **pigment** is a material that gives a substance its color by absorbing some colors of light and reflecting others.

Answers to QuickLab

2–4. The answers will vary depending on the object chosen by the student and the order in which the different filters are used. Students should notice that a colored object seems to change colors when viewed through different filters or combinations of filters.

5. The colors changed because different colors of light are allowed to pass through the different filters. If you use more than one filter, fewer colors are allowed to pass through.

Almost everything contains pigments. In fact, pigments give objects color. Chlorophyll and melanin are two examples of pigments. Chlorophyll gives plants a green color, and melanin gives your skin its color.

Color Subtraction   Each pigment absorbs at least one color of light. When you mix pigments together, more colors of light are absorbed, or subtracted. Therefore, mixing colors of pigments is called color subtraction.

The *primary pigments* are yellow, cyan, and magenta. They can be combined to produce any other color. In fact, all the colors in this book were produced by using just the primary pigments and black ink. The black ink was used to provide contrast to the images. **Figure 27** shows how the four pigments combine to produce many different colors.

Geology CONNECTION

Minerals are naturally occurring crystalline solids. A blue mineral called azurite was once used by European painters as a pigment in paint. But these painters didn't realize that azurite changes into another mineral over time. The new mineral, malachite, is green. So some paintings that once had beautiful blue skies now have skies that look greenish.

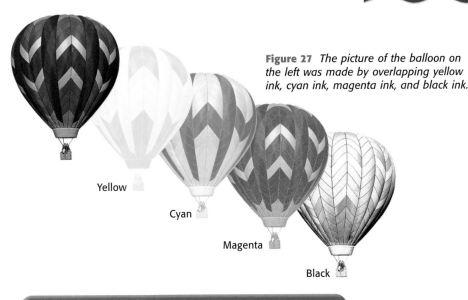

Figure 27 *The picture of the balloon on the left was made by overlapping yellow ink, cyan ink, magenta ink, and black ink.*

Yellow

Cyan

Magenta

Black

SECTION REVIEW

1. Describe three different ways light interacts with matter.

2. What are the primary colors of light, and why are they called primary colors?

3. Describe the difference between the primary colors of light and the primary pigments.

4. **Applying Concepts**   Explain what happens to the different colors of light when white light shines on a violet object.

internet**connect**

SCI**LINKS.**
NSTA

TOPIC: Colors
GO TO: www.scilinks.org
*sci*LINKS NUMBER: HSTP550

83

Answers to Section Review

1. Light may be reflected (light bounces off matter), absorbed (energy from light is transferred to matter), or transmitted (light passes through matter) by matter.

2. The primary colors of light—red, blue, and green—are called primary colors because all other colors of light can be made by combining them.

3. The primary colors of light combine by color addition to form white light. The primary pigments combine by color subtraction to form black.

4. When white light shines on a violet object, violet light is reflected. All other colors of light are absorbed.

4 **Close**

CROSS-DISCIPLINARY FOCUS

Art   Encourage students to find information about the pointillist artists Georges Seurat, Henri Edmond Cross, and Paul Signac. In art, pointillism is the theory or practice of applying small strokes or dots of color to a surface so that when viewed from a distance, the dots or strokes blend to form an image.

Quiz

1. Is the color of a purple racing car determined the same way as the color of a clear purple perfume bottle? Explain. (No; the purple car reflects purple light and absorbs all other colors; the clear purple bottle transmits purple light and absorbs the other colors.)

2. What color of light will you produce if you mix green light with magenta light? Why? (White; magenta light is a combination of red and blue light, and adding green to it combines all three primary colors to make white light.)

3. In a television show, a doctor gets some yellow roses from a grateful patient. How is that yellow color produced on your television screen? (Yellow is produced by mixing the colors emitted by the red and green phosphor dots on the screen.)

ALTERNATIVE ASSESSMENT

Concept Mapping   Have students make a concept map that shows the three ways that light interacts with matter. The map should include how the color of objects is determined for each interaction.

Mixing Colors
Teacher's Notes

Time Required

One or two 45-minute class periods

Lab Ratings

EASY ────────→ HARD

TEACHER PREP 🧪🧪
STUDENT SET-UP 🧪🧪
CONCEPT LEVEL 🧪🧪
CLEAN UP 🧪🧪

MATERIALS

Materials listed are for each group of 2–4 students. If a sufficient number of flashlights is not available, consider using the spotlights on the school stage or portable floodlight holders instead. Each group should have a set of watercolors that includes red, blue, and green.

Safety Caution

Students should wear aprons when doing Part B of this lab.

Answers

6. Mixing two colors of light together results in a color that is brighter than the original colors.

7. Mixing three colors of light results in a color that is much brighter than the color produced by mixing two colors because more wavelengths are present.

8. The result would be bright white light because all the wavelengths of light would be combined.

Skill Builder Lab

Mixing Colors

Mix two colors, such as red and green, and you create a new color. Is the new color brighter or darker? Color and brightness depend on the light that reaches your eye. And what reaches your eye depends on whether you are adding colors (combining wavelengths by mixing colors of light) or subtracting colors (absorbing wavelengths by mixing colors of pigments). In this activity, you will do both types of color formation and see the results firsthand!

MATERIALS

Part A
- 3 flashlights
- colored filters–red, green, and blue
- white paper
- masking tape

Part B
- 2 small plastic or paper cups
- water
- paintbrush
- watercolor paints
- masking tape
- white paper
- metric ruler

Datasheets for LabBook

Part A: Color Addition

Procedure

1. Tape a colored filter over each flashlight lens.

2. In a darkened room, shine the red light on a sheet of clean white paper. Then shine the blue light next to the red light. You should have two circles of light, one red and one blue, next to each other.

3. Move the flashlights so that the circles overlap by about half their diameter. What color is formed in the area? Is the mixed area brighter or darker than the single-color areas? Record your observations.

4. Repeat steps 2 and 3 with the red and green lights.

5. Now shine all three lights at the same point on the paper. Record your observations.

Analysis

6. In general, when you mixed two colors, was the result brighter or darker than the original colors?

7. In step 5, you mixed all three colors. Was the resulting color brighter or darker than when you mixed two colors? Explain your answer in terms of color addition.

Red   ?   Green

8. What do you think would happen if you mixed together all the colors of light? Explain your answer.

Barry Bishop
San Rafael Junior High
Ferron, Utah

84

Part B: Color Subtraction

Procedure

9 Place a piece of masking tape on each cup. Label one cup "Clean" and the other cup "Dirty." Fill each cup about half full with water.

10 Wet the paintbrush thoroughly in the Clean cup. Using the watercolor paints, paint a red circle on the white paper. The circle should be approximately 4 cm in diameter.

11 Clean the brush by rinsing it first in the Dirty cup and then in the Clean cup.

12 Paint a blue circle next to the red circle. Then paint half the red circle with the blue paint.

13 Examine the three areas: red, blue, and mixed. What color is the mixed area? Does it appear brighter or darker than the red and blue areas? Record your observations in your ScienceLog.

14 Clean the brush. Paint a green circle 4 cm in diameter, and then paint half the blue circle with green paint.

15 Examine the green, blue, and mixed areas. Record your observations.

16 Now add green paint to the mixed red-blue area so that you have an area that is a mixture of red, green, and blue paint. Clean your brush.

17 Record your observations of this new mixed area.

Analysis

18 In general, when you mixed two colors, was the result brighter or darker than the original colors?

19 In step 16, you mixed all three colors. Was the result brighter or darker than the result from mixing two colors? Explain your answer in terms of color subtraction.

20 Based on your results, what do you think would happen if you mixed all the colors of paint? Explain your answer.

Procedure Notes

For further reinforcement in Part B, students can continue to mix colors to confirm their findings about color subtraction (provided their watercolor sets include more than the three required colors).

Answers

18. Mixing two colors of paint together results in a color that is darker than the original colors.

19. Mixing three colors of paint results in a color that is darker than the color that results from mixing two colors. Because each color of paint absorbs some light, colors that have been mixed together absorb even more light.

20. If you mixed all the colors of paint, all colors of light would be absorbed, and a black spot would result.

Disposal Information

Have plenty of paper towels on hand to wipe up water and paint spills. Make sure students clean their brushes thoroughly. Students should use soap and water to clean any watercolor smudges off their lab tables.

Chapter Highlights

SECTION 1

electromagnetic wave a wave that can travel through space or matter and consists of changing electric and magnetic fields.

radiation the emission of energy in the form of electromagnetic waves

SECTION 2

electromagnetic spectrum the entire range of electromagnetic waves

SECTION 1

Vocabulary

electromagnetic wave *(p. 62)*
radiation *(p. 63)*

Section Notes

- Light is an electromagnetic (EM) wave. An electromagnetic wave is a wave that travels as vibrating electric and magnetic fields. EM waves require no medium through which to travel.

- Electromagnetic waves are produced by the vibration of electrically charged particles.

- The speed of light in a vacuum is 300,000,000 m/s.

SECTION 2

Vocabulary

electromagnetic spectrum *(p. 65)*

Section Notes

- All EM waves travel at the speed of light. EM waves differ only by wavelength and frequency.

- The entire range of EM waves is called the electromagnetic spectrum.

- Radio waves are most often used for communication.

- Microwaves are used for cooking and in radar.

- Infrared waves have shorter wavelengths and higher frequencies than microwaves. The absorption of infrared waves is felt as an increase in temperature.

- Visible light is the very narrow range of wavelengths that humans can see. Different wavelengths are seen as different colors.

- Ultraviolet light is useful for killing bacteria and for producing vitamin D in the body, but overexposure can cause health problems.

- X rays and gamma rays are EM waves that are often used in medicine. Overexposure to these EM waves can damage or kill living cells.

☑ Skills Check

Math Concepts

DISTANCE To calculate the distance that light travels in space, multiply the amount of time light travels by the speed of light in a vacuum. The speed of light in a vacuum is 300,000,000 m/s. If light from a star travels for 192 seconds before reaching a planet, then the distance the light traveled can be calculated as follows:

distance = speed of light × time

distance = 300,000,000 m/s × 192 s

distance = 57,600,000,000 m

Visual Understanding

THE PRODUCTION OF LIGHT Light is produced by the vibration of electrically charged particles. Repeated vibrations of these particles, or electrons, release tiny "packets" of energy called photons. Review Figure 2 on page 63 to see how light and other electromagnetic waves are the result of electron movement.

Lab and Activity Highlights

Mixing Colors **PG 84**

What Color of Light Is Best for Green Plants? **PG 132**

Which Color Is Hottest? **PG 133**

 Datasheets for LabBook
(blackline masters for these labs)

SECTION 3

Vocabulary
> **reflection** *(p. 73)*
> **law of reflection** *(p. 73)*
> **absorption** *(p. 74)*
> **scattering** *(p. 75)*
> **refraction** *(p. 75)*
> **diffraction** *(p. 77)*
> **interference** *(p. 77)*

Section Notes

- Two types of reflection are regular and diffuse reflection.

- Absorption and scattering cause light beams to become dimmer with distance.

- How much a light beam bends during refraction depends on the light's wavelength.

- Light waves diffract more when traveling through a narrow opening.

- Interference of light waves can cause bright and dark bands.

SECTION 4

Vocabulary
> **transmission** *(p. 79)*
> **transparent** *(p. 80)*
> **translucent** *(p. 80)*
> **opaque** *(p. 80)*
> **pigment** *(p. 82)*

Section Notes

- Objects are classified as transparent, translucent, or opaque depending on their ability to transmit light.

- Colors of opaque objects are determined by the color of light they reflect. White opaque objects reflect all colors and black opaque objects absorb all colors.

- Colors of transparent and translucent objects are determined by the color of light they transmit. All other colors are absorbed.

- White light is a mixture of all colors of light. The primary colors of light are red, blue, and green.

- Pigments give objects color. The primary pigments are magenta, cyan, and yellow.

Labs
> **What Color of Light Is Best for Green Plants?** *(p. 132)*
> **Which Color Is Hottest?** *(p. 133)*

SECTION 3

reflection what happens when light or any other wave bounces off an object

law of reflection the law that states that the angle of incidence is equal to the angle of reflection

absorption the transfer of energy carried by light waves to particles of matter

scattering the release of light energy by particles of matter that have absorbed energy

refraction the bending of a wave as it passes at an angle from one medium to another

diffraction the bending of waves around barriers or through openings

interference a wave interaction that occurs when two or more waves overlap and combine

SECTION 4

transmission the passing of light through matter

transparent describes matter through which light is easily transmitted

translucent describes matter that transmits light but also scatters the light as it passes through the matter

opaque describes matter that does not transmit any light

pigment a material that gives a substance its color by absorbing some colors of light and reflecting others

---

 internetconnect

go.hrw.com

GO TO: go.hrw.com

Visit the **HRW** Web site for a variety of learning tools related to this chapter. Just type in the keyword:

KEYWORD: HSTLGT

SC*i*LINKS℠
NSTA

GO TO: www.scilinks.org

Visit the **National Science Teachers Association** on-line Web site for Internet resources related to this chapter. Just type in the *sci*LINKS number for more information about the topic:

TOPIC: Using Light	*sci*LINKS NUMBER: HSTP528
TOPIC: Light Energy	*sci*LINKS NUMBER: HSTP529
TOPIC: The Electromagnetic Spectrum	*sci*LINKS NUMBER: HSTP530
TOPIC: Reflection and Refraction	*sci*LINKS NUMBER: HSTP545
TOPIC: Colors	*sci*LINKS NUMBER: HSTP550

87

Lab and Activity Highlights

LabBank

 Long-Term Projects & Research Ideas, The Image of the Future

Interactive Explorations CD-ROM

 CD3, Exploration 7, "In the Spotlight"

 Vocabulary Review Worksheet

 Blackline masters of these Chapter Highlights can be found in the **Study Guide.**

Chapter Review Answers

USING VOCABULARY

1. Radiation
2. opaque
3. Interference
4. electromagnetic wave
5. transmission

UNDERSTANDING CONCEPTS

Multiple Choice

6. d
7. c
8. c
9. c
10. a
11. c
12. b
13. d
14. c

Short Answer

15. Electromagnetic waves differ by their wavelength and frequency (and by the amount of energy they carry).
16. An electromagnetic wave is produced when a charged particle vibrates. This creates a vibrating electric field, which creates a vibrating magnetic field. The two vibrating fields make up an electromagnetic wave.
17. Frost is translucent, so the light traveling through it is scattered as it passes through.

Chapter Review

USING VOCABULARY

To complete the following sentences, choose the correct term from each pair of terms listed below:

1. __?__ is the transfer of energy by electromagnetic waves. *(Radiation* or *Scattering)*

2. This book is a(n) __?__ object. *(translucent* or *opaque)*

3. __?__ is a wave interaction that occurs when two or more waves overlap and combine. *(Diffraction* or *Interference)*

4. Light is a type of __?__. *(electromagnetic wave* or *electromagnetic spectrum)*

5. Light travels through an object during __?__. *(absorption* or *transmission)*

UNDERSTANDING CONCEPTS

Multiple Choice

6. Electromagnetic waves transmit
   a. charges.   c. matter.
   b. fields.   d. energy.

7. Objects that transmit light easily are
   a. opaque.   c. transparent.
   b. translucent.   d. colored.

8. You can see yourself in a mirror because of
   a. absorption.   c. regular reflection.
   b. scattering.   d. diffuse reflection.

9. Shadows have blurry edges because of
   a. diffuse reflection.   c. diffraction.
   b. scattering.   d. refraction.

10. Microwaves are often used for
    a. cooking.
    b. broadcasting AM radio.
    c. cancer treatment.
    d. All of the above

11. What color of light is produced when red light is added to green light?
    a. cyan   c. yellow
    b. blue   d. white

12. Prisms produce rainbows through
    a. reflection.   c. diffraction.
    b. refraction.   d. interference.

13. Which type of electromagnetic wave travels the fastest in a vacuum?
    a. radio waves
    b. visible light
    c. gamma rays
    d. They all travel at the same speed.

14. Electromagnetic waves are made of
    a. vibrating particles.
    b. vibrating charged particles.
    c. vibrating electric and magnetic fields.
    d. electricity and magnetism.

Short Answer

15. Name two ways EM waves differ from one another.

16. Describe how an electromagnetic wave is produced.

17. Why is it difficult to see through glass that has frost on it?

Concept Mapping

18. Use the following terms to create a concept map: light, matter, reflection, absorption, scattering, transmission.

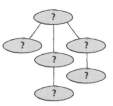

CRITICAL THINKING AND PROBLEM SOLVING

19. A tern is a type of bird that dives underwater to catch fish. When a young tern begins learning to catch fish, it is rarely successful. The tern has to learn that when a fish appears to be in a certain place underwater, the fish is actually in a slightly different place. Explain why the tern sees the fish in the wrong place.

20. Radio waves and gamma rays are both types of electromagnetic waves. Exposure to radio waves does not harm the human body, whereas exposure to gamma rays can be extremely dangerous. What is the difference between these types of EM waves? Why are gamma rays more dangerous?

21. If you look around a parking lot during the summer, you might notice sun shades set up in the windshields of cars. Explain how the sun shades help keep the inside of a car cool.

MATH IN SCIENCE

22. Calculate the time it takes for light from the sun to reach Mercury. Mercury is 54,900,000,000 m away from the sun.

INTERPRETING GRAPHICS

23. Each of the pictures below shows the effects of a wave interaction of light. Identify the interaction involved.

a

b

c

Reading Check-up

Take a minute to review your answers to the Pre-Reading Questions found at the bottom of page 60. Have your answers changed? If necessary, revise your answers based on what you have learned since you began this chapter.

89

Background

Luciferase assays have a number of relevant uses in medicine as well. Bacterial infections can be deadly. Researchers have developed luciferase assays to measure bacteria in the urine and blood. Antibiotics, the medicines used to treat bacterial infections, are not always effective. Luciferase tests can be used to evaluate the effectiveness of antibiotic therapy on particular patients.

ATP is one of the most significant sources of energy in biological compounds. ATP has three phosphate bonds; when these bonds are broken, they give off energy. If one phosphate is cleaved off the ATP molecule, it yields ADP, or adenosine diphosphate. This converts chemical energy into light energy by exciting the electrons in luciferin.

Science, Technology, and Society

Fireflies Light the Way

Just as beams of light from coastal lighthouses warn boats of approaching danger, scientists are using the light of an unlikely source—fireflies—to warn food inspectors of life-threatening bacterial contamination! Thousands of people die each year from meat contaminated with bacteria. The light from fireflies is being used to study several diseases, waste-water treatment, and environmental protection as well!

Nature's Guiding Light

A number of organisms, including some fishes, squids, beetles, and bacteria, emit light. Fireflies, in particular, use this light to attract mates. How do these organisms use energy to emit light?

Remarkably, all of these organisms use one enzyme to make light, an enzyme called *luciferase*. This enzyme breaks down *adenosine triphosphate* (ATP) to create energy. This energy is used to excite electrons to produce light in the form of a glow or flash. Fireflies are very effective light bulbs. Nearly 100 percent of the energy they get from ATP is given off as light. Only 10 percent of energy given off by electrical light bulbs is in the form of light; the other 90 percent is thermal energy!

Harnessing Life's Light

How have scientists harnessed the firefly's ability to produce light to find bacteria? Researchers have found the gene responsible for making luciferase. Scientists have taken the gene from fireflies that makes luciferase and inserted it into a virus that preys on bacteria. The virus isn't harmful to humans and can be mixed into meat to help scientists detect bacteria. When the virus infects the bacteria, it transfers the gene into the genetic machinery of the bacteria. This bacteria then produces luciferase and glows!

▲ *The firefly* (Photuris pyralis) *is helping food inspectors save thousands of lives each year!*

This process is being used to find a number of dangerous bacteria that contaminate foods, including *Salmonella* and *Escherichia coli*. These bacteria are responsible for thousands of deaths each year. Not only is the test effective, it is fast. Before researchers developed this test, it took up to 3 days to determine whether food was contaminated by bacteria. By that time, the food was already at the grocery store!

Think About It!

▶ What color of light would you hypothesize gives plants the most energy? Investigate, and see if your hypothesis is right!

90

Answer to Think About It!

Given the information on light energy in this chapter, students may hypothesize that light toward the blue end of the spectrum will provide the most energy to plants. Students will find out that photosynthesis is much more complex than this and requires a variety of light.

Eureka!

It's a Heat Wave!

Percy L. Spencer never stopped looking for answers. In fact, he patented 120 inventions in his 39 years with the company Raytheon. During a routine visit to one of the Raytheon laboratories in 1946, Spencer found that a candy bar had melted inside his coat pocket. He could have just chalked this up to body heat, but he didn't. Instead, he took a closer look at his surroundings and noticed a nearby magnetron—a tube he designed to produce microwaves for radar systems.

A Popping Test

This made Spencer curious. Did the microwaves from the magnetron melt the candy bar, and if so, could microwaves be used to heat other things? Spencer answered his questions by putting a bag of unpopped corn kernels next to a magnetron. The kernels popped! Spencer had just made the first "microwave" popcorn! The test was a huge success. This simple experiment showed that a magnetron could heat foods with microwaves, and it could heat them quickly. When Spencer patented his invention in 1953, he called it a "High Frequency Dielectric Heating Apparatus."

Perfect Timing!

Spencer originally designed magnetrons for radar machines used in World War II. Discovering another use for them was well timed. After the war, the military had little use for the 10,000 magnetrons a week that Raytheon could manufacture. So Raytheon decided to use the magnetrons to power Spencer's "High Frequency Dielectric

Heating Apparatus." But first the company had to come up with a simpler name! The winning entry in the renaming contest was "Radar Range," which later became one word, *Radarange*.

An Inconvenient Convenience

The first Radaranges had a few drawbacks. For one thing, they were very expensive. They also weighed over 340 kg and were 1.6 m tall. Try fitting that on your kitchen counter! Because the Radarange was so large and expensive, only restaurants, railroad companies, and cruise ships used them. By 1967, improvements in the design made the Radarange compact and affordable, similar to the microwave ovens of today.

The first microwave oven, known as a "Radarange," 1953 ▲

Now You're Cooking!

Just how do microwave ovens cook food? It just so happens that microwaves are absorbed by water molecules in the food being cooked. When water molecules throughout the food absorb microwaves, they start to move faster. As a result, the food's temperature increases. Leftovers anyone?

Find Out for Yourself

▶ Microwaves make water molecules in food move faster. This is what increases the temperature of food that is cooked in a microwave. But did you know that most dishes will not heat up in a microwave oven if there is no food on them? To discover why, find out what most dishes are made of. Then infer why empty dishes do not heat up in a microwave.

91

Answer to Find Out for Yourself

Most dishes are made of materials that do not have water molecules. If the dishes have no water molecules to absorb microwaves, the dishes will not get hot.

Background

Microwave radiation is very different from radioactive radiation. The radiation that microwave ovens use is called *nonionizing radiation*. This is not to be confused with the ionizing radiation of X rays, gamma rays, and cosmic rays that can cause damage to living cells (including genetic mutations and tissue damage) and alter the molecular structure of matter. Examples of nonionizing radiation are radio waves, infrared radiation, and visible light. These waves have lower frequencies and less energy than ionizing radiation.

Chapter Organizer

CHAPTER ORGANIZATION	TIME MINUTES	OBJECTIVES	LABS, INVESTIGATIONS, AND DEMONSTRATIONS
Chapter Opener pp. 92–93	45	National Standards: UCP 2, 3, SAI 1, ST 1, SPSP 5, HNS 1, 3	**Start-Up Activity,** Mirror, Mirror, p. 93
Section 1 Light Sources	90	▶ Compare luminous and illuminated objects. ▶ Name four ways light can be produced. UCP 1, 2, SPSP 5, HNS 1, 3, PS 3a, 3c, 3e, 3f	**Demonstration,** Neon Light, p. 96 in ATE
Section 2 Mirrors and Lenses	90	▶ Illustrate how mirrors and lenses form images using ray diagrams. ▶ Explain the difference between real and virtual images. ▶ Compare plane mirrors, concave mirrors, and convex mirrors. ▶ Explain how concave and convex lenses form images. UCP 2, SPSP 5, PS 3c; Labs UCP 3, PS 3c	**Skill Builder,** Mirror Images, p. 114 **Datasheets for LabBook,** Mirror Images **Discovery Lab,** Images from Convex Lenses, p. 134 **Datasheets for LabBook,** Images from Convex Lenses **Inquiry Labs,** Eye Spy
Section 3 Light and Sight	90	▶ Identify the parts of the human eye, and describe their functions. ▶ Describe some common vision problems, and explain how they can be corrected. UCP 2, SPSP 1, PS 3c	**Whiz-Bang Demonstrations,** Light Humor
Section 4 Light Technology	90	▶ Explain how optical instruments use lenses and mirrors to form images. ▶ Explain how lasers work and what makes laser light different from non-laser light. ▶ Identify uses for lasers. ▶ Describe how optical fibers and polarizing filters work. UCP 5, ST 2, SPSP 2, 5, PS 3c	**Demonstration,** p. 108 in ATE **QuickLab,** Now You See, Now You Don't, p. 113 **Labs You Can Eat,** Fiber-Optic Fun **EcoLabs & Field Activities,** Photon Drive **Long-Term Projects & Research Ideas,** Island Vacation

See page **T23** for a complete correlation of this book with the

NATIONAL SCIENCE EDUCATION STANDARDS.

TECHNOLOGY RESOURCES

 Guided Reading Audio CD English or Spanish, Chapter 4

 One-Stop Planner CD-ROM with Test Generator

 CNN **Science, Technology & Society,** Correcting Colorblindness, Segment 2

 Science Discovery Videodiscs: Image and Activity Bank with Lesson Plans: Light Fantastic

Science Sleuths: The Fogged Photos

CLASSROOM WORKSHEETS, TRANSPARENCIES, AND RESOURCES	SCIENCE INTEGRATION AND CONNECTIONS	REVIEW AND ASSESSMENT
Directed Reading Worksheet **Science Puzzlers, Twisters & Teasers**		
Directed Reading Worksheet, Section 1	**Astronomy Connection,** p. 94 **Cross-Disciplinary Focus,** p. 95 in ATE **Science, Technology, and Society:** Traffic Lights, p. 120	**Homework,** p. 96 in ATE **Section Review,** p. 97 **Quiz,** p. 97 in ATE **Alternative Assessment,** p. 97 in ATE
Transparency 295, How a Mirror Works **Directed Reading Worksheet,** Section 2 **Transparency 296,** The Optical Axis, Focal Point, and Focal Length **Transparency 297,** Creating Virtual Images and Real Images with a Concave Mirror **Transparency 298,** Thick and Thin Convex Lenses **Transparency 298,** A Concave Lens **Reinforcement Worksheet,** Mirror, Mirror	**Real-World Connection,** p. 99 in ATE **Real-World Connection,** p. 101 in ATE **Apply,** p. 102 **Math and More,** p. 102 in ATE **Cross-Disciplinary Focus,** p. 104 in ATE	**Homework,** pp. 99, 101 in ATE **Section Review,** p. 102 **Section Review,** p. 104 **Quiz,** p. 104 in ATE **Alternative Assessment,** p. 104 in ATE
Transparency 299, How Your Eyes Work **Directed Reading Worksheet,** Section 3	**Connect to Life Science,** p. 105 in ATE **Cross-Disciplinary Focus,** p. 106 in ATE **Biology Connection,** p. 107	**Section Review,** p. 107 **Quiz,** p. 107 in ATE **Alternative Assessment,** p. 107 in ATE
Transparency 299, How a Camera Works **Directed Reading Worksheet,** Section 4 **Transparency 2,** Compound Light Microscope **Transparency 300,** How Telescopes Work **Critical Thinking Worksheet,** Light That Heals	**Cross-Disciplinary Focus,** p. 108 in ATE **Connect to Earth Science,** p. 109 in ATE **Cross-Disciplinary Focus,** p. 109 in ATE **Multicultural Connection,** p. 111 in ATE **Connect to Life Science,** p. 111 in ATE **Real-World Connection,** p. 112 in ATE **Eye on the Environment:** Light Pollution, p. 121	**Self-Check,** p. 109 **Homework,** p. 110 in ATE **Section Review,** p. 113 **Quiz,** p. 113 in ATE **Alternative Assessment,** p. 113 in ATE

END-OF-CHAPTER REVIEW AND ASSESSMENT

Chapter Review in Study Guide
Vocabulary and Notes in Study Guide
Chapter Tests with Performance-Based Assessment, Chapter 4 Test
Chapter Tests with Performance-Based Assessment, Performance-Based Assessment 4
Concept Mapping Transparency 23

  internet**connect**

go.hrw.com **Holt, Rinehart and Winston On-line Resources**

go.hrw.com

For worksheets and other teaching aids related to this chapter, visit the HRW Web site and type in the keyword: **HSTLOW**

 *sci*LINKS NSTA **National Science Teachers Association**

www.scilinks.org

Encourage students to use the *sci*LINKS numbers listed in the internet connect boxes to access information and resources on the **NSTA** Web site.

Chapter Resources & Worksheets

Visual Resources

TEACHING TRANSPARENCIES

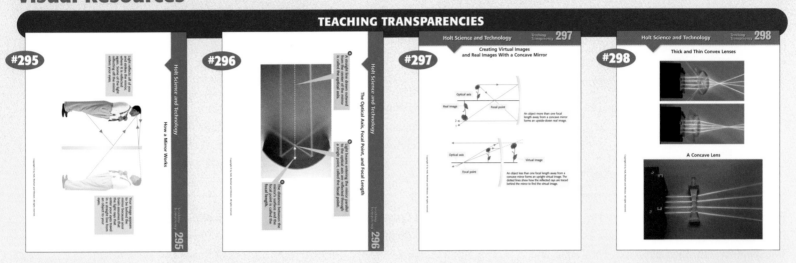

#295 — Holt Science and Technology — How a Mirror Works — Teaching Transparency 295

#296 — Holt Science and Technology — The Optical Axis, Focal Point, and Focal Length — Teaching Transparency 296

#297 — Holt Science and Technology — Teaching Transparency 297 — Creating Virtual Images and Real Images With a Concave Mirror

#298 — Holt Science and Technology — Teaching Transparency 298 — Thick and Thin Convex Lenses / A Concave Lens

TEACHING TRANSPARENCIES

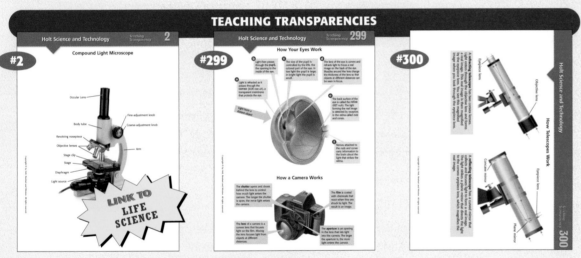

#2 — Holt Science and Technology — Teaching Transparency 2 — Compound Light Microscope — LINK TO LIFE SCIENCE

#299 — Holt Science and Technology — Teaching Transparency 299 — How Your Eyes Work / How a Camera Works

#300 — Holt Science and Technology — How Telescopes Work — Teaching Transparency 300

CONCEPT MAPPING TRANSPARENCY

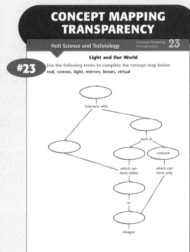

#23 — Holt Science and Technology — Concept Mapping Transparency 23 — Light and Our World
Use the following terms to complete the concept map below: real, convex, light, mirrors, lenses, virtual

Meeting Individual Needs

DIRECTED READING

#4 — DIRECTED READING WORKSHEET — Light and Our World

Chapter Introduction
As you begin this chapter, answer the following.
1. Read the title of the chapter. List three things that you already know about this subject.

2. Write two questions about this subject that you would like answered by the time you finish this chapter.

Section 1: Light Sources (p. 94)
3. Visible light
   a. covers the entire electromagnetic spectrum.
   b. covers most of the electromagnetic spectrum.
   c. covers a small part of the electromagnetic spectrum.
   d. is not a part of the electromagnetic spectrum.

Light Source or Reflection? (p. 94)
4. Look at the Astronomy Connection on page 94. The sun and the moon are two celestial objects visible from Earth. Which one is luminous, and which one is illuminated?

REINFORCEMENT & VOCABULARY REVIEW

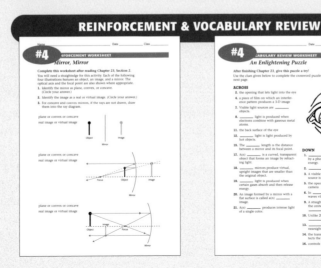

#4 — REINFORCEMENT WORKSHEET — Mirror, Mirror

Complete this worksheet after reading Chapter 23, Section 2.
You will need a straightedge for this activity. Each of the following four illustrations features an object, an image, and a mirror. The optical axis and the focal point are also shown where appropriate.
1. Identify the mirror as plane, convex, or concave.
   (Circle your answer.)
2. Identify the image as a real or virtual image. (Circle your answer.)
3. For concave and convex mirrors, if the rays are not drawn, draw them into the ray diagram.

plane or convex or concave
real image or virtual image

plane or convex or concave
real image or virtual image

plane or convex or concave
real image or virtual image

#4 — VOCABULARY REVIEW WORKSHEET — An Enlightening Puzzle

After finishing Chapter 23, give this puzzle a try!
Use the clues given below to complete the crossword puzzle on the next page.

ACROSS
2. the opening that lets light into the eye
4. a piece of film on which an interference pattern produces a 3-D image
7. Visible light sources are _____ objects.
8. _____ light is produced when electrons combine with gaseous metal atoms.
11. the back surface of the eye
12. _____ light is light produced by hot objects.
15. The _____ length is the distance between a mirror and its focal point.
17. A(n) _____ is a curved, transparent object that forms an image by refracting light.
18. _____ mirrors produce virtual, upright images that are smaller than the original object.
19. _____ light is produced when certain gases absorb and then release energy.
20. An image formed by a mirror with a flat surface is called a(n) _____ image.
21. A(n) _____ produces intense light of a single color.

DOWN
1. _____ light is visible light emitted by a phosphor particle when it absorbs energy.
2. _____ mirrors have a flat surface.
3. A visible object that is not a light source is being _____.
5. the opening that lets light into a camera
6. In _____ light, all of the light waves vibrate in the same plane.
9. a straight line drawn outward from the center of a lens or mirror is the _____ axis.
10. Unlike 20 across, light passes through _____ images.
13. _____ lenses are used to correct nearsightedness.
14. the transparent membrane that protects the eye
16. controls the size of the pupil

SCIENCE PUZZLERS, TWISTERS & TEASERS

#4 — SCIENCE PUZZLERS, TWISTERS & TEASERS — Light and Our World

Riddle-Eye-O
1. "See" if you can answer the riddles below. Write each item in the space provided.
   a. In bright light I hardly show, but dimness causes me to grow.
   b. Brown, green, hazel, or blue, I provide the eye its hue.
   c. I focus light to the back of the eye, and change shape for things far and nigh.
   d. I'm clear on my role to protect the eye and refract the light as it passes by.
   e. The back of the eye is where I am found; the real image forms on me, upside down.

Sound Alikes
2. Each clue below will lead you to one or two short words. Combine the syllables to find the hidden terms, which are used in the study of light.
   a. another word for hotel — tunafish package — going down a hill, or a plane going down to land
   b. a machine for making rugs or fabric — not nut but _____ — She/ her He/him We/ _____
   c. what you mop in the kitchen — it comes between R and T. — a smell or odor

Word Connections
3. Each of the following sentences includes a hidden vocabulary word from the chapter. These words can be found by looking at part of one word and connecting it to the beginning of the next word. For example, dog could be hidden in Judo games. Circle the hidden words below.
   a. I eat popcorn each time I go to the movie theater.
   b. I rise very early in the morning.

Chapter 4 • Light and Our World

Review & Assessment

STUDY GUIDE

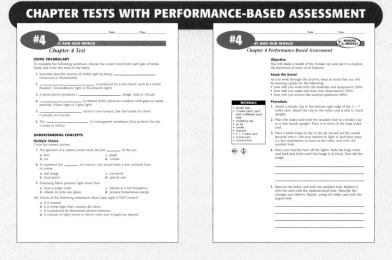

CHAPTER TESTS WITH PERFORMANCE-BASED ASSESSMENT

Lab Worksheets

INQUIRY LABS

LABS YOU CAN EAT

ECOLABS & FIELD ACTIVITIES

LONG-TERM PROJECTS & RESEARCH IDEAS

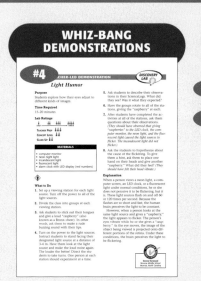

WHIZ-BANG DEMONSTRATIONS

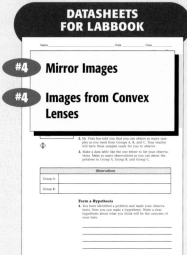

DATASHEETS FOR LABBOOK

#4 Mirror Images

#4 Images from Convex Lenses

Applications & Extensions

CRITICAL THINKING & PROBLEM SOLVING

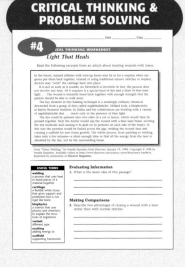

SCIENCE, TECHNOLOGY & SOCIETY

SECTION 1

Light Sources

▶ **Photons**

Light is produced when an electron in an atom shifts from an excited or energized energy level back to its unexcited level. The electron emits a quantum of energy called a *photon.*

▶ **Artificial Light Sources**

There are two basic ways to produce light from artificial sources. Both methods use electrons to increase the energy of electrons in other materials.

- One way is to use electrons to excite the electrons in a solid filament until they begin to emit photons. We say that the filament is so hot that it glows. This is the principle behind incandescent and fluorescent light bulbs.

- The second method is to pass electrons through a gas so that the electrons in the atoms of the gas are excited to the point that they begin to emit photons. This is the principle behind neon lights and mercury and sulfur lamps.

▶ **Street Lights**

The color of street lights depends on the material inside the tube. Sodium lights contain sodium vapor, which glows a bright yellow-orange when electrons pass through it. Mercury vapor lights give off a bluish white light.

IS THAT A FACT!

- ➤ Light bulb filaments are made of long spirals of tungsten that glow white-hot and will not melt at 2,500°C. The bulbs also contain an inert gas, such as argon, to keep the metal from combining with the oxygen in the air and burning up.

- ➤ Fluorescent lights were developed in 1939 by General Electric.

SECTION 2

Mirrors and Lenses

▶ **History of Mirrors**

Natural mirrors made of obsidian were used in Turkey 7,500 years ago. Bronze mirrors were used in Egypt as early as 3500 to 3000 B.C. Later, polished mirrors of copper, brass, bronze, tin, and silver were used.

- Metal mirrors were luxury items because it was difficult to make a flat, highly polished metal surface that would reflect light well enough to form images.

- The Venetians found a way to use polished silver to make mirrors in the 1200s, but the silvering process used on mirrors today was founded by a German chemist, Justus von Liebig (1803–1873), in 1835.

IS THAT A FACT!

- ➤ The Keck and Keck II telescopes, in Mauna Kea, Hawaii, are 10 m in diameter. They are the largest reflecting telescopes in the world today. Each uses 36 mirror segments fitted together so seamlessly that they act as one large mirror. The segments are realigned about 1,000 times a second by computers to counteract the effects of gravity and other distortions.

▶ **Early Uses of Lenses**

The use of lenses is first known from references to the Roman emperor Nero. As Nero watched performances in the arena, he used a piece of emerald that happened to be the perfect shape to correct his poor eyesight. Convex lenses in eyeglasses came into use in Italy in about 1287.

SECTION 3

Light and Sight

▶ Correcting Vision

Adapting lasers for medical use enables doctors to correct previously untreatable eye problems. Laser surgery can repair the retina and is used in cataract surgery, cornea replacement, and vision corrective surgery. Most of these treatments have been developed in just the last 20–30 years.

▶ Stereoscopic Vision

Having two eyes allows humans to judge depth, distance, and speed effectively. Each eye receives a slightly different view of the same object, and the brain combines these views to give a three-dimensional interpretation. People who suffer from strabismus, a defect in which the eyes are not used together, often have difficulty judging distances to objects.

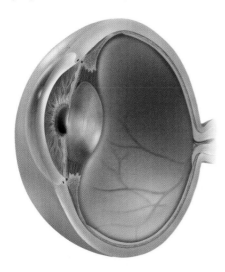

IS THAT A FACT!

- ☛ The human eye is so sensitive to light that in the dark it can see a lighted candle 1.6 km away.

- ☛ The human body needs vitamin A to produce the light-sensitive protein *rhodopsin* in the rods of the eye. The structure of the rods and rhodopsin enable the eyes to see in dim light. Carrots are an excellent source of vitamin A, which helps prevent night blindness.

SECTION 4

Light Technology

▶ Holograms

The word hologram is a compound word derived from two Greek words. *Holo* is Greek for "whole," and *gram* is Greek for "message."

- In 1948, Dennis Gabor (1900–1979) invented the process for making holograms. The first holograms were of poor quality because a good source of coherent light was not available. When lasers were perfected in the 1960s, holography surged in popularity.

- If a hologram is made from a source with a short wavelength, such as ultraviolet rays, then viewed in visible light with its longer wavelengths, the image produced appears greatly magnified. The amount of magnification is proportional to the ratio of the increase in wavelengths.

▶ Endoscopes

In use since 1958, endoscopes are medical tools used to look inside the body with fiber optics. The long, thin tubes carry light without distortion to and from the area being observed. Observation is made through an eyepiece. Fiber optic threads can be thinner than human hair.

IS THAT A FACT!

- ☛ In fiber optics, total internal reflection depends on the shallow angle (critical angle) at which the light waves reflect off the walls of the optical fiber. The critical angle when water acts as the prism is 49°; for crown glass (a type of optical glass), it is 41.1°.

> **For background information about teaching strategies and issues, refer to the *Professional Reference for Teachers*.**

CHAPTER

4

Light in Our World

 Pre-Reading Questions

Students may not know the answers to these questions before reading the chapter, so accept any reasonable response.

Suggested Answers

1. Accept all reasonable answers. Possible answers include incandescent light, fluorescent light, neon light, and vapor light.

2. Mirrors and lenses form images by focusing light or by making it appear that light is focused.

3. Light is refracted as it passes through the cornea and enters the eye through the pupil. The size of the pupil is controlled by the iris. The lens of the eye focuses light on the retina. Light is detected by the rods and cones in the retina. Nerves attached to the rods and cones carry information to the brain, where an image is formed.

Sections

 **Pre-Reading Questions**

1. Name three sources of light.
2. How do mirrors and lenses form images?
3. How does the human eye detect light?

92

Light in Our World

BRIGHT LIGHTS, NEON LIGHTS

Look at the multicolored arcs of light in this photo. These "neon" lights are made by passing electricity through tubes filled with certain gases. Neon, argon, krypton, helium, and mercury gases each light up as a different dazzling color. In this chapter, you will learn how different kinds of light are produced and how images that reflect or focus light are formed. You will also learn how mirrors, lenses, and high-tech instruments focus or transmit light energy.

---

 internetconnect

 HRW On-line Resources

go.hrw.com

For worksheets and other teaching aids, visit the HRW Web site and type in the keyword: **HSTLOW**

 SCiLINKS NSTA

www.scilinks.com

Use the *sci*LINKS numbers at the end of each chapter for additional resources on the **NSTA** Web site.

Smithsonian Institution

www.si.edu/hrw

Visit the Smithsonian Institution Web site for related on-line resources.

 CNNfyi.com

www.cnnfyi.com

Visit the CNN Web site for current events coverage and classroom resources.

MIRROR, MIRROR

In this activity, you will explore images formed by plane mirrors.

Procedure

1. **Tape** a sheet of **graph paper** on your desk. Stand a **plane mirror** straight up in the middle of the paper. Hold the mirror in place with small pieces of **modeling clay.**

2. Count four grid squares from the mirror, and place a **pencil** there. Look in the mirror. How many squares behind the mirror is the image of the pencil? Move the pencil farther away from the mirror. How did the image change?

3. Replace the mirror with **colored glass.** Look at the pencil image in the glass. Compare it with the image you saw in the mirror.

4. Use a pencil to draw a square on the graph paper in front of the glass. Looking through the glass, trace the image of the square on the paper behind the glass. Using a **metric ruler,** measure and compare the sizes of the two squares.

Analysis

5. How does the distance from an object to a plane mirror compare with the apparent distance from the mirror to the object's image behind the mirror?

6. In general, how does the size of an object compare with that of its image in a plane mirror?

93

MIRROR, MIRROR

MATERIALS
FOR EACH GROUP: • graph paper, 1 cm squares • plane mirror • modeling clay • pencil • colored glass • metric ruler

Safety Caution

Caution students to wear safety goggles while doing this activity. Also caution students to handle the mirrors and pieces of colored glass very carefully. Tape the edges of the glass with masking tape.

Answers to START-UP Activity

2. The pencil should be four squares behind the mirror. The pencil should appear farther behind the mirror than before.

3. The image in the glass should be the same size and same distance behind the glass as the image was in the mirror.

4. The length of the sides of both squares should be identical.

5. In general, the distance from an object to a plane mirror and the distance from the mirror to the image is the same.

6. In general, the size of an object and the size of its image in a plane mirror are identical.

Focus

Light Sources

Students learn the difference between luminous objects and illuminated objects. Students also learn how incandescent, fluorescent, neon, and vapor light are produced and how these different types of light may be used.

Bellringer

Give students the following:

Most people use some sort of light from the moment they wake up until they go to bed at night. In your ScienceLog, list the many different sources of light you use in a typical day. Explain why you need each source of light.

1) Motivate

DISCUSSION

Ask students to think about how different light sources can be used to create different moods. Ask them to imagine that they are the lighting director for a movie or a play. Have them describe a scene and explain what kind of light source they would use to create the proper mood. Ask them to share their ideas with the class.

 Directed Reading Worksheet Section 1

Terms to Learn

luminous
illuminated
incandescent light
fluorescent light
neon light
vapor light

What You'll Do

◆ Compare luminous and illuminated objects.
◆ Name four ways light can be produced.

Astronomy CONNECTION

Sometimes the moon shines so brightly that you might think there is a lot of "moonlight." But did you know that moonlight is actually sunlight? The moon does not give off light. You can see the moon because it is illuminated by light from the sun. You see different phases of the moon because light from the sun shines only on the part of the moon that faces the sun.

Light Sources

Although visible light represents only a small portion of the electromagnetic spectrum, it has a huge effect on your life. Visible light from the sun gives plants the energy necessary for growth and reproduction. Without plants at the base of the food chain, few other life-forms could exist. And of course, without visible light, you could not see anything. Your eyes are totally useless without sources of visible light.

Light Source or Reflection?

If you look at a television in a bright room, you see the cabinet around the television as well as the image on the screen. But if you look at the same television in the dark, only the image on the screen shows up. The difference is that the screen is a light source, while the cabinet around the television isn't.

You can see a light source even in the dark because its light passes directly into your eyes. Flames, light bulbs, fireflies, and the sun are all light sources. Scientists describe objects that produce visible light as being **luminous** (LOO muh nuhs). **Figure 1** shows examples of luminous objects.

Most of the objects around you are not light sources. But you can still see them because light from a light source reflects off the objects and then travels to your eyes. Scientists describe a visible object that is not a light source as being **illuminated** (i LOO muh NAYT ed).

Figure 1 *Television screens, fires, and fireflies are luminous objects.*

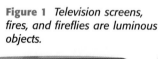

WEIRD SCIENCE

There are about 175 species of fireflies in the United States and perhaps 2,000 species worldwide. Fireflies (really a type of beetle) are luminous animals. They produce flashes of light by means of a chemical reaction that happens inside photocytes (special cells in their abdomen). Inside the photocytes, two chemicals, luciferin (named after Lucifer, the fallen angel of light) and the enzyme luciferase, combine with oxygen, ATP, and magnesium to produce energy in the form of light. Read the feature about fireflies at the end of Chapter 3.

Producing Light

Light sources produce light in many ways. For example, if you heat a piece of metal enough, it will visibly glow red hot. Light can also be produced chemically, like the light produced by a firefly. Light can even be produced by sending an electric current through certain gases.

Incandescent Light If you have ever looked inside a toaster while toasting a piece of bread, you may have seen thin wires or bars glowing red. The wires give off energy as light when heated to a high temperature. Light produced by hot objects is called **incandescent** (IN kuhn DES uhnt) **light. Figure 2** shows a source of incandescent light that you have in your home.

Sources of incandescent light also release a large amount of thermal energy. Sometimes this thermal energy is useful because it can be used to cook food or to warm a room. But often this thermal energy is not used for anything. For example, the thermal energy given off by a light bulb is not very useful.

Halogen lights are another type of incandescent light. They were originally developed for use on the wings of airplanes, but they are now used in homes and in car headlights. **Figure 3** shows how halogen lights work.

Figure 2 *Light bulbs produce incandescent light.*

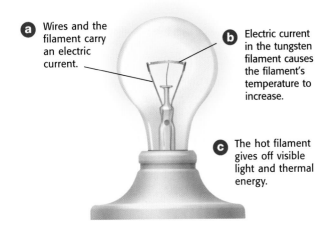

a Wires and the filament carry an electric current.

b Electric current in the tungsten filament causes the filament's temperature to increase.

c The hot filament gives off visible light and thermal energy.

Figure 3 *The way in which the tungsten from the filament can be used over and over again prevents the bulb from burning out too quickly.*

A tungsten filament, heated to about 3,000°C, glows very brightly and vaporizes.

The tungsten vapor (red particles) travels to the glass wall, where it cools to about 800°C.

At the lower temperature, tungsten combines with a halogen gas (blue particles) to form a new compound.

The new compound travels back to the filament, where it breaks down because of the high temperature. Tungsten from the compound is deposited on the filament and can be used again.

95

IS THAT A FACT!

Thomas Edison (1847–1931) is usually credited with the invention of the electric light bulb in 1879. However, in 1860, almost 20 years before Edison, British chemist and physicist Joseph Swan (1828–1914) demonstrated a carbon-filament incandescent bulb in London.

Swan improved his bulb in 1878. The next year, Edison independently created a carbon-filament incandescent vacuum light bulb that burned for nearly 50 hours. Swan's 1878 improved bulb was better than Edison's, and Edison subsequently bought the rights to Swan's design.

2 Teach

READING 📖 STRATEGY

Predicting Before students read this section, discuss with them the many kinds of artificial lighting that humans use. Most artificial lighting involves electrical energy. But are all electric lights the same? Have students identify some different types of artificial light. Are the lights in the classroom the same kind as the ones at home? Are street lamps or lights at sports stadiums different from other types of artificial lights?

BRAIN FOOD

The moon's *albedo*, or reflectivity, is about the same as a piece of coal. Both reflect only about 7 percent of the sunlight that strikes them. Yet the moon is often the brightest object in the night sky, and a full moon is sometimes almost bright enough to read by. Imagine what life would be like if the moon were twice as bright as it is?

CROSS-DISCIPLINARY FOCUS

History A Greek scientist, Hipparchus (147–126 B.C.), is considered the father of astronomy. Hipparchus measured the distance from the Earth to the moon and calculated the coordinates of stars. His catalog of 850 stars, the first such list ever compiled, gave each star's coordinates and approximate brightness relative to other stars.

MEETING INDIVIDUAL NEEDS

Advanced Learners Have students compare incandescent lighting and fluorescent lighting for home use and for use in business, commercial, school, and manufacturing buildings. Encourage them to be creative in presenting their findings; some students may want to create models to demonstrate the advantages and disadvantages of each type of lighting.
Sheltered English

DEMONSTRATION

Neon Light You will need a screwdriver-type circuit tester (available in hardware stores) with a small neon bulb. Remove the neon light from the handle. Hold one end of the bulb in your hand, and rub the other end against a piece of Styrofoam™ or hard foam insulation. The bulb will light due to static electricity.

Homework

Have students research the history of neon lighting or the making of neon signs. The basic principles of neon lighting go back to 1675 and the French astronomer Jean Picard. Georges Claude (1870–1960), a French inventor, engineer, and chemist, was the first to make a neon lamp in about 1902. Eight years later, Claude presented his lamp to the public, and the neon sign industry was born. Neon signs today are made in much the same way as they were 90 years ago.

Fluorescent Light The light that comes from the long, cylindrical bulbs in your classroom is called fluorescent light. **Fluorescent** (FLOO uh RES uhnt) **light** is visible light emitted by a phosphor particle when it absorbs energy such as ultraviolet light. Fluorescent light is sometimes called cool light because less thermal energy is produced than with incandescent light. **Figure 4** shows how a fluorescent light bulb works.

Figure 4 Fluorescent Light

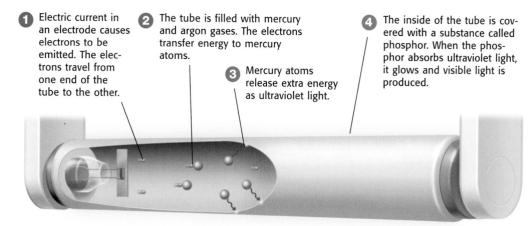

① Electric current in an electrode causes electrons to be emitted. The electrons travel from one end of the tube to the other.

② The tube is filled with mercury and argon gases. The electrons transfer energy to mercury atoms.

③ Mercury atoms release extra energy as ultraviolet light.

④ The inside of the tube is covered with a substance called phosphor. When the phosphor absorbs ultraviolet light, it glows and visible light is produced.

Neon Light The visible light emitted by atoms of certain gases, such as neon, when they absorb and then release energy is called **neon light**. **Figure 5** shows how neon light is produced.

A true neon light—one in which the tube is filled with neon gas—glows red. Other colors are produced when the tubes are filled with different gases. For example, sodium gas produces yellow light, and krypton gas produces purple light. A mixture of argon gas and mercury gas produces blue light.

Figure 5 Neon Light

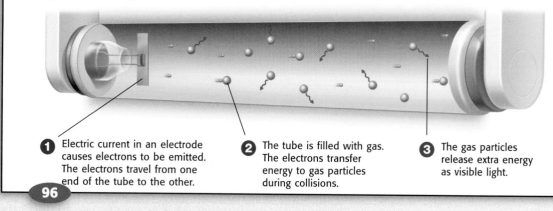

① Electric current in an electrode causes electrons to be emitted. The electrons travel from one end of the tube to the other.

② The tube is filled with gas. The electrons transfer energy to gas particles during collisions.

③ The gas particles release extra energy as visible light.

IS THAT A FACT!

Combustible gases have been known since the seventeenth century. The use of gas for heat and light was pioneered by French chemist Philippe Lebon (1767–1804). Lebon demonstrated gas lighting to the public in 1801 when he used flammable gas derived from wood.

SCIENCE HUMOR

Q: Where was Edison when the lights went out?

A: in the dark

Vapor Light Another type of incandescent light, called **vapor light,** is produced when electrons combine with gaseous metal atoms. Street lamps usually contain either mercury vapor or sodium vapor. You can tell the difference by the color of the light. If the light is bluish, the lamp contains mercury vapor. If the light is orange, the lamp contains sodium vapor. Both kinds of vapor lamps produce light in similar ways, as described in **Figure 6.**

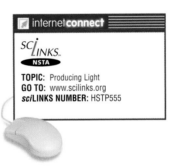

Stop! and go read about the invention of traffic lights on page 120.

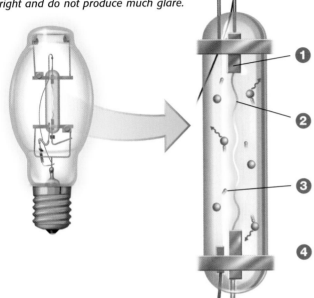

Figure 6 *Sodium vapor lights are very bright and do not produce much glare.*

1 High-voltage electric current creates an arc of electrons between two electrodes.

2 The arc passes through a gas called xenon, heating the gas to a high temperature.

3 The hot xenon vaporizes sodium in the tube and causes the sodium atoms to lose electrons.

4 When the electrons recombine with sodium, light is produced.

SECTION REVIEW

1. Identify five illuminated objects in your classroom, and name the luminous object (or objects) providing the light.

2. Describe places where you might use incandescent light, fluorescent light, neon light, and vapor light.

3. Describe how fluorescent light is similar to neon light.

4. **Applying Concepts** Halogen bulbs emit bright light from small bulbs. They also emit thermal energy. Would you use a halogen bulb to study by? Why or why not?

internetconnect

*SCi*LINKS
NSTA

TOPIC: Producing Light
GO TO: www.scilinks.org
*sci*LINKS NUMBER: HSTP555

▼ **Answers to Section Review**

1. Accept all reasonable answers. Possible answers: illuminated objects—books, people, pencils; luminous objects—the sun, lights in room, emergency lights.

2. Accept all reasonable answers. Possible answers: incandescent light—in bedrooms, living rooms, kitchens; fluorescent light—in classrooms, office buildings, malls; neon light—signs, advertising in store windows; vapor light—street lights, stadium lights.

3. Both types of light bulbs use electrodes to emit electrons that transfer energy to gas particles during collisions.

4. Accept all reasonable answers. Halogen lights emit both bright light and thermal energy.

---

3) Extend

DISCUSSION

Writing Have students write a short story about a city without electric lights of any kind. Encourage them to illustrate their stories. Ask for volunteers to share their stories with the class. Finish by discussing what life would be like in factories, schools, stores, and homes without electric lights.

4) Close

Quiz

1. Consider the sun and the moon. Which is a light source? Explain how that light source allows us to see the other body. (The sun is a light source. Its light strikes the moon and is reflected to Earth, where we see the moon.)

2. How does an incandescent lamp produce light? What other form of energy is produced in an incandescent bulb? (When there is electric current in the filament in an incandescent bulb, the filament releases energy as visible light when it is heated to a high temperature. Thermal energy is also produced.)

ALTERNATIVE ASSESSMENT

Have students use colored pencils to draw and label illustrations of four ways light is produced.

internetconnect

*SCi*LINKS
NSTA

TOPIC: Producing Light
GO TO: www.scilinks.org
*sci*LINKS NUMBER: HSTP555

Focus

Mirrors and Lenses

In this section, students learn how mirrors and lenses form images and how ray diagrams are used to determine where the images are. This section covers plane mirrors, concave mirrors, convex mirrors, convex lenses, and concave lenses. Students learn uses for the different kinds of mirrors and lenses.

🔔 Bellringer

Ask students:

What is the difference between a mirror and a lens? What is the difference between a convex mirror and a concave mirror? Can you think of one common use for convex and concave lenses? Write your answers in your ScienceLog.

1 Motivate

ACTIVITY

MATERIALS
FOR EACH SMALL GROUP:
• flashlight
• 1 or 2 small hand mirrors

Give each group of students one or two small hand mirrors and a flashlight. Allow students to experiment with the mirrors and flashlights to find out how light waves travel and what mirrors do to light waves. Dim the class-room lights so students can see the beams from their flashlight better. Students should discover that light waves seem to travel in straight lines, and that they continue to travel in straight lines after they have been reflected by a mirror.

Terms to Learn

plane mirror	lens
concave mirror	convex lens
focal point	concave lens
convex mirror	

What You'll Do

- ◆ Illustrate how mirrors and lenses form images using ray diagrams.
- ◆ Explain the difference between real and virtual images.
- ◆ Compare plane mirrors, concave mirrors, and convex mirrors.
- ◆ Explain how concave and convex lenses form images.

Mirrors and Lenses

Look at the letters on the front of the ambulance shown at right. Do you notice anything strange about them? Some of the letters are backward, and they don't seem to spell a word.

The letters spell the word AMBULANCE when viewed in a mirror. Images in mirrors are reversed left to right. The word *ambulance* is spelled backward so that people driving cars can read it when they see the ambulance in their rearview mirror. To understand how images are formed in mirrors, you must first learn how to use rays to trace the path of light waves.

Rays Show the Path of Light Waves

Light is an electromagnetic wave. Light waves travel from their source in all directions. If you could trace the path of one wave as it travels away from a light source, you would find that the path is a straight line. Because light waves travel in straight lines, you can use an arrow called a *ray* to show the path and the direction of a light wave. **Figure 7** shows some rays coming from a light bulb.

Rays can also be used to show the path of light waves after the waves have been reflected or refracted. Therefore, rays in ray diagrams are often used to show changes in the direction light travels after being reflected by mirrors or refracted by lenses. You'll learn more about ray diagrams a little later in this section.

Figure 7 *Rays from this light bulb show the path and direction of some light waves produced by the bulb.*

98

SCIENTISTS AT ODDS

Sir Isaac Newton (1642–1727) did not accept the theory of his colleague Robert Hooke (1635–1703) that light is a wave. Newton believed that white light was composed of particles, or "corpuscles."

Newton knew that if light were a wave, it should bend around corners. When Newton could not prove that light bends around corners, he disagreed with Hooke.

Mirrors Reflect Light

Have you ever looked at your reflection in a metal spoon? The polished metal of the spoon acts like a mirror, but not like the mirror in your bathroom! If you look on one side of the spoon, your face is upside down. But if you look on the other side, your face is right side up. Why?

The shape of a reflecting surface affects the way light reflects from it. Therefore, the image you see in your bathroom mirror differs from the image you see in a spoon. Mirrors are classified by their shape. The different shapes are called plane, concave, and convex.

Plane Mirrors Most mirrors, such as the one in your bathroom, are plane mirrors. A **plane mirror** is a mirror with a flat surface. When you look in a plane mirror, your reflection is upright and is the same size as you are. Images in plane mirrors are reversed left to right, as shown in **Figure 8.**

When you look in a plane mirror, your image appears to be the same distance behind the mirror as you are in front of it. Why does your image seem to be behind the mirror? Because mirrors are opaque objects, light does not travel through them. But when light reflects off the mirror, your brain interprets the reflected light as if it travels in a straight line from behind the mirror. A *virtual image* is an image through which light does not actually travel. The image formed by a plane mirror is a virtual image. The ray diagram in **Figure 9** explains how light travels when you look into a mirror.

Figure 8 *Rearview mirrors in cars are plane mirrors.*

Figure 9 *The rays show how light reaches your eyes. The dotted lines show where the light appears to come from.*

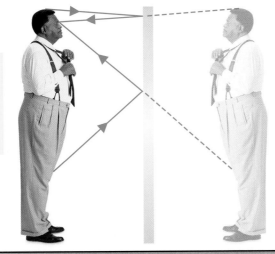
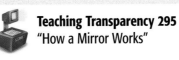

Light reflects off of you and strikes the mirror, where it is reflected again. Some of the light reflecting off the mirror enters your eyes.

Your image appears to be behind the mirror because your brain assumes that the light rays that enter your eyes travel in a straight line from an object to your eyes.

99

Teaching Transparency 295
"How a Mirror Works"

Directed Reading Worksheet Section 2

---

2 Teach

MEETING INDIVIDUAL NEEDS

Advanced Learners Have students use what they know about reflection to explain why a plane mirror must be at least half a person's height for the person to see his or her full image in the mirror. Have students use diagrams or mirrors in their explanations. (The angle of incidence equals the angle of reflection, so a person can see the top of his or her head by looking at a point on the mirror halfway between his or her eyes and the top of his or her head. A person can see his or her feet by looking at a point on the mirror halfway between his or her eyes and feet. Together, these two images add up to half the person's height.)

REAL-WORLD CONNECTION

Up to 40 percent of the summertime heat that builds up in a house is a direct result of sunlight that shines through the windows. Special coatings can be applied to windows that reflect up to 80 percent of the incoming sunlight. These coatings are partially reflective, much like a plane mirror. They do transmit enough light that a person can still see through the window. Adding a reflective coating to windows that receive direct sunlight can reduce the amount of energy needed to cool a home.

Homework

Have students make periscopes using materials of their choice. Each student should draw a diagram explaining how his or her periscope works. Challenge students to think of ways in which periscopes can be used.

READING STRATEGY

Mnemonics Students are learning about concave and convex mirrors and lenses and about the types of images each produces. Have students create mnemonic devices to help them recall the differences between concave and convex. For example: Concave curves inward because it has caved in.

ACTIVITY

MATERIALS
FOR EACH STUDENT: • shiny metal spoon

Before handing out spoons to students, have them predict what type of image they will see when they look at themselves in the front of the spoon. Ask them to draw in their ScienceLog the image they predict they will see. Then give students the spoons, and have them look at their reflection. Have them draw what they actually see. Then have students move the spoon closer and closer to their eye and describe what they see. Ask them if they can explain how the spoon reflects light rays.

Repeat the activity with the back of the spoon. Sheltered English

USING THE FIGURE

After students have done the activity above, use **Figure 10** to help them understand how the image in the front (concave) part of the spoon is formed.

Concave Mirrors Mirrors that are curved inward, such as the inside of a spoon, are called **concave mirrors**. Because the surfaces of concave mirrors are curved, the images formed by concave mirrors differ from the images formed by plane mirrors. To understand how concave mirrors form images, you must learn the terms illustrated in **Figure 10**.

Figure 10 *The image formed by a concave mirror depends on its optical axis, its focal point, and its focal length.*

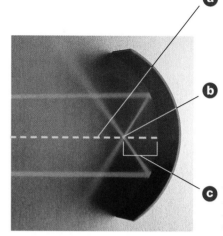

a A straight line drawn outward from the center of the mirror is called the *optical axis*.

b Light beams entering the mirror parallel to the optical axis are reflected through a single point, called the **focal point**.

c The distance between the mirror's surface and the focal point is called the *focal length*.

You already learned that plane mirrors can form only virtual images. Concave mirrors also form virtual images, but they can form *real images* too. A real image is an image through which light actually passes. A real image can be projected onto a screen; a virtual image cannot. To find out what kind of image a concave mirror forms, you can create a ray diagram. Just remember the following three rules when drawing ray diagrams for concave mirrors:

1 Draw a ray from the top of the object parallel to the optical axis. This ray will reflect through the focal point.

2 If the object is more than one focal length away from the mirror, draw a ray from the top of the object through the focal point. This ray will reflect parallel to the optical axis.

3 If the object is less than one focal length away from the mirror, draw a ray through the top of the object as if it came from the focal point. This ray will reflect parallel to the optical axis.

IS THAT A FACT!

In 1663, Scottish astronomer James Gregory (1638–1675) was the first to describe using a concave mirror to focus light rays in a telescope. In 1688, Isaac Newton used Gregory's idea to build the first reflecting telescope. Astronomers found that reflecting telescopes were much more powerful than refracting telescopes. Today's most powerful telescopes use giant concave mirrors.

Real or Virtual For each ray diagram, you need to draw only two rays from the top of the object to find what kind of image is formed. If the reflected rays cross in front of the mirror, a real image is formed. The point where the rays cross is the top of the image. If the reflected rays do not cross, trace the reflected rays in straight lines behind the mirror. Those lines will cross to show where a virtual image is formed. Study **Figure 11** to better understand ray diagrams.

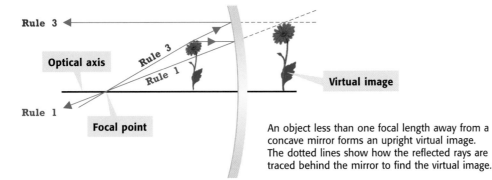

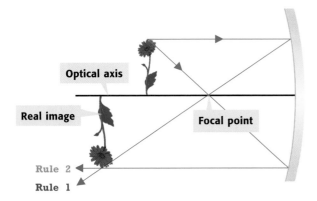

Figure 11 *The type of image formed by a concave mirror depends on the distance between the object and the mirror as well as the focal length.*

An object more than one focal length away from a concave mirror forms an upside-down real image.

Virtual image

An object less than one focal length away from a concave mirror forms an upright virtual image. The dotted lines show how the reflected rays are traced behind the mirror to find the virtual image.

Neither Real Nor Virtual If an object is placed at the focal point of a concave mirror, no image will form. Rule 2 explains why this happens—all rays that pass through the focal point on their way to the mirror will reflect parallel to the optical axis. Because all the reflected rays are parallel, they will never cross in front of or behind the mirror. If you place a light source at the focal point of a concave mirror, the light will reflect outward in a powerful light beam. Therefore, concave mirrors are used in car headlights and flashlights.

101

Homework

Some lighthouses use a strong light source placed at or near the focal point of a concave mirror. Ask students to research both ancient and modern lighthouses. Have them make a poster or do a presentation showing a particular lighthouse and how it operates.

internet**connect**

SCi**LINKS**
NSTA

TOPIC: Mirrors
GO TO: www.scilinks.org
*sci***LINKS NUMBER:** HSTP560

DISCUSSION

Concept Mapping As a class, make a concept map and ray diagrams for mirrors on the board. Help students classify mirrors and the types of images they make. Then have students copy the completed concept map and ray diagrams in their ScienceLog to use as a study aid.
Sheltered English

MATH and MORE

An object is one half the focal length away from a concave mirror. Will the image be virtual or real? Draw a ray diagram to find the answer. (The image is upright and virtual. The diagram should look like the bottom image in Figure 11 on page 101.)

MEETING INDIVIDUAL NEEDS

Learners Having Difficulty
Help students make a ray diagram by using a ruler and a compass to show an object reflected in a convex mirror.
Sheltered English

Answer to APPLY

The images in convex mirrors are always smaller than the original objects. Because the images are smaller than the original objects, the objects look like they are farther away. It is important for drivers to remember that approaching cars are actually closer than they appear. This warning helps drivers to remember and to avoid accidents.

Convex Mirrors If you look at your reflection in the back of a spoon, you will notice that your image is right side up and small. The back of a spoon is a **convex mirror**—a mirror that curves out toward you. **Figure 12** shows how an image is formed by a convex mirror. All images formed by convex mirrors are virtual, upright, and smaller than the original object. Convex mirrors are useful because they produce images of a large area. This is the reason convex mirrors are often used for security in stores and factories. Convex mirrors are also used as side mirrors in cars and trucks.

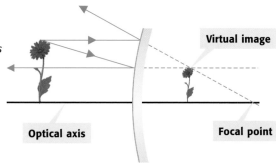

Figure 12 *All images formed by convex mirrors are formed behind the mirror. Therefore, all images formed by convex mirrors are virtual.*

Convex Mirrors Help Drivers

The passenger side mirrors of most cars and trucks are convex mirrors. Convex mirrors are used because they help the driver see more of the traffic around the car than a plane mirror would. However, these mirrors are often stamped with the words "Objects in Mirror Are Closer Than They Appear." What property of convex mirrors makes this warning necessary? Why do you think the warning is important for drivers?

internetconnect

SC**LINKS**
NSTA

TOPIC: Mirrors
GO TO: www.scilinks.org
*sci*LINKS NUMBER: HSTP560

SECTION REVIEW

1. How is a concave mirror different from a convex mirror?

2. Draw a ray diagram showing how a concave mirror forms a real image.

3. **Applying Concepts** Plane mirrors, concave mirrors, and convex mirrors are useful at different times. Describe a situation in which you would use each type of mirror.

▼ *Answers to Section Review*

1. A concave mirror is curved inward like the inside of a spoon. A concave mirror can form a real image, a virtual image, or no image at all, depending on the mirror's focal length and the distance from the object to the mirror. A convex mirror is curved outward like the back of a spoon, and can form only a virtual image.

2. Students' diagrams should look like the top image in Figure 11 on page 101.

3. Accept all reasonable answers. Possible answers: Plane mirrors are useful when you comb your hair or as rearview mirrors in cars. Concave mirrors are useful to create strong beams of light, such as in car headlights and flashlights. Convex mirrors are useful for security purposes in stores and as side mirrors on cars.

Lenses Refract Light

What do cameras, binoculars, telescopes, and movie projectors have in common? They all use lenses to create images. A **lens** is a curved, transparent object that forms an image by refracting, or bending, light. Like mirrors, lenses are classified by their shape. There are two types of lenses—convex and concave.

Convex Lenses A **convex lens** is thicker in the middle than at the edges. When light rays enter a convex lens, they refract toward the center. Light rays that enter a convex lens parallel to the optical axis are refracted so that they go through a focal point. The amount of refraction and the focal length depend on the curvature of the lens, as shown in **Figure 13.** Light rays that pass through the center of a lens are not refracted.

Convex lenses form many different kinds of images, depending on the focal length of the lens and the position of the object. For example, whenever you use a magnifying glass, you are using a convex lens to form an enlarged, virtual image. **Figure 14** illustrates how a magnifying lens works.

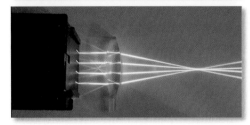

Figure 13 *Light rays refract more through convex lenses with greater curvature than through convex lenses with less curvature.*

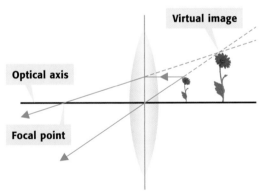

Figure 14 *If an object is less than one focal length away from a convex lens, a virtual image is formed. The image is larger than the object and can be seen only by looking into the lens.*

MISCONCEPTION ALERT

The amount that a lens refracts light, and therefore its focal point and focal length, depends mostly on the curvature of the lens and not its thickness. If the thin lens in **Figure 13** had the same curvature as the thick lens, it would refract light just as much as the thick lens. The material of which a lens is made may also affect the amount it refracts light.

LabBook **PG 134**
Images from Convex Lenses

Teaching Transparency 298
"Thick and Thin Convex Lenses"
"A Concave Lens"

3 Extend

MEETING INDIVIDUAL NEEDS

Advanced Learners Glass lenses are made from a high-quality type of glass known as optical glass. Have students research the history of grinding glass to make lenses, the development of optical glass, and the way lenses are made, ground, and polished. Have them compare and contrast making lenses with making mirrors. Encourage students to be creative with their presentations.

ACTIVITY

Each group of students will need a small comb, some tape, a flashlight, a small index card, a piece of white paper on top of a textbook, a convex lens, a concave lens (eyeglass lens), and a pair of scissors.

Have students cut a 2 cm hole in the card and tape the comb to it. Then have students stand the card up and shine the light through the card and the comb onto the sheet of paper. Have them place the convex lens in front of the paper and observe what happens to the light. Ask students to draw their observations in their ScienceLog. Then have students remove the convex lens and put the concave lens in front of the paper. Ask them to observe the difference in the light pattern. Have students again draw their observations in their ScienceLog.

GUIDED PRACTICE

Have students use a ruler and a compass to make simple ray diagrams for a magnifying glass, a movie projector, camera, and a plain convex lens.
Sheltered English

Mathematics In 1610, Johannes Kepler (1571–1630), a German mathematician and astronomer, was the first scientist to describe the properties of lenses. A year later, he presented a new design for the telescope using two convex lenses.

Quiz

1. What is the difference between a real image and a virtual image? (Light actually passes through a real image, and a real image can be projected onto a screen. Neither is true of a virtual image.)

2. What is the difference between a mirror and a lens? (Mirrors reflect light; lenses refract light.)

3. Use ray diagrams to explain the difference between convex lenses and concave lenses. (Students' ray diagrams should look like the diagrams on pages 103 and 104.)

ALTERNATIVE ASSESSMENT

Concept Mapping Have students make a concept map explaining the properties of lenses and the images they form.

Reinforcement Worksheet
"Mirror, Mirror"

internet**connect**

SC*LINKS*
NSTA
TOPIC: Lenses
GO TO: www.scilinks.org
*sci*LINKS NUMBER: HSTP565

Convex lenses can also form real images. Movie projectors use convex lenses to focus real images on a screen. Cameras use convex lenses to focus real images on a piece of film. Both types of images are shown in **Figure 15.**

Figure 15 *Convex lenses can also form real images.*

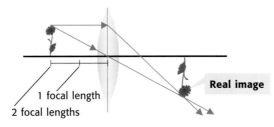

a If the object is located between one and two focal lengths away from the lens, a real, enlarged image is formed far away from the lens. This is how movie projectors produce images on large screens.

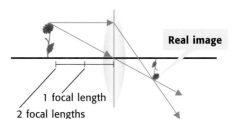

b If the object is located more than two focal lengths away from the lens, a real, reduced image is formed close to the lens. This is how the lens of a camera forms images on the film.

Figure 16 *Concave lenses form reduced virtual images. If you trace the refracted rays in a straight line behind a concave lens, you can determine where the virtual image is formed.*

Concave Lenses A **concave lens** is thinner in the middle than at the edges. Light rays entering a concave lens parallel to the optical axis always bend away from each other toward the edges of the lens; the rays never meet. Therefore, concave lenses can never form a real image. Instead, they form virtual images, as shown in **Figure 16.** Concave lenses are sometimes combined with other lenses in telescopes. The combination of lenses produces clearer images of distant objects. You will read about another, more common use for concave lenses in the next section.

internet**connect**

SC*LINKS*
NSTA
TOPIC: Lenses
GO TO: www.scilinks.org
*sci*LINKS NUMBER: HSTP565

SECTION REVIEW

1. Draw a ray diagram showing how a magnifying glass forms a virtual image.

2. Explain why a concave lens cannot form a real image.

3. **Applying Concepts** Your teacher sometimes uses an overhead projector to show transparencies on a screen. What type of lens does an overhead projector use?

104

▼ **Answers to Section Review**

1. Students' ray diagrams should look like the one in Figure 14 at the bottom of page 103.

2. A concave lens cannot form real images because light rays passing through it bend away from each other and never meet.

3. Overhead projectors must use convex lenses because real images that can be projected onto a screen can only be formed by convex lenses.

Terms to Learn

cornea   iris
pupil   retina

What You'll Do

◆ Identify the parts of the human eye, and describe their functions.

◆ Describe some common vision problems, and explain how they can be corrected.

Light and Sight

When you look around, you can see objects both near and far. You can also see the different colors of the objects. You see luminous objects because they produce their own light, which is detected by your eyes. You see all other objects (illuminated objects) because light reflecting off the objects enters your eyes. But how do your eyes work, and what causes people to have problems with their vision? Read on to find out.

How You Detect Light

Visible light is the part of the electromagnetic spectrum that can be detected by your eyes. The process by which your eye gathers light to form the images that you see involves several steps, as shown in **Figure 17**.

Figure 17 How Your Eyes Work

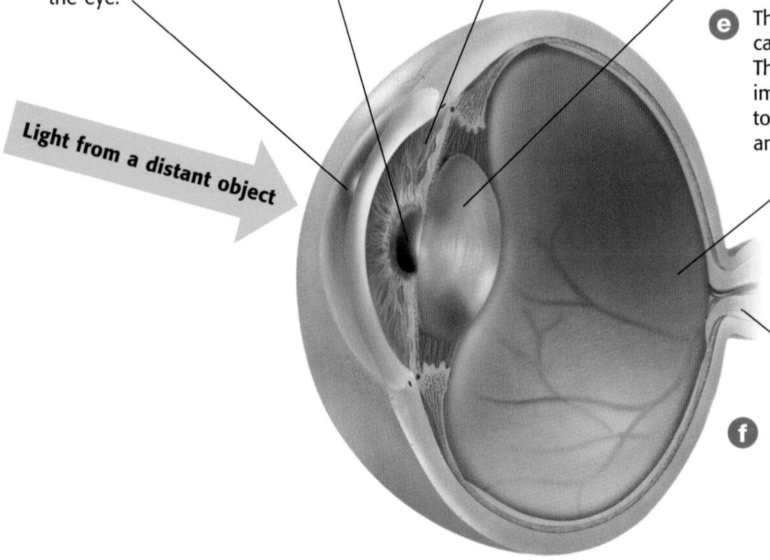

b Light then passes through the **pupil,** the opening to the inside of the eye.

c The size of the pupil is controlled by the **iris,** the colored part of the eye. In low light the pupil is large; in bright light the pupil is small.

d The lens of the eye is convex and refracts light to focus a real image on the back of the eye. Muscles around the lens change the thickness of the lens so that objects at different distances can be seen in focus.

a Light is refracted as it passes through the **cornea** (KOR nee uh), a transparent membrane that protects the eye.

e The back surface of the eye is called the **retina** (RET nuh). The light forming the real image is detected by receptors in the retina called *rods* and *cones*.

Light from a distant object

f Nerves attached to the rods and cones carry information to the brain about the light that strikes the retina.

105

CONNECT TO
LIFE SCIENCE

In some people, the lens of the eye gets cloudy. This is called a cataract. Eye surgeons correct cataracts by making a tiny incision in the eye and inserting a slender instrument that uses sound waves to break up the cloudy lens. The surgeon then vacuums out the pieces. Once the cataract is removed, a new, clear-plastic implant lens is inserted through the incision and positioned inside the eye. The surgery takes about an hour, and the patient can go home the same day.

Focus

Light and Sight

This section identifies the parts of the human eye and explains how they function. It also describes some common vision problems and how they are corrected.

🔔 Bellringer

Ask students the following:

If you were going to design a camera, would you make it work like the human eye? Why or why not? Explain your answer.

1 Motivate

ACTIVITY

Have pairs of students observe one another's eyes. Turn off the lights, and have them observe what happens to the pupils. Then turn the lights on, and have students observe the pupils. Ask students why the pupils change size. Sheltered English

BRAIN FOOD

In 1604, Johannes Kepler (1571–1630) gave the first correct explanation of how the human eye works, including why the image formed on the retina is upside down. Kepler's interest in light and optics led to his study of the eye.

Teaching Transparency 299 "How Your Eyes Work"

Directed Reading Worksheet Section 3

ACTIVITY

To simulate normal vision, have students focus an image from an overhead projector onto a screen. Have them measure and record the distance from the projector to the screen. Then, to simulate a nearsighted eye, have students increase the distance between the projector and the screen. The image becomes blurry because it is focused in front of the screen. Then have students move the projector closer to the screen than the original distance. This simulates farsightedness: the image is now focused behind the screen, making it blurry. **Sheltered English**

One explanation offered as to why red contacts reduce chickens' aggressiveness is that when chickens see a spot of blood on another chicken, they will peck that chicken, and even kill it. Red contact lenses keep chickens from seeing blood on other chickens and thereby reduce aggressive behavior.

GOING FURTHER

Some animals' eyes seem to glow in the dark, while other animals have highly specialized eyes. Have students research unusual eyes in the animal kingdom. Encourage students to find creative ways to present the results of their research.

Some chickens wear red contact lenses. The lenses don't improve the chickens' vision—they just make the chickens see everything in red! Chickens that see in red are less aggressive and produce more eggs. But it is difficult to fit a chicken for contact lenses properly, and chickens often lose their contacts quickly.

Common Vision Problems

A person with normal vision can clearly see objects both close up and far away and can distinguish all colors of visible light. However, because the eye is complex, it's no surprise that many people have defects in their eyes that affect their vision. Luckily, some common vision problems can be easily corrected.

Nearsightedness and Farsightedness The lens of a properly working eye focuses light on the retina, so the images formed are always clear. Two common vision problems—nearsightedness and farsightedness—occur when light is not focused on the retina. A nearsighted person can see objects clearly only if the objects are nearby. Objects that are farther away look blurry. A farsighted person can see faraway objects clearly, but objects nearby look blurry. **Figure 18** explains how nearsightedness and farsightedness occur and how they can be corrected.

Figure 18 *Nearsightedness and farsightedness are common vision problems that can be corrected easily with glasses or contact lenses.*

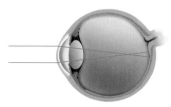
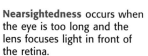

Nearsightedness occurs when the eye is too long and the lens focuses light in front of the retina.

A concave lens placed in front of the eye refracts the light outward. The lens in the eye can then focus the light on the retina.

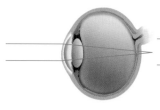
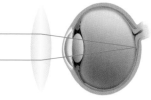

Farsightedness occurs when the eye is too short and the lens focuses light behind the retina.

A convex lens placed in front of the eye refracts the light and focuses it slightly. The lens in the eye can then focus the light on the retina.

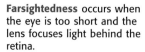

internet connect

SCiLINKS **TOPIC:** The Eye
GO TO: www.scilinks.org
*sci*LINKS NUMBER: HSTP570

CROSS-DISCIPLINARY FOCUS

Language Arts French author Antoine de Saint-Exupéry (1900–1944), in his book *The Little Prince,* wrote, "It is only with the heart one can see rightly; what is essential is invisible to the eye." Have students write an explanation of what they think this quote means. Ask students to discuss their ideas.

Color Deficiency Roughly 5 to 8 percent of men and 0.5 percent of women in the world have *color deficiency,* often referred to as colorblindness. True colorblindness, in which a person can see only in black and white, is very rare. The majority of people with color deficiency have trouble distinguishing shades of red and green, or distinguishing red from green.

Color deficiency occurs when the cones in the retina do not receive the right instructions. The three types of cones are named for the colors they detect most—red, green, and blue. Each type of cone reacts to a range of wavelengths of light. A person with normal color vision can see all colors. But in some people, the cones get the wrong instructions and respond to the wrong wavelengths. That person may have trouble seeing certain colors. For example, he or she may see too much red or too much green, and not enough of the other color. **Figure 19** shows one type of test for color deficiency.

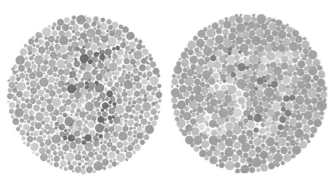

Figure 19 *Doctors use images like these to detect red-green color deficiency. Can you see a number in each image?*

Biology CONNECTION

Whether a person is colorblind depends on his or her genes. Certain genes give instructions to the cones for detecting certain wavelengths of light. If the genes give the wrong instructions, the person will have a color deficiency. A person needs one set of the genes that give the right instructions. Genes for color vision are on the X chromosome. Women have two X chromosomes, but men have only one. Therefore, men are more likely to be lacking a set of these genes and are more likely than women to be colorblind.

SECTION REVIEW

1. Name the parts of the human eye, and describe what each part does.

2. What kind of lens would help a person who is nearsighted? What kind would help someone who is farsighted?

3. **Inferring Conclusions** Why do you think colorblindness cannot be corrected?

4. **Applying Concepts** Sometimes people are both nearsighted and farsighted. They wear glasses with two different kinds of lenses. Why are two lenses necessary?

internet connect

SC*LINKS*
NSTA

TOPIC: The Eye
GO TO: www.scilinks.org
*sci***LINKS NUMBER:** HSTP570

4) Close

Quiz

1. Which vision problem occurs when the eye is too short? when it is too long? (farsightedness; nearsightedness)

2. In the eye, rods respond to movement and light but not colors, while the cones detect colors. Which do you think is more important? Why? (Accept all reasonable answers.)

ALTERNATIVE ASSESSMENT

Concept Mapping Have students make a concept map using the following terms:

retina, cornea, lens, optic nerve, farsightedness, nearsightedness, convex lens, and concave lens

Answers to Colorblind Test

Note: It is difficult to reproduce color vision tests accurately. Figure 19 may indicate that some students have color vision problems, but it is only an example. Students should see a professional to answer any questions. Students with normal color vision should be able to see *5* in the left-hand circle and *57* in the right-hand circle.

▼ *Answers to Section Review*

1. cornea—transparent membrane that protects the eye and refracts light; pupil—lets light pass into the eye; iris—controls the size of the pupil; lens—refracts light to create an image on the retina; retina—back surface of the eye that detects light; nerves—carry information from the retina to the brain

2. Concave lenses help nearsighted people; convex lenses help farsighted people.

3. Colorblindness is not correctable because it is not now possible to change or replace the genes that send the wrong messages to a person's cones.

4. Two lenses are necessary because a concave lens is needed to correct nearsightedness and a convex lens is needed to correct farsightedness. (Note: Such glasses are called bifocals.)

Focus

Light Technology

This section describes some optical instruments that make use of lenses and mirrors. It also explains how lasers work and discusses some uses for lasers. Students also learn about fiber optics and polarized light.

 Bellringer

Ask students if they have ever taken or seen a blurry photograph. Ask them what they think might have caused the problem.

1) Motivate

DEMONSTRATION

If you have them, demonstrate a Polaroid™ camera and a classroom laser. Ask students what the two items have in common and how they are different. Display other optical instruments, especially a microscope and a telescope, where students can see them. Discuss each instrument with students. Ask them what they know about each instrument and if they can explain how each one works.

Teaching Transparency 299 "How a Camera Works"

Directed Reading Worksheet Section 4

Terms to Learn

laser   hologram

What You'll Do

◆ Explain how optical instruments use lenses and mirrors to form images.
◆ Explain how lasers work and what makes laser light different from non-laser light.
◆ Identify uses for lasers.
◆ Describe how optical fibers and polarizing filters work.

Light Technology

So far in this chapter, you have learned some ways light can be produced, how mirrors and lenses affect light, and some ways that people use mirrors and lenses. In this section, you will learn how different technological devices rely on mirrors and lenses and how mirrors help produce a type of light called laser light.

Optical Instruments

Optical instruments are devices that use arrangements of mirrors and lenses to help people make observations. Some optical instruments help you see objects that are very far away, and some help you see objects that are very small. Some optical instruments record images. The optical instrument that you are probably most familiar with is the camera.

Cameras The way a camera works is similar to the way your eye works. A camera has a lens that focuses light and has an opening that lets in light. The main difference between a camera and the eye is that the film in a camera permanently stores the images formed on it, but the images formed on the retina disappear when you stop looking at an object. **Figure 20** shows the parts of a camera and their functions.

Figure 20 The Parts of a Camera

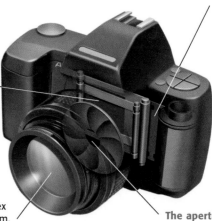

The shutter opens and closes behind the lens to control how much light enters the camera. The longer the shutter is open, the more light enters the camera.

The film is coated with chemicals that react when they are struck by light. The result is an image stored on the film.

The lens of a camera is a convex lens that focuses light on the film. Moving the lens focuses light from objects at different distances.

The aperture is an opening in the lens that lets light into the camera. The larger the aperture is, the more light enters the camera.

108

CROSS-DISCIPLINARY FOCUS

Math (Challenging) Two numbers are very important to photographers: shutter speed and f-stop. Have students research both, and have them make a concept map, diagram, or other presentation to explain their findings to the class. Encourage them to be creative.

Telescopes Astronomers use telescopes to study objects in space, such as the moon, planets, and stars. Telescopes are classified as either refracting or reflecting. Refracting telescopes use lenses to collect light, while reflecting telescopes use mirrors. **Figure 21** illustrates how simple refracting and reflecting telescopes work.

Figure 21 *Both refracting and reflecting telescopes are used to see objects that are far away.*

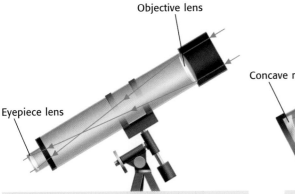

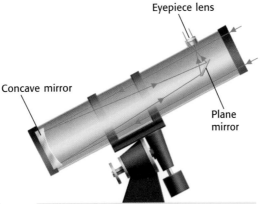

A **refracting telescope** has two convex lenses. Light enters through the objective lens and forms a real image. This real image is then magnified by the eyepiece lens. You see this magnified image when you look through the eyepiece lens.

A **reflecting telescope** has a concave mirror that collects and focuses light to form a real image. The light strikes a plane mirror that directs the light to the convex eyepiece lens, which magnifies the real image.

Light Microscopes Simple light microscopes are similar to refracting telescopes. They have two convex lenses—an objective lens, which is close to the object being studied, and an eyepiece lens, which you look through. The difference between microscopes and telescopes is that microscopes are used to see magnified images of tiny, nearby objects rather than images of large, distant objects.

> ✓ **Self-Check**
>
> Explain why the objective lens of a telescope cannot be a concave lens. *(See page 152 to check your answer.)*

Lasers and Laser Light

Have you ever seen a laser light show? Laser light beams flash through the air and sometimes form pictures on surfaces. A **laser** is a device that produces intense light of only one color and wavelength. Laser light is different from non-laser light in many ways. One important difference is that laser light is *coherent.* When light is coherent, light waves move together as they travel away from their source. The crests and troughs of coherent light waves line up, and the individual waves behave as one single wave. Other differences between laser light and non-laser light are shown in **Figure 22,** on the next page.

109

CROSS-DISCIPLINARY FOCUS

Art Photography is a combination of art and science. A photographer must understand how film, light, and lenses work together to produce images. And a good photographer must know how light will interact with the subject of a photograph, what the camera lens will do to the light, and how the light will affect the film.

Answer to Self-Check

Concave lenses do not form real images. Only a real image can be magnified by another lens, such as the eyepiece lens.

USING THE FIGURE

Use **Figure 23** to explain the two special properties of laser light: it is light of a single wavelength and color, and it is *coherent*. Light is coherent when the peaks and troughs of light waves are aligned through interference. This causes the individual light waves to act as a single wave. Soon the laser light has enough energy to escape through the partially coated mirror in an intense and concentrated beam. Non-laser light sources emit light waves of many different wavelengths and colors whose peaks are not aligned.

MEETING INDIVIDUAL NEEDS

Learners Having Difficulty

Have students make a model of a laser by using construction paper for the tube and aluminum foil for the mirrors. They can use fishing weights for neon atoms and red holes from a hole punch for the photons. Have students explain their model.

Homework

Have students research the many ways argon, carbon dioxide, helium-neon, and other lasers are used for medical diagnosis and treatment.

internetconnect

SciLINKS
NSTA

TOPIC: Lasers
GO TO: www.scilinks.org
*sci*LINKS NUMBER: HSTP575

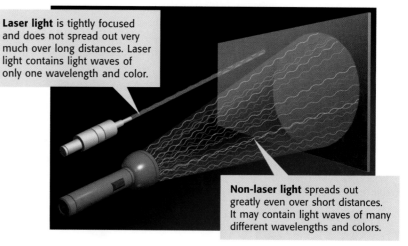

Figure 22 Laser Light Versus Non-laser Light

Laser light is tightly focused and does not spread out very much over long distances. Laser light contains light waves of only one wavelength and color.

Non-laser light spreads out greatly even over short distances. It may contain light waves of many different wavelengths and colors.

How Lasers Produce Light The word *laser* stands for light amplification by stimulated emission of radiation. You already know what light and radiation are. *Amplification* is the increase in the brightness of the light.

What is stimulated emission? In an atom, an electron can move from one energy level to another. A photon is released when an electron moves from a higher energy level to a lower energy level. This process is called *emission. Stimulated emission* occurs when a photon strikes an atom in an excited state and makes that atom emit another photon. The newly emitted photon is identical to the first photon, and they travel away from the atom together. **Figure 23** shows how stimulated emission works to produce laser light.

Figure 23 A Helium-Neon Laser

a The inside of the laser is filled with helium and neon gases. An electric current in the gases excites the atoms of the gases.

b Excited neon atoms release photons of red light. When these photons strike other excited neon atoms, stimulated emission occurs.

c Plane mirrors on both ends of the laser reflect photons traveling the length of the laser back and forth along the tube.

d Because the photons travel back and forth many times, many stimulated emissions occur, making the laser light brighter.

e One mirror is only partially coated, so some of the photons "leak" out and form a laser light beam.

⚛ WEIRD SCIENCE

Laser light can be produced in a variety of ways. Gas lasers, such as the one in **Figure 23,** produce laser light from excited gas atoms. Solid-state lasers have a solid, rather than a gas, between the two mirrors to produce photons for the laser beam. Semiconductor lasers use the same material that is found in computer chips to produce laser light. Most CD and DVD players use semiconductor lasers.

Holograms Lasers are used to produce holograms. A **hologram** is a piece of film on which an interference pattern produces a three-dimensional image of an object. You have probably seen holograms on magazine covers or baseball cards. **Figure 24** shows how light from a laser is split into two beams. These two beams combine to form an interference pattern on the film, which results in a hologram.

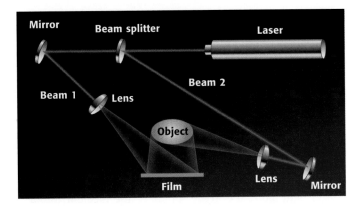

Figure 24 Light from one beam shines directly on the film, and light from the other beam shines on an object and is reflected onto the film.

Holograms, like the one shown in **Figure 25,** are similar to photographs because they are images permanently recorded on film. However, unlike photographs, the images you see are not on the surface of the film. They appear either in front of or behind the film. And if you move the image around, you will see it from different angles.

Figure 25 After the film is developed, the interference pattern reconstructs a three-dimensional image of the object.

Other Uses for Lasers In addition to making holograms, lasers are used for a wide variety of tasks. For example, lasers are used to cut materials such as metal and cloth. Surgeons sometimes use lasers to cut through human tissue. Laser surgery on the cornea of the eye can correct nearsightedness and farsightedness. And, as you read at the beginning of this chapter, lasers can also be used as extremely accurate rulers. You even use a laser when you listen to music from a CD player.

111

SCIENTISTS AT ODDS

Two American physicists, Arthur Schawlow and Charles Townes, received a patent for the working principles of a laser in 1958. But Gordon Gould claimed that he not only had discovered how to produce laser light but also had named the process in 1957. Finally, in 1987, after many bitter court battles, Gould's claim was upheld.

CONNECT TO
LIFE SCIENCE

Biologists use laser devices called optical tweezers to handle organisms without damaging them. Biologists also use optical tweezers to manipulate organelles within living cells without breaking the cell membrane, to move chromosomes within a cell nucleus, and to manipulate single strands of DNA.

Although many systems that transmit information now use fiber optic cables, these thin threads are not perfect. The advantages of fiber optics—that they carry more data, are less susceptible to interference, are thinner and lighter than copper wires, and transmit data digitally—must be weighed against the disadvantages. Fiber optics are more expensive to install and are much more fragile than copper wires.

BRAIN FOOD

Polarized light is used in liquid crystal displays. When the polarized light passes through the liquid crystal material, the liquid crystals cause the polarized light to twist. When a weak electric voltage is applied to the liquid crystals, it no longer twists or affects the polarized light. This lets part of the display go dark and leaves a segment to form a number or letter.

ACTIVITY

Place a polarizing filter over the face of a liquid-crystal display calculator. An overhead calculator gives excellent results. Rotate the filter; have students observe what happens. Ask students to speculate on what causes these changes. (As the filter is rotated, the display blacks out. This means there must be another polarizing filter inside the device because two polarizing filters are needed to block out light.)

Fiber Optics

Imagine a glass thread as thin as a human hair that can transmit more than 1,000 telephone conversations at the same time with only flashes of light. It might sound impossible, but such glass threads are at work all over the world. These threads, called *optical fibers,* are thin, flexible glass wires that can transmit light over long distances. Some optical fibers are shown at left. The use of optical fibers is called *fiber optics.* The transmission of information through telephone cables is the most common use of fiber optics. Optical fibers carry information faster and more clearly than older copper telephone cables. Optical fibers are also used to network computers and to allow doctors to see inside patients' bodies without performing major surgery.

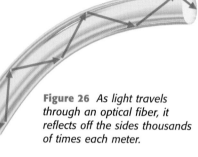

Light in a Pipe Optical fibers transmit light over long distances because they act like pipes for light. Just as a good water pipe doesn't let water leak out, a good light pipe doesn't let light leak out. Light stays inside an optical fiber because of total internal reflection. *Total internal reflection* is the complete reflection of light along the inside surface of the medium through which it travels. **Figure 26** shows total internal reflection in an optical fiber.

Figure 26 *As light travels through an optical fiber, it reflects off the sides thousands of times each meter.*

Polarized Light

Next time you go shopping for sunglasses, look for those that have lenses that polarize light. Sunglasses that contain polarizing lenses reduce glare better than sunglasses that do not. *Polarized light* consists of light waves that vibrate in only one plane. **Figure 27** illustrates how light is polarized.

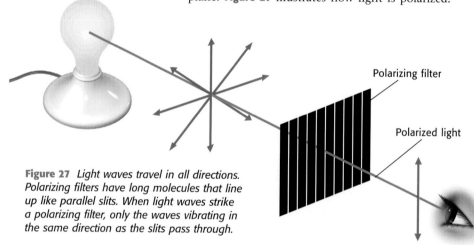

Polarizing filter

Polarized light

Figure 27 *Light waves travel in all directions. Polarizing filters have long molecules that line up like parallel slits. When light waves strike a polarizing filter, only the waves vibrating in the same direction as the slits pass through.*

 Critical Thinking Worksheet, "Light That Heals"

IS THAT A FACT!

Have you used a laser today? If you've played a CD or DVD, the answer is yes. And you probably used a laser the last time you picked up the phone. Many phone lines are now made of fiber optic cables, and lasers are the source of the light that transmits information through fiber optic cables.

When light reflects at a certain angle from a smooth surface, it is completely polarized parallel to that surface. If the surface is parallel to the ground, the light is polarized horizontally. This is what causes the bright glare from bodies of water and car hoods.

Polarizing sunglasses reduce glare from horizontal surfaces because the sunglasses have lenses with vertically polarized filters. These filters allow only vertically vibrating light waves to pass through them. So when you wear polarizing sunglasses, the reflected light that is horizontally polarized does not reach your eyes. Polarizing filters are also used by photographers to reduce glare and reflection in their photographs. Examine **Figure 28** to see the effect of a polarizing filter on a camera.

Figure 28 *These two photos were taken by the same camera from the same angle. There is less reflected light in the photo at right because a polarizing filter was placed over the lens of the camera.*

SECTION REVIEW

1. How is a camera similar to the human eye?

2. What is the difference between a refracting telescope and a reflecting telescope?

3. How is a beam of laser light different from non-laser light?

4. Why are fiber optics useful for transmitting information?

5. **Applying Concepts** Why do you think lasers are used to cut cloth and metal and to perform surgery?

---

4 Close

QuickLab

MATERIALS

FOR EACH GROUP:
• 2 polarizing lenses

Answers to QuickLab

3. As one lens is rotated, the room becomes progressively darker until, when one lens is rotated 90° relative to the other lens, students will not be able to see the room.

4. The first lens polarizes light so that only waves vibrating in, for example, the vertical plane are able to pass through. When the second lens is rotated 90° from the first lens, it polarizes light in the horizontal plane (90° from the first lens). The vertically polarized light from the first lens can't pass through the second (horizontal) lens. No light gets through, and the room looks completely dark.

Quiz

1. Name three optical instruments that use lenses or mirrors. (microscopes, telescopes, cameras)

2. What is one use of fiber optics? (endoscopy; computer networking)

3. How do polarized sunglass lenses work? (They have filters that allow only vertical waves to pass through, reducing the amount of glare.)

ALTERNATIVE ASSESSMENT

Have each student write seven questions with answers from this section. Play a game with the class. Each student should answer at least one question.

▼ **Answers to Section Review**

1. Answers will vary; they should cover the information from Figure 17 on page 105.

2. refracting telescope—two convex lenses; reflecting telescope—one concave mirror and one convex lens

3. Laser light is coherent, has only one color and wavelength, and stays focused over long distances. Non-laser light is not coherent and may have light waves of many different colors and wavelengths.

4. Fiber optics transmit information faster and more clearly than older metal cables.

5. Accept all reasonable answers. Possible answers: Lasers produce tightly focused beams of light that can deliver a large amount of energy to a small space.

Mirror Images
Teacher's Notes

Time Required

One or two 45-minute class periods

Lab Ratings

EASY ————————→ HARD

TEACHER PREP
STUDENT SET-UP
CONCEPT LEVEL
CLEAN UP

MATERIALS

Mirrors with a focal length around 50 cm work well.

Safety Caution

Caution students about working near an open flame. Any loose hair or clothing should be tied back before beginning the experiment.

Kevin McCurdy
Elmwood Junior High
Rogers, Arkansas

Skill Builder Lab

Mirror Images

When light actually passes through an image, the image is a real image. When light does not pass through the image, the image is a virtual image. Recall that plane mirrors produce only virtual images because the image appears to be behind the mirror where no light can pass through it.

In fact, all mirrors can form virtual images, but only some mirrors can form real images. In this experiment, you will explore the virtual images formed by concave and convex mirrors, and you will try to find a real image using both types of mirrors.

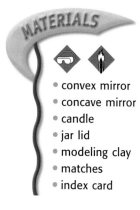

MATERIALS

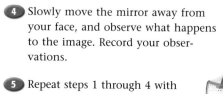

- convex mirror
- concave mirror
- candle
- jar lid
- modeling clay
- matches
- index card

Part A: Finding Virtual Images

Make Observations

1. Hold the convex mirror at arm's length away from your face. Observe the image of your face in the mirror.

2. Slowly move the mirror toward your face, and observe what happens to the image. Record your observations in your ScienceLog.

3. Move the mirror very close to your face. Record your observations in your ScienceLog.

4. Slowly move the mirror away from your face, and observe what happens to the image. Record your observations.

5. Repeat steps 1 through 4 with the concave mirror.

114

Answers

6. Students should find a virtual image for both kinds of mirrors. The virtual image appears to be behind the mirror, where no light rays can pass through the image.

7. Images in a convex mirror will be smaller and upright. Images in a concave mirror will be larger and upright when the mirror is close and smaller and inverted when the mirror is farther from the student's face.

8. Accept all reasonable answers. Convex mirrors are used for wide-angle views in side-view mirrors on cars and to see around corners in busy hallways. Concave mirrors are used for make-up and shaving mirrors. Concave mirrors are also used in telescopes.

Analyze Your Results

6 For each mirror, did you find a virtual image? How can you tell?

7 Describe the images you found. Were they smaller, larger, or the same size as your face? Were they upright or inverted?

Draw Conclusions

8 Describe at least one use for each type of mirror. Be creative, and try to think of inventions that might use the properties of the two types of mirrors.

Part B: Finding a Real Image

Make Observations

9 In a darkened room, place a candle in a jar lid near one end of a table. Use modeling clay to hold the candle in place. Light the candle.
Caution: Use extreme care around an open flame.

10 Use more modeling clay to make a base to hold the convex mirror upright. Place the mirror at the other end of the table, facing the candle.

11 Hold the index card between the candle and the mirror but slightly to one side so that you do not block the candlelight, as shown below.

12 Move the card slowly from side to side and back and forth to see whether you can focus an image of the candle on it. Record your results in your ScienceLog.

13 Repeat steps 10–12 with the concave mirror.

Analyze Your Results

14 For each mirror, did you find a real image? How can you tell?

15 Describe the real image you found. Was it smaller, larger, or the same size as the object? Was it upright or inverted?

Draw Conclusions

16 Astronomical telescopes use large mirrors to reflect light to form a real image. Based on your results, would a concave or convex mirror be better for this instrument? Explain your answer.

Answers

14. A real image can be observed with the concave mirror but not with the convex mirror. The real image is "real" because the light reflects off the mirror and forms a visible image on the card.

15. The image is smaller and inverted.

16. A concave mirror would be better than a convex mirror. A real image cannot be formed with a convex mirror.

 Datasheets for LabBook

Chapter Highlights

VOCABULARY DEFINITIONS

SECTION 1

luminous describes objects that are visible light sources

illuminated describes visible objects that are not light sources

incandescent light light produced by hot objects

fluorescent light visible light emitted by a phosphor particle when it absorbs energy, such as ultraviolet light

neon light visible light emitted by atoms of certain gases when they absorb and then release energy

vapor light light produced when electrons combine with gaseous metal atoms

SECTION 2

plane mirror a mirror with a flat surface

concave mirror a mirror that is curved inward like the inside of a spoon

focal point the point on the axis of a mirror or lens through which light beams entering the mirror or lens parallel to the axis are focused

convex mirror a mirror that curves out toward you, like the back of a spoon

lens a curved, transparent object that forms an image by refracting light; the part of the eye that refracts light to focus an image on the retina

convex lens a lens that is thicker in the middle than at the edges

concave lens a lens that is thinner in the middle than at the edges

Chapter Highlights

SECTION 1

Vocabulary

  luminous (p. 94)
  illuminated (p. 94)
  incandescent light (p. 95)
  fluorescent light (p. 96)
  neon light (p. 96)
  vapor light (p. 97)

Section Notes

- You see objects either because they are luminous (produce their own light) or because they are illuminated (reflect light).

- Light produced by hot objects is incandescent light. Ordinary light bulbs are a common source of incandescent light.

- Fluorescent light is visible light emitted by a particle when it absorbs ultraviolet light. Little energy is wasted by fluorescent light bulbs.

- Neon light results from an electric current in certain gases.

- Vapor light is produced when electrons combine with gaseous metal atoms.

SECTION 2

Vocabulary

  plane mirror (p. 99)
  concave mirror (p. 100)
  focal point (p. 100)
  convex mirror (p. 102)
  lens (p. 103)
  convex lens (p. 103)
  concave lens (p. 104)

Section Notes

- Rays are arrows that show the path and direction of a single light wave. Ray diagrams can be used to determine where images are formed by mirrors and lenses.

- Plane mirrors produce virtual images that are the same size as the objects. These images are reversed left to right.

☑ Skills Check

Visual Understanding

OPTICAL AXIS, FOCAL POINT, AND FOCAL LENGTH To understand how concave and convex mirrors and lenses work, you need to know what the terms *optical axis*, *focal point*, and *focal length* mean. Figure 10 on page 100 explains these terms.

LASERS Laser light is different from ordinary non-laser light in several ways. Look back at Figure 22 on page 110 to review some differences between the two types of light.

THE EYE Study Figure 17 on page 105 to review the parts of the eye and review the process by which your eye gathers light to form the images that you see.

Lab and Activity Highlights

Mirror Images `PG 114`

Images from Convex Lenses `PG 134`

 Datasheets for LabBook (blackline masters for these labs)

SECTION 2

- Concave mirrors can produce real images and virtual images. They can also be used to produce a powerful light beam.

- Convex mirrors produce only virtual images.

- Convex lenses can produce real images and virtual images. A magnifying glass is an example of a convex lens.

- Concave lenses produce only virtual images.

Labs
Images from Convex Lenses (p. 134)

SECTION 3

Vocabulary
cornea (p. 105)
pupil (p. 105)
iris (p. 105)
retina (p. 105)

Section Notes

- Your eye has several parts, such as the cornea, the pupil, the iris, the lens, and the retina.

- Nearsightedness and farsightedness occur when light is not focused on the retina. Both problems can be corrected with glasses or contact lenses.

- Color deficiency is a genetic condition in which cones in the retina are given the wrong instructions. Color deficiency cannot be corrected.

SECTION 4

Vocabulary
laser (p. 109)
hologram (p. 111)

Section Notes

- Optical instruments, such as cameras, telescopes, and microscopes, are devices that use mirrors and lenses to help people make observations.

- Lasers are devices that produce intense, coherent light of only one wavelength and color. Lasers produce light by a process called stimulated emission.

- Optical fibers can transmit light over long distances because of total internal reflection.

- Polarized light contains light waves that vibrate in only one direction.

VOCABULARY DEFINITIONS, *continued*

SECTION 3

cornea a transparent membrane that protects the eye and refracts light

pupil the opening to the inside of the eye

iris the colored part of the eye

retina the back surface of the eye

SECTION 4

laser a device that produces intense light of only one wavelength and color

hologram a piece of film on which an interference pattern produces a three-dimensional image of an object

Vocabulary Review Worksheet

Blackline masters of these Chapter Highlights can be found in the **Study Guide.**

internetconnect

GO TO: go.hrw.com

Visit the **HRW** Web site for a variety of learning tools related to this chapter. Just type in the keyword:

KEYWORD: HSTLOW

SCI LINKS
NSTA

GO TO: www.scilinks.org

Visit the **National Science Teachers Association** on-line Web site for Internet resources related to this chapter. Just type in the *sci*LINKS number for more information about the topic:

TOPIC: Producing Light   *sci*LINKS NUMBER: HSTP555
TOPIC: Mirrors   *sci*LINKS NUMBER: HSTP560
TOPIC: Lenses   *sci*LINKS NUMBER: HSTP565
TOPIC: The Eye   *sci*LINKS NUMBER: HSTP570
TOPIC: Lasers   *sci*LINKS NUMBER: HSTP575

117

Lab and Activity Highlights

LabBank

Labs You Can Eat,
Fiber-Optic Fun

EcoLabs & Field Activities,
Photon Drive

Whiz-Bang Demonstrations,
Light Humor

Inquiry Labs, Eye Spy

Long-Term Projects & Research Ideas,
Island Vacation

Chapter Review
Answers

USING VOCABULARY

1. Incandescent light
2. concave mirror
3. retina
4. laser
5. illuminated

UNDERSTANDING CONCEPTS

Multiple Choice

6. c
7. a
8. d
9. d
10. d
11. c
12. c
13. c

Short Answer

14. Convex lenses should be prescribed. Convex lenses focus light slightly before it enters the eye so that the lens of the eye can focus the light properly on the retina.

15. Holograms produce three-dimensional images that appear in front of or behind the hologram. Photographs have two-dimensional images on the surface of the film.

16. The North Pole is covered with snow that reflects a great deal of light. The reflected light is polarized and can be eliminated by using sunglasses with polarized lenses.

Chapter Review

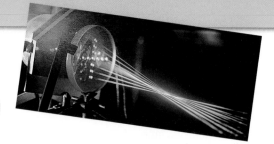

USING VOCABULARY

To complete the following sentences, choose the correct term from each pair of terms listed below:

1. __?__ is commonly used in homes and produces a lot of thermal energy. *(Incandescent light* or *Fluorescent light)*

2. A __?__ is curved inward, like the inside of a spoon. *(convex mirror* or *concave mirror)*

3. You can see an object when light is focused on the __?__ of your eye. *(pupil* or *retina)*

4. A __?__ is a device that produces coherent, intense light of only one color. *(laser* or *lens)*

5. You can see this book because it is a(n) __?__ object. *(luminous* or *illuminated)*

UNDERSTANDING CONCEPTS

Multiple Choice

6. When you look at yourself in a plane mirror, you see a
   a. real image behind the mirror.
   b. real image on the surface of the mirror.
   c. virtual image that appears to be behind the mirror.
   d. virtual image that appears to be in front of the mirror.

7. A vision problem that occurs when light is focused in front of the retina is
   a. nearsightedness.
   b. farsightedness.
   c. color deficiency.
   d. None of the above

8. Which part of the eye refracts light?
   a. iris   c. lens
   b. cornea   d. both (b) and (c)

9. Visible light produced when electrons combine with gaseous metal atoms is
   a. incandescent light.
   b. fluorescent light.
   c. neon light.
   d. vapor light.

10. You see less of a glare when you wear certain sunglasses because the lenses
    a. produce total internal reflection.
    b. create holograms.
    c. produce coherent light.
    d. polarize light.

11. What kind of mirrors provide images of large areas and are used for security?
    a. plane mirrors   c. convex mirrors
    b. concave mirrors   d. all of the above

12. A simple refracting telescope has
    a. a convex lens and a concave lens.
    b. a concave mirror and a convex lens.
    c. two convex lenses.
    d. two concave lenses.

13. Light waves in a laser beam interact and act as one wave. This light is called
    a. red.   c. coherent.
    b. white.   d. emitted.

Short Answer

14. What type of lens should be prescribed for a person who cannot focus on nearby objects? Explain.

15. How is a hologram different from a photograph?

16. Why might a scientist at the North Pole need polarizing sunglasses?

Concept Mapping

17. Use the following terms to create a concept map: lens, telescope, camera, real image, virtual image, optical instrument.

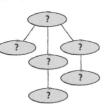

CRITICAL THINKING AND PROBLEM SOLVING

18. Stoplights are usually mounted so that the red light is on the top and the green light is on the bottom. Explain why it is important for a person who has red-green color deficiency to know this arrangement.

19. Some companies are producing fluorescent light bulbs that will fit into sockets on lamps designed for incandescent light bulbs. Although fluorescent bulbs are more expensive, the companies hope that people will use them because they are better for the environment. Explain why fluorescent light bulbs are better for the environment than incandescent light bulbs.

20. Imagine you are given a small device that produces a beam of red light. You want to find out if the device is producing laser light or if it is just a red flashlight. To do this, you point the beam of light against a wall across the room. What would you expect to see if the device is producing laser light? Explain.

INTERPRETING GRAPHICS

21. Examine the ray diagrams below, and identify the type of mirror or lens that is being used and the kind of image that is being formed.

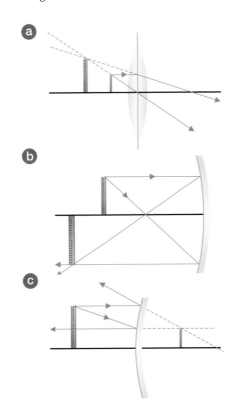

Reading Check-up

Take a minute to review your answers to the Pre-Reading Questions found at the bottom of page 92. Have your answers changed? If necessary, revise your answers based on what you have learned since you began this chapter.

Concept Mapping

17. An answer to this exercise can be found at the front of this book.

CRITICAL THINKING AND PROBLEM SOLVING

18. People who are red-green color-blind cannot distinguish between red and green. If they do not know the arrangement of lights on stoplights, they can't use the stoplight to determine when it is safe to cross an intersection or when they need to stop.

19. Fluorescent lights are better than incandescent lights for the environment because they waste less thermal energy, and less energy is needed to make fluorescent light bulbs glow.

20. You would expect to see a small dot of light because focused laser light does not spread out very much over long distances.

INTERPRETING GRAPHICS

21. a. convex lens; a virtual image
    b. concave mirror; a real image
    c. convex mirror; a virtual image

Concept Mapping Transparency 23

Blackline masters of this Chapter Review can be found in the **Study Guide.**

Background

Traffic lights are crucial to modern transportation because in most situations they are far more effective at regulating traffic than other methods of traffic control. And although color-blind drivers cannot distinguish the color of each light, they can respond to the signal by memorizing the position of each color.

In addition to the traffic light, Morgan also invented a woman's hat fastener, a friction-drive clutch, and a safety hood—a gas mask—that protected the wearer from dangerous airborne materials.

Morgan's safety hood was tested in 1916 when an explosion in a Cleveland tunnel left 32 men trapped amid smoke and toxic gases. Morgan and his brother heard of the disaster, raced to the scene, donned their gas masks, and went into the tunnel. Although not all of the men survived, Morgan and his brother retrieved every single man from the tunnel. For his actions, Morgan received a medal from a group of Cleveland citizens as well as an award from the International Association of Fire Engineers.

Science, Technology, and Society

Traffic Lights

One day in the 1920s, an automobile collided with a horse and carriage. The riders were thrown from their carriage, the driver of the car was knocked unconscious, and the horse was fatally injured. A man named Garrett Morgan (1877–1963) witnessed this scene, and the accident gave him an idea.

A Bright Idea

Morgan's idea was a signal that included signs to direct traffic at busy intersections. The signal could be seen from a distance and could be clearly understood.

Morgan patented the first traffic signal in 1923. His signal looked very different from those used today. Unlike the small, three-bulb signal boxes that now hang over most busy intersections, the early versions were T-shaped, with the words *stop* and *go* printed on them.

Morgan's traffic signal was operated by a preset timing system. An electric motor turned a system of gears that operated a timing dial. As the timing dial rotated, it turned the switches on and off.

Morgan's invention was an immediate success, and he sold the patent to General Electric Corporation for $40,000—quite a large sum in those days. Since then, later versions of Morgan's traffic signal have been the mainstay of urban traffic control.

Light Technology

The technology of traffic lights continues to improve. For example, in some newer models the timing can be changed, depending on the traffic needs for a particular time of day. Some models have sensors installed in the street to monitor traffic flow. In other models, sensors can be triggered from inside an ambulance so that the light automatically turns green, allowing the ambulance to pass.

More About Morgan

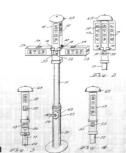

Garrett Morgan, the son of former slaves, was born in Paris, Kentucky. He was one of 11 children, and his formal education ended at the sixth grade. At age 14, with no money and few skills, Morgan left home to work in Cincinnati, Ohio. He soon moved to Cleveland and quickly taught himself enough about sewing machines to get a job repairing them. Morgan saw how important the rest of his education was, so he taught himself and he hired tutors to help him complete his education. By 1907, Morgan opened his own sewing-machine repair shop. He was on his way!

Not only was Morgan an inventor, he was a hero. Gas masks that Morgan invented in 1912 were used in WWI to protect soldiers from chlorine gas fumes. Morgan himself, wearing one of his masks, later helped save several men trapped in a tunnel after a gas explosion.

Think About It

► Traffic control is not the only system in which light is used as a signal. What are some other systems that do so, and what makes light so useful for communication?

▲ *Morgan's patent for the first traffic light*

Answer to Think About It

Other systems that use light for communication include Morse code (such as when ships communicate with flashing lights), spotlights, lighthouses, crosswalk signals, and advertisements. In addition, aisles in theaters and airplanes are often equipped with lights to guide foot traffic. Light is a good method of communication because it is not affected by noise, it works well in all lighting conditions, and it is fairly inexpensive.

EYE ON THE ENVIRONMENT

Light Pollution

At night, large cities are often visible from far away. Soft light from windows outlines buildings. Bright lights from stadiums and parking lots shine like beacons. Scattered house lights twinkle like jewels. The sight is stunning!

Unfortunately, astronomers consider all these lights a form of pollution. Around the world, light pollution is reducing astronomers' ability to see beyond our atmosphere.

Sky Glow

Twenty years ago, stars were very visible above even large cities. The stars are still there, but now they are obscured by city lights. This glow, called sky glow, is created when light reflects off dust and other particles suspended in the atmosphere. Sky glow affects the entire atmosphere to some degree. Today, even remote locations around the globe are affected by light pollution.

The majority of light pollution comes from outdoor lights such as headlights, street lights, porch lights, and bright parking-lot and stadium lights. Other sources include forest fires and gas burn-offs in oil fields. Air pollution makes the situation worse, adding more particles to the air so that reflection is even greater.

A Light of Hope

Unlike other kinds of pollution, light pollution has some simple solutions. In fact, light pollution can be reduced in as little time as it takes to turn off a light! While turning off most city lights is impractical, several simple strategies can make a surprising difference. For example, using covered outdoor lights keeps the light angled downward, preventing most of the light from reaching particles in the sky. Also, using motion-sensitive lights and timed lights helps eliminate unnecessary light.

▲ *Lights from cities can be seen from space, as shown in this photograph taken from the space shuttle* Columbia. *Bright, uncovered lights (inset) create a glowing haze in the night sky above most cities in the United States.*

Many of these strategies also save money by saving energy.

Astronomers hope that public awareness will help improve the visibility of the night sky in and around major cities. Some cities, including Boston and Tucson, have already made some progress in reducing light pollution. Scientists have projected that if left unchecked, light pollution will affect every observatory on Earth within the next decade.

See for Yourself

▶ With your parents' permission, go outside at night and find a place where you can see the sky. Count the number of stars you can see. Now turn on a flashlight or porch light. How many stars can you see now? Compare your results. How much was your visibility reduced?

Background

Many observatories in the United States are in danger of becoming inoperative as cities near them continue to grow. Some ways in which an individual can help reduce light pollution include installing low-wattage bulbs in porch lights, using outdoor light sources only when necessary, and joining an organization such as the International Dark-Sky Association, which helps educate the public through lectures and newspaper articles.

One solution is to put telescopes and other instruments in orbit around the Earth. But launching satellites is very expensive, and the observatories can have collisions with orbiting debris.

121

Answer to See for Yourself

Student responses will vary depending on how dark the sky is. In a medium to large city, they may be able to see only a handful of stars, and any nearby light will reduce the number even more. In the countryside, students may see a sky full of stars. (Ironically, brightly lit skies can aid some observatories, because then only the very brightest stars are visible, thus aiding their identification.)

SAFETY FIRST!

Exploring, inventing, and investigating are essential to the study of science. However, these activities can also be dangerous. To make sure that your experiments and explorations are safe, you must be aware of a variety of safety guidelines.

You have probably heard of the saying, "It is better to be safe than sorry." This is particularly true in a science classroom where experiments and explorations are being performed. Being uninformed and careless can result in serious injuries. Don't take chances with your own safety or with anyone else's.

Following are important guidelines for staying safe in the science classroom. Your teacher may also have safety guidelines and tips that are specific to your classroom and laboratory. Take the time to be safe.

Safety Rules!

Start Out Right

Always get your teacher's permission before attempting any laboratory exploration. Read the procedures carefully, and pay particular attention to safety information and caution statements. If you are unsure about what a safety symbol means, look it up or ask your teacher. You cannot be too careful when it comes to safety. If an accident does occur, inform your teacher immediately, regardless of how minor you think the accident is.

Safety Symbols

All of the experiments and investigations in this book and their related worksheets include important safety symbols to alert you to particular safety concerns. Become familiar with these symbols so that when you see them, you will know what they mean and what to do. It is important that you read this entire safety section to learn about specific dangers in the laboratory.

If you are instructed to note the odor of a substance, wave the fumes toward your nose with your hand. Never put your nose close to the source.

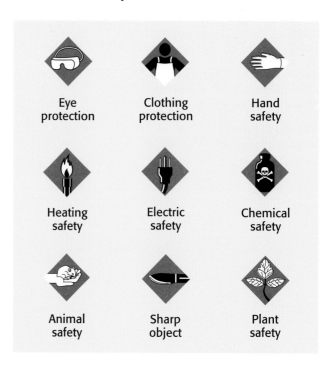

Eye protection	Clothing protection	Hand safety
Heating safety	Electric safety	Chemical safety
Animal safety	Sharp object	Plant safety

Eye Safety

Wear safety goggles when working around chemicals, acids, bases, or any type of flame or heating device. Wear safety goggles any time there is even the slightest chance that harm could come to your eyes. If any substance gets into your eyes, notify your teacher immediately, and flush your eyes with running water for at least 15 minutes. Treat any unknown chemical as if it were a dangerous chemical. Never look directly into the sun. Doing so could cause permanent blindness.

Avoid wearing contact lenses in a laboratory situation. Even if you are wearing safety goggles, chemicals can get between the contact lenses and your eyes. If your doctor requires that you wear contact lenses instead of glasses, wear eye-cup safety goggles in the lab.

Safety Equipment

Know the locations of the nearest fire alarms and any other safety equipment, such as fire blankets and eyewash fountains, as identified by your teacher, and know the procedures for using them.

Be extra careful when using any glassware. When adding a heavy object to a graduated cylinder, tilt the cylinder so the object slides slowly to the bottom.

Neatness

Keep your work area free of all unnecessary books and papers. Tie back long hair, and secure loose sleeves or other loose articles of clothing, such as ties and bows. Remove dangling jewelry. Don't wear open-toed shoes or sandals in the laboratory. Never eat, drink, or apply cosmetics in a laboratory setting. Food, drink, and cosmetics can easily become contaminated with dangerous materials.

Certain hair products (such as aerosol hair spray) are flammable and should not be worn while working near an open flame. Avoid wearing hair spray or hair gel on lab days.

Sharp/Pointed Objects

Use knives and other sharp instruments with extreme care. Never cut objects while holding them in your hands. Place objects on a suitable work surface for cutting.

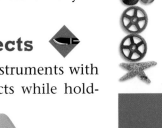

Heat

Wear safety goggles when using a heating device or a flame. Whenever possible, use an electric hot plate as a heat source instead of an open flame. When heating materials in a test tube, always angle the test tube away from yourself and others. In order to avoid burns, wear heat-resistant gloves whenever instructed to do so.

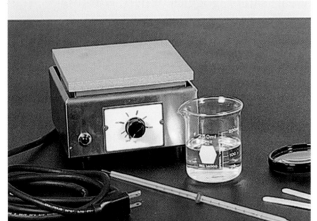

Electricity

Be careful with electrical cords. When using a microscope with a lamp, do not place the cord where it could trip someone. Do not let cords hang over a table edge in a way that could cause equipment to fall if the cord is accidentally pulled. Do not use equipment with damaged cords. Be sure your hands are dry and that the electrical equipment is in the "off" position before plugging it in. Turn off and unplug electrical equipment when you are finished.

Chemicals

Wear safety goggles when handling any potentially dangerous chemicals, acids, or bases. If a chemical is unknown, handle it as you would a dangerous chemical. Wear an apron and safety gloves when working with acids or bases or whenever you are told to do so. If a spill gets on your skin or clothing, rinse it off immediately with water for at least 5 minutes while calling to your teacher.

Never mix chemicals unless your teacher tells you to do so. Never taste, touch, or smell chemicals unless you are specifically directed to do so. Before working with a flammable liquid or gas, check for the presence of any source of flame, spark, or heat.

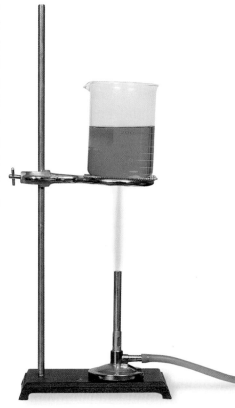

Animal Safety

Always obtain your teacher's permission before bringing any animal into the school building. Handle animals only as your teacher directs. Always treat animals carefully and with respect. Wash your hands thoroughly after handling any animal.

Plant Safety

Do not eat any part of a plant or plant seed used in the laboratory. Wash hands thoroughly after handling any part of a plant. When in nature, do not pick any wild plants unless your teacher instructs you to do so.

Glassware

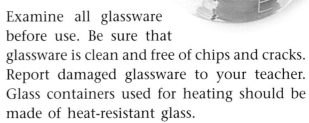

Examine all glassware before use. Be sure that glassware is clean and free of chips and cracks. Report damaged glassware to your teacher. Glass containers used for heating should be made of heat-resistant glass.

Wave Speed, Frequency, and Wavelength
Teacher's Notes

Time Required

One or two 45-minute class periods

Lab Ratings

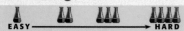

EASY ————————→ HARD

TEACHER PREP 🧪

STUDENT SET-UP 🧪

CONCEPT LEVEL 🧪🧪

CLEAN UP 🧪

MATERIALS

The materials listed for this lab are for each group of 3 students. This lab can also be done as a teacher demonstration if space or materials are limited.

Safety Caution

Remind all students to review all safety cautions and icons before beginning this lab activity.

Lab Notes

You may need to demonstrate step 3 in Part A. Do all of Part A before beginning Part B.

Wave Speed, Frequency, and Wavelength

Wave speed, frequency, and wavelength are three related properties of waves. In this lab you will make observations and collect data to determine the relationship among these properties.

Part A—Wave Speed

Procedure

1. Copy Table 1 into your ScienceLog.

Table 1 Wave Speed Data			
Trial	Length of spring (m)	Time for wave (s)	Speed of wave (m/s)
1			
2			
3			
Average			

DO NOT WRITE IN BOOK

2. On the floor or a table, two students should stretch the spring to a length of 2 to 4 m. A third student should measure the length of the spring. Record the length in Table 1.

3. One student should pull part of the spring sideways with one hand, as shown at right, and release the pulled-back portion. This will cause a wave to travel down the spring.

4. Using a stopwatch, the third student should measure how long it takes for the wave to travel down the length of the spring and back. Record this time in Table 1.

5. Repeat steps 3 and 4 two more times.

Analyze Your Results

6. Calculate and record the wave speed for each trial. (Hint: Speed equals distance divided by time; distance is twice the spring length.)

7. Calculate and record the average time and the average wave speed.

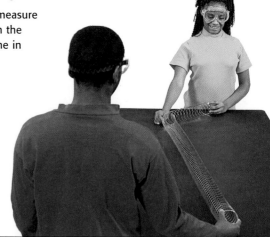

Materials

- coiled spring toy
- meterstick
- stopwatch

 Datasheets for LabBook

126

Part B—Wavelength and Frequency

Procedure

8. Keep the spring the same length that you used in Part A.

9. Copy Table 2 into your ScienceLog.

Table 2 Wavelength and Frequency Data				
Trial	Length of spring (m)	Time for 10 cycles (s)	Wave frequency (Hz)	Wavelength (m)
1				
2				
3				
Average				

DO NOT WRITE IN BOOK

10. One of the two students holding the spring should start shaking the spring from side to side until a wave pattern appears that resembles one of those shown below.

11. Using the stopwatch, the third group member should measure and record how long it takes for 10 cycles of the wave pattern to occur. (One back-and-forth shake is one cycle.) Keep the pattern going so that measurements for three trials can be made.

Analyze Your Results

12. Calculate the frequency for each trial by dividing the number of cycles (10) by the time. Record the answers in Table 2.

13. Determine the wavelength using the equation at right that matches your wave pattern. Record your answer in Table 2.

14. Calculate and record the average time and frequency.

Draw Conclusions—Parts A and B

15. To discover the relationship among speed, wavelength, and frequency, try multiplying or dividing any two of them to see if the result equals the third. (Use the average speed, wavelength, and average frequency from your data tables.) In your ScienceLog, write the equation that shows the relationship.

16. Reread the definitions for *frequency* and *wavelength* in the chapter titled "The Energy of Waves." Use these definitions to explain the relationship that you discovered.

Wave Patterns

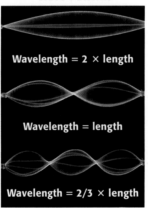

Wavelength = 2 × length

Wavelength = length

Wavelength = 2/3 × length

Answers

15. Accept all answers with correct calculations. Correct forms of the equation are: speed = wavelength × frequency; wavelength = speed/frequency; or frequency = speed/wavelength.

Lab Notes

In answer 15, students will be using numbers from their data to do the calculations. However, when students write their equation, they should use the terms, not their numbers.

16. Sample answer: The frequency of a wave is the number of waves that pass a certain point in a given amount of time. The wavelength is how long a wave is. So the speed of a wave must be wavelength (how long it is) times frequency (how many pass by per second).

Kevin McCurdy
Elmwood Junior High
Rogers, Arkansas

Easy Listening
Teacher's Notes

Time Required

One or two 45-minute class periods

Lab Ratings

EASY —————————————→ HARD

TEACHER PREP

STUDENT SET-UP

CONCEPT LEVEL

CLEAN UP

MATERIALS

FOR EACH GROUP OF 3 TO 4 STUDENTS:
- 4 tuning forks of different frequencies
- pink rubber eraser (or tuning fork mallet)
- meterstick
- graph paper

Answer

2. Answers will vary. Accept all reasonable hypotheses.

Datasheets for LabBook

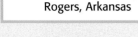

Terry Rakes
Elmwood Junior High
Rogers, Arkansas

DISCOVERY LAB

Easy Listening

Pitch describes how low or high a sound is. A sound's pitch is related to its frequency—the number of waves per second. Frequency is expressed in hertz (Hz), where 1 Hz equals one wave per second. Most humans can hear frequencies from 20 Hz to 20,000 Hz. However, not everyone detects all pitches equally well at all distances. In this activity you will collect data to see how well you and your classmates hear different frequencies at different distances.

Materials

- 4 tuning forks of different frequencies
- pink rubber eraser
- meterstick
- graph paper

Ask a Question

1. Do students in your classroom hear low-, mid-, or high-frequency sounds better?

Form a Hypothesis

2. In your ScienceLog, write a hypothesis that answers the question above. Explain your reasoning.

Test the Hypothesis

3. Choose one member of your group to be the sound maker. The others will be the listeners.

4. Copy the data table below into your ScienceLog. Be sure to include a column for every listener in your group.

Data Collection Table				
	Distance (m)			
Frequency	Listener 1	Listener 2	Listener 3	Average
1 (___Hz)				
2 (___Hz)				
3 (___Hz)				
4 (___Hz)				

DO NOT WRITE IN BOOK

5. Record the frequency of one of the tuning forks in the top row of the first column of the data table.

128

6. The listeners should stand in front of the sound maker with their backs turned.

7. The sound maker will create a sound by striking the tip of the tuning fork gently with the eraser.

8. The listeners who hear the sound should take one step away from the sound maker. The listeners who do not hear the sound should stay where they are.

9. Repeat steps 7 and 8 until none of the listeners can hear the sound or the listeners reach the edge of the room.

10. Using the meterstick, the sound maker should measure the distance from his or her position to each of the listeners. All group members should record this data in their tables.

11. Repeat steps 5 through 10 with a different tuning fork.

12. Continue until all four tuning forks have been tested.

Analyze the Results

13. Calculate the average distance for each frequency. Share your group's data with the rest of the class to make a data table for the whole class.

14. Calculate the average distance for each frequency for the class.

15. Make a graph of the class results, plotting average distance (*y*-axis) versus frequency (*x*-axis).

Draw Conclusions

16. Was everyone in the class able to hear all frequencies equally? (Hint: Was the average distance for each frequency the same?)

17. If the answer to question 16 is no, which frequency had the largest average distance? Which frequency had the smallest average distance?

18. Based on your graph, do your results support your hypothesis? Explain your answer.

19. Do you think your class sample is large enough to confirm your hypothesis for all humans of all ages? Explain your answer.

Lab Notes

You may wish to use the classroom graph to have students practice interpreting a graph. For instance, you could ask students to try and pinpoint the distances at which other frequencies might be heard based on the graph.

Answers

13. You may wish to provide a table on the board or on an overhead transparency for students to record their data. The table should include a column for each group and a row for the distance measurement for each tuning fork.

14. Calculate the class average for each frequency. All students should have the same averages.

15. The graph will vary depending on what frequencies are used, surrounding noise levels, and individual hearing abilities. See the sample graph below:

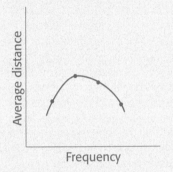

16. The average distance for each frequency should be different.

17. Answers will depend on which frequencies were used. Accept all answers that agree with class data.

18. Answers will vary depending on hypotheses. Accept all reasonable responses.

19. The class sample is not enough to confirm the hypothesis for all humans of all ages, because most people in the classroom are the same age. In addition, the number of students in an average classroom is just too small to provide results that can be extended to the general population.

The Speed of Sound
Teacher's Notes

Time Required

One 45-minute class period

Lab Ratings

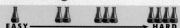

EASY ———————————→ HARD

TEACHER PREP 🍶🍶
STUDENT SET-UP 🍶🍶
CONCEPT LEVEL 🍶🍶
CLEAN UP 🍶

MATERIALS

Students will need stopwatches, measuring tapes, and various types of noise makers (cymbals, wood blocks, drums, horns, etc.). You will need an area where students can hear an echo. A long hall will do, but this lab generally works better outside. To make this lab even more interesting, you might have a contest with awards for the most creative experiment, the most accurate experiment, and the experiment with the least spread in the data for multiple measurements.

Safety Caution

Be sure that you have approved all experimental designs before students proceed.

Answers

4. Answers may vary. Factors that could cause a different value include air temperature and accuracy of distance and time measurements.

5. Several trials are necessary in order to confirm results and to rule out the possibility of reporting an error with just one measurement.

6. Answers will vary. Accept all reasonable responses.

The Speed of Sound

In the chapter titled "The Nature of Sound," you learned that the speed of sound in air is 343 m/s at 20°C (approximately room temperature). In this lab you'll design an experiment to measure the speed of sound yourself—and you'll determine if you're "up to speed"!

Materials

• materials of your choice, approved by your teacher

Procedure

1. Brainstorm with your teammates to come up with a way to measure the speed of sound. Consider the following as you design your experiment:

   a. You must have a method of making a sound. Some simple examples include speaking, clapping your hands, and hitting two boards together.

   b. Remember that speed is equal to distance divided by time. You must devise methods to measure the distance that a sound travels and to measure the amount of time it takes for that sound to travel that distance.

   c. Sound travels very rapidly. A sound from across the room will reach your ears almost before you can start recording the time! You may wish to have the sound travel a long distance.

   d. Remember that sound travels in waves. Think about the interactions of sound waves. You might be able to include these interactions in your design.

2. Discuss your experimental design with your teacher, including any equipment you need. Your teacher may have questions that will help you improve your design.

Conduct an Experiment

3. Once your design is approved, carry out your experiment. Be sure to perform several trials. Record your results in your ScienceLog.

Draw Conclusions

4. Was your result close to the value given in the introduction to this lab? If not, what factors may have caused you to get such a different value?

5. Why was it important for you to perform several trials in your experiment?

Communicate Your Results

6. Compare your results with those of your classmates. Determine which experimental design provided the best results. In your ScienceLog, explain why you think this design was so successful.

 Datasheets for LabBook

Paul Boyle
Perry Heights Middle School
Evansville, Indiana

Tuneful Tube

If you have seen a singer shatter a crystal glass simply by singing a note, you have seen an example of resonance. For this to happen, the note has to match the resonant frequency of the glass. A column of air within a cylinder can also resonate if the air column is the proper length for the frequency of the note. In this lab you will investigate the relationship between the length of an air column, the frequency, and the wavelength during resonance.

Procedure

1. Copy the data table below into your ScienceLog.

Data Collection Table

Frequency (Hz)				
Length (cm)				

DO NOT WRITE IN BOOK

2. Fill the graduated cylinder with water.

3. Hold a plastic tube in the water so that about 3 cm is above the water.

4. Record the frequency of the first tuning fork. Gently strike the tuning fork with the eraser, and hold it so that the prongs are just above the tube, as shown at right. Slowly move the tube and fork up and down until you hear the loudest sound.

5. Measure the distance from the top of the tube to the water. Record this length in your data table.

6. Repeat steps 3–5 using the other three tuning forks.

Analysis

7. Calculate the wavelength (in centimeters) of each sound wave by dividing the speed of sound in air (343 m/s at 20°C) by the frequency and multiplying by 100.

8. Make the following graphs: air column length versus frequency and wavelength versus frequency. On both graphs, plot the frequency on the x-axis.

9. Describe the trend between the length of the air column and the frequency of the tuning fork.

10. How are the pitches you heard related to the wavelengths of the sounds?

Materials

- 100 mL graduated cylinder
- water
- plastic tube, supplied by your teacher
- metric ruler
- 4 tuning forks of different frequencies
- pink rubber eraser
- graph paper

Jennifer Ford
North Ridge Middle School
North Richland Hills, Texas

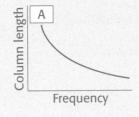

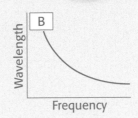

Datasheets for LabBook

131

Tuneful Tube
Teacher's Notes

Time Required
One 45-minute class period

Lab Ratings

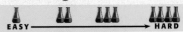
EASY ———————————➤ HARD

TEACHER PREP 🧪🧪🧪
STUDENT SET-UP 🧪
CONCEPT LEVEL 🧪🧪🧪
CLEAN UP 🧪🧪

MATERIALS

The length of tube needed (PVC pipe works well) equals 25 times the speed of sound in air (343 m/s at 20°C) divided by the lowest frequency of the tuning forks used. (The answer is one-fourth the wavelength of the sound wave expressed in centimeters.) Cut each tube at least 5 cm longer than the calculated length. You may want to demonstrate the resonance point so students can hear the change in volume.

Answers

7. Answers will depend on the frequency of the tuning forks.

8. Graphs will depend on results. Sample graphs are shown at left.

9. As the frequency decreases, the length of the air column increases.

10. The pitches (which are determined by the frequencies) are inversely related to the wavelengths of the sounds. As the pitch gets lower (when the frequency decreases), the wavelength increases.

What Color of Light Is Best for Green Plants?
Teacher's Notes

Time Required

One 45-minute class period, plus 5 minutes/day for 5 days

Lab Ratings

EASY ——————————→ HARD

TEACHER PREP 🧪🧪🧪
STUDENT SET-UP 🧪🧪
CONCEPT LEVEL 🧪🧪🧪🧪
CLEAN UP 🧪

MATERIALS

Seeds may be purchased at a garden store and should be germinated several days before this activity. At least green and red lights should be used. Colored bulbs or bulbs with theatrical gels can be used. For best results, give seedlings light of only one color.

Safety Caution

Caution students to use care when working near hot bulbs.

Answers

2. Accept all reasonable hypotheses.

8. Other than natural light, red light is the best, and green light is the worst.

9. Green plants reflect green light and use other colors to grow. Red is best because it is reflected the least.

10. Purple plants do not grow well under purple light because all the light is reflected.

11. Accept all reasonable summaries.

DISCOVERY LAB

What Color of Light Is Best for Green Plants?

Plants grow well outdoors under natural sunlight. However, some plants are grown indoors under artificial light. A wide variety of colored lights are available for helping plants grow indoors. In this experiment, you'll test several colors of light to discover which color best meets the energy needs of green plants.

Materials

- masking tape
- marker
- Petri dishes and covers
- water
- paper towels
- bean seedlings
- variety of colored lights, supplied by your teacher

Ask a Question

1. What color of light is the best for growing green plants?

Form a Hypothesis

2. In your ScienceLog, write a hypothesis that answers the question above. Explain your reasoning.

Test the Hypothesis

3. Use the masking tape and marker to label the side of each Petri dish with your name and the type of light you will place the dish under.

4. Place a moist paper towel in each Petri dish. Place five seedlings on top of the paper towel. Cover each dish.

5. Record your observations of the seedlings, such as length, color, and number of leaves, in your ScienceLog.

6. Place each dish under the appropriate light.

7. Observe the Petri dishes every day for at least 5 days. Record your observations in your ScienceLog.

Analyze the Results

8. Based on your results, which color of light is the best for growing green plants? Which color of light is the worst?

Draw Conclusions

9. Remember that the color of an opaque object (such as a plant) is determined by the colors the object reflects. Use this information to explain your answer to question 8.

10. Would a purple light be good for growing purple plants? Explain.

Communicate Results

11. Write a short paragraph summarizing your conclusions.

132

Datasheets for LabBook

CLASSROOM TESTED & APPROVED

Edith C. McAlanis
Socorro Middle School
El Paso, Texas

Which Color Is Hottest?

Will a navy blue hat or a white hat keep your head warmer in cool weather? Colored objects absorb energy, which can make the objects warmer. How much energy is absorbed depends on the object's color. In this experiment you will test several colors under a bright light to determine which colors absorb the most energy.

Procedure

1. Copy the table below into your ScienceLog. Be sure to have one column for each color of paper you have and enough rows to end at 3 minutes.

Data Collection Table

Time (s)	White	Red	Blue	Black
0				
15				
30				
45				
etc.				

DO NOT WRITE IN BOOK

2. Tape a piece of colored paper around the bottom of a thermometer and hold it under the light source. Record the temperature every 15 seconds for 3 minutes.

3. Cool the thermometer by removing the piece of paper and placing the thermometer in the cup of room-temperature water. After 1 minute, remove the thermometer, and dry it with a paper towel.

4. Repeat steps 2 and 3 with each color, making sure to hold the thermometer at the same distance from the light source.

Analyze the Results

5. Prepare a graph of temperature (*y*-axis) versus time (*x*-axis). Plot all data on one graph using a different colored pencil or pen for each set of data.

6. Rank the colors you used in order from hottest to coolest.

Materials

- tape
- squares of colored paper
- thermometer
- light source
- cup of room-temperature water
- paper towels
- graph paper
- colored pencils or pens

Draw Conclusions

7. Compare the colors based on the amount of energy each absorbs.

8. In this experiment a white light was used. How would your results be different if you used a red light? Explain.

9. Use the relationship between color and energy absorbed to explain why different colors of clothing are used for different seasons.

Which Color Is Hottest?
Teacher's Notes

Time Required

One or two 45-minute class periods

Lab Ratings

EASY ————————→ HARD

TEACHER PREP	🧪🧪
STUDENT SET-UP	🧪🧪
CONCEPT LEVEL	🧪🧪🧪🧪
CLEAN UP	🧪

MATERIALS

A 75 W or 100 W incandescent bulb is a good light source. For best results, a single type of paper should be used. Each group needs one square of each color. Be sure to use at least black, blue, red, and white.

Safety Caution

Caution students to wear safety goggles and aprons while performing this activity.

Procedure Notes

To conserve class time, prepare 2 × 2 cm squares of colored paper in advance.

Answers

5. A sample graph is shown at right. (Red and blue may be reversed.)

Temp. (°C)

Black
Red
Blue
White

Time (s)

6. Black, red, blue, and white.

7. Black absorbs the most energy. Red absorbs more energy than blue. White absorbs the least energy.

8. The red and white papers would be coolest because they reflect red light.

9. Sample answer: Black clothes absorb energy and can help keep a person warm in winter. White clothes reflect energy and can help keep a person cool in summer.

 Datasheets for LabBook

Tracy Jahn
Berkshire Junior–Senior High School
Canaan, New York

Images from Convex Lenses
Teacher's Notes

Time Required
One or two 45-minute class periods

Lab Ratings

EASY ——————→ HARD

TEACHER PREP 🝧
STUDENT SET-UP 🝧
CONCEPT LEVEL 🝧🝧🝧
CLEAN UP 🝧

MATERIALS
Lenses with a focal length of around 25 cm work well.

Safety Caution
Caution students about working near an open flame. Any loose hair or clothing should be tied back before beginning the experiment.

Lab Notes
Image 1 forms when the distance between the candle and the card is 4 times the focal length of the lens. However, students do NOT need to know the focal length of the lens to perform the procedure.

Using Scientific Methods

Images from Convex Lenses

A convex lens is thicker in the center than at the edges. Light rays passing through a convex lens come together at a point. Under certain conditions, a convex lens will create a real image of an object. This image will have certain characteristics, depending on the distance between the object and the lens. In this experiment you will determine the characteristics of real images created by a convex lens—the kind of lens used as a magnifying lens.

Materials
- index card
- modeling clay
- candle
- jar lid
- matches
- convex lens
- meterstick

Ask a Question

1. What are the characteristics of real images created by a convex lens? How do these characteristics depend on the location of the object and the lens?

Conduct an Experiment

2. Copy the table below into your ScienceLog.

	Data Collection			
Image	Orientation (upright/inverted)	Size (larger/smaller)	Image distance (cm)	Object distance (cm)
1				
2				
3				

3. Use some modeling clay to make a base for the lens. Place the lens and base in the middle of the table.

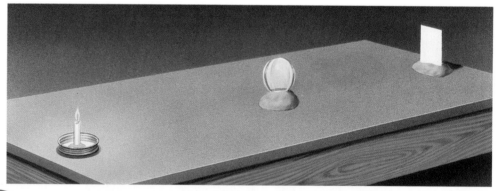

 Datasheets for LabBook

Patricia McFarlane Soto
George Washington Carver Middle School
Miami, Florida

4. Stand the index card upright in some modeling clay on one side of the lens.

5. Place the candle in the jar lid, and anchor it with some modeling clay. Place the candle on the table so that the lens is halfway between the candle and the card. Light the candle. **Caution:** Use extreme care around an open flame.

Collect Data

6. In a darkened room, slowly move the card and the candle away from the lens while keeping the lens exactly halfway between the card and the candle. Continue until you see a clear image of the candle flame on the card. This is image 1.

7. Measure and record the distance between the lens and the card (image distance) and between the lens and the candle (object distance).

8. Is image 1 upright or inverted? Is it larger or smaller than the candle? Record this information in the table.

9. Slide the lens toward the candle to get a new image (image 2) of the candle on the card. Leave the lens in this position.

10. Repeat steps 7 and 8 for image 2.

11. Move the lens back to the middle, and then move the lens toward the card to get a third image (image 3).

12. Repeat steps 7 and 8 for image 3.

Analyze Your Results

13. Describe the trend between image distance and image size.

14. What are the similarities between the real images formed by a convex lens?

Draw Conclusions

15. The lens of your eye is a convex lens. Use the information you collected to describe the image projected on the back of your eye when you look at an object.

16. Convex lenses are used in film projectors. Explain why your favorite movie stars are truly "larger than life" on the screen in terms of the image distance and the object distance.

Communicate Your Results

17. Write a paragraph to summarize your answer to the question in step 1. Be sure to include the roles that image distance and object distance have in determining the characteristics of the images.

Answers

13. When the image distance gets larger, the image size gets larger.

14. The images are inverted.

15. The image projected on the back of your eye is a real image that is smaller than the object and inverted.

16. The object distance (from the film to the lens) is much smaller than the image distance (from the lens to the screen). Thus, the image projected on the screen will be very large compared with the size of the image on the film itself.

17. Accept all reasonable answers. Sample summary: At certain combinations of object distance and image distance, a convex lens will form a real image. The image size varies with the distances. When the image distance is small (and the object distance is large) the image size is small. When the image distance is large, the image size is large. When the image distance and object distance are the same, the image is the same size as the object. All of the real images were inverted, which did not depend on distance at all.

Concept Mapping: A Way to Bring Ideas Together

What Is a Concept Map?

Have you ever tried to tell someone about a book or a chapter you've just read and found that you can remember only a few isolated words and ideas? Or maybe you've memorized facts for a test and then weeks later discovered you're not even sure what topics those facts covered.

In both cases, you may have understood the ideas or concepts by themselves but not in relation to one another. If you could somehow link the ideas together, you would probably understand them better and remember them longer. This is something a concept map can help you do. A concept map is a way to see how ideas or concepts fit together. It can help you see the "big picture."

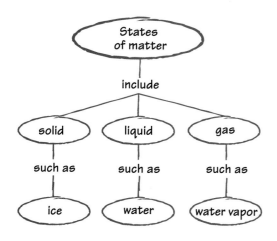

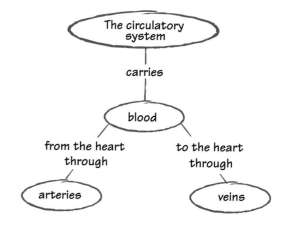

How to Make a Concept Map

❶ Make a list of the main ideas or concepts.

It might help to write each concept on its own slip of paper. This will make it easier to rearrange the concepts as many times as necessary to make sense of how the concepts are connected. After you've made a few concept maps this way, you can go directly from writing your list to actually making the map.

❷ Arrange the concepts in order from the most general to the most specific.

Put the most general concept at the top and circle it. Ask yourself, "How does this concept relate to the remaining concepts?" As you see the relationships, arrange the concepts in order from general to specific.

❸ Connect the related concepts with lines.

❹ On each line, write an action word or short phrase that shows how the concepts are related.

Look at the concept maps on this page, and then see if you can make one for the following terms:

plants, water, photosynthesis, carbon dioxide, sun's energy

One possible answer is provided at right, but don't look at it until you try the concept map yourself.

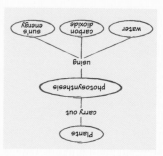

SI Measurement

The International System of Units, or SI, is the standard system of measurement used by many scientists. Using the same standards of measurement makes it easier for scientists to communicate with one another.

SI works by combining prefixes and base units. Each base unit can be used with different prefixes to define smaller and larger quantities. The table below lists common SI prefixes.

SI Prefixes			
Prefix	**Abbreviation**	**Factor**	**Example**
kilo-	k	1,000	kilogram, 1 kg = 1,000 g
hecto-	h	100	hectoliter, 1 hL = 100 L
deka-	da	10	dekameter, 1 dam = 10 m
		1	meter, liter
deci-	d	0.1	decigram, 1 dg = 0.1 g
centi-	c	0.01	centimeter, 1 cm = 0.01 m
milli-	m	0.001	milliliter, 1 mL = 0.001 L
micro-	μ	0.000 001	micrometer, 1 μm = 0.000 001 m

SI Conversion Table		
SI units	**From SI to English**	**From English to SI**
Length		
kilometer (km) = 1,000 m	1 km = 0.621 mi	1 mi = 1.609 km
meter (m) = 100 cm	1 m = 3.281 ft	1 ft = 0.305 m
centimeter (cm) = 0.01 m	1 cm = 0.394 in.	1 in. = 2.540 cm
millimeter (mm) = 0.001 m	1 mm = 0.039 in.	
micrometer (μm) = 0.000 001 m		
nanometer (nm) = 0.000 000 001 m		
Area		
square kilometer (km^2) = 100 hectares	1 km^2 = 0.386 mi^2	1 mi^2 = 2.590 km^2
hectare (ha) = 10,000 m^2	1 ha = 2.471 acres	1 acre = 0.405 ha
square meter (m^2) = 10,000 cm^2	1 m^2 = 10.765 ft^2	1 ft^2 = 0.093 m^2
square centimeter (cm^2) = 100 mm^2	1 cm^2 = 0.155 in.^{2}	1 in.^{2} = 6.452 cm^2
Volume		
liter (L) = 1,000 mL = 1 dm^3	1 L = 1.057 fl qt	1 fl qt = 0.946 L
milliliter (mL) = 0.001 L = 1 cm^3	1 mL = 0.034 fl oz	1 fl oz = 29.575 mL
microliter (μL) = 0.000 001 L		
Mass		
kilogram (kg) = 1,000 g	1 kg = 2.205 lb	1 lb = 0.454 kg
gram (g) = 1,000 mg	1 g = 0.035 oz	1 oz = 28.349 g
milligram (mg) = 0.001 g		
microgram (μg) = 0.000 001 g		

Scientific Method

The series of steps that scientists use to answer questions and solve problems is often called the **scientific method.** The scientific method is not a rigid procedure. Scientists may use all of the steps or just some of the steps of the scientific method. They may even repeat some of the steps. The goal of the scientific method is to come up with reliable answers and solutions.

Six Steps of the Scientific Method

1 **Ask a Question** Good questions come from careful **observations.** You make observations by using your senses to gather information. Sometimes you may use instruments, such as microscopes and telescopes, to extend the range of your senses. As you observe the natural world, you will discover that you have many more questions than answers. These questions drive the scientific method.

Questions beginning with *what, why, how,* and *when* are very important in focusing an investigation, and they often lead to a hypothesis. (You will learn what a hypothesis is in the next step.) Here is an example of a question that could lead to further investigation.

Question: How does acid rain affect plant growth?

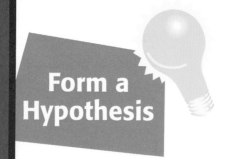

2 **Form a Hypothesis** After you come up with a question, you need to turn the question into a **hypothesis.** A hypothesis is a clear statement of what you expect the answer to your question to be. Your hypothesis will represent your best "educated guess" based on your observations and what you already know. A good hypothesis is testable. If observations and information cannot be gathered or if an experiment cannot be designed to test your hypothesis, it is untestable, and the investigation can go no further.

Here is a hypothesis that could be formed from the question, "How does acid rain affect plant growth?"

Hypothesis: Acid rain causes plants to grow more slowly.

Notice that the hypothesis provides some specifics that lead to methods of testing. The hypothesis can also lead to predictions. A **prediction** is what you think will be the outcome of your experiment or data collection. Predictions are usually stated in an "if . . . then" format. For example, **if** meat is kept at room temperature, **then** it will spoil faster than meat kept in the refrigerator. More than one prediction can be made for a single hypothesis. Here is a sample prediction for the hypothesis that acid rain causes plants to grow more slowly.

Prediction: If a plant is watered with only acid rain (which has a pH of 4), then the plant will grow at half its normal rate.

3 **Test the Hypothesis** After you have formed a hypothesis and made a prediction, you should test your hypothesis. There are different ways to do this. Perhaps the most familiar way is to conduct a **controlled experiment.** A controlled experiment tests only one factor at a time. A controlled experiment has a **control group** and one or more **experimental groups.** All the factors for the control and experimental groups are the same except for one factor, which is called the **variable.** By changing only one factor, you can see the results of just that one change.

Sometimes, the nature of an investigation makes a controlled experiment impossible. For example, dinosaurs have been extinct for millions of years, and the Earth's core is surrounded by thousands of meters of rock. It would be difficult, if not impossible, to conduct controlled experiments on such things. Under such circumstances, a hypothesis may be tested by making detailed observations. Taking measurements is one way of making observations.

Test the Hypothesis

4 **Analyze the Results** After you have completed your experiments, made your observations, and collected your data, you must analyze all the information you have gathered. Tables and graphs are often used in this step to organize the data.

Analyze the Results

5 **Draw Conclusions** Based on the analysis of your data, you should conclude whether or not your results support your hypothesis. If your hypothesis is supported, you (or others) might want to repeat the observations or experiments to verify your results. If your hypothesis is not supported by the data, you may have to check your procedure for errors. You may even have to reject your hypothesis and make a new one. If you cannot draw a conclusion from your results, you may have to try the investigation again or carry out further observations or experiments.

Draw Conclusions

Do they support your hypothesis?

No

Yes

6 **Communicate Results** After any scientific investigation, you should report your results. By doing a written or oral report, you let others know what you have learned. They may want to repeat your investigation to see if they get the same results. Your report may even lead to another question, which in turn may lead to another investigation.

Communicate Results

Scientific Method in Action

The scientific method is not a "straight line" of steps. It contains loops in which several steps may be repeated over and over again, while others may not be necessary. For example, sometimes scientists will find that testing one hypothesis raises new questions and new hypotheses to be tested. And sometimes, testing the hypothesis leads directly to a conclusion. Furthermore, the steps in the scientific method are not always used in the same order. Follow the steps in the diagram below, and see how many different directions the scientific method can take you.

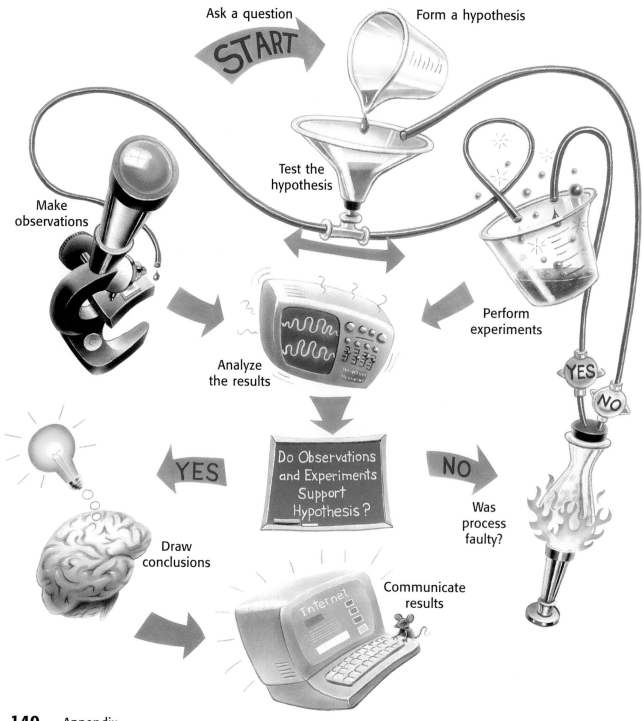

Ask a question

START

Form a hypothesis

Test the hypothesis

Make observations

Perform experiments

Analyze the results

YES

NO

YES   Do Observations and Experiments Support Hypothesis?   NO

Was process faulty?

Draw conclusions

Communicate results

Making Charts and Graphs

Circle Graphs

A circle graph, or pie chart, shows how each group of data relates to all of the data. Each part of the circle represents a category of the data. The entire circle represents all of the data. For example, a biologist studying a hardwood forest in Wisconsin found that there were five different types of trees. The data table at right summarizes the biologist's findings.

Wisconsin Hardwood Trees	
Type of tree	Number found
Oak	600
Maple	750
Beech	300
Birch	1,200
Hickory	150
Total	3,000

How to Make a Circle Graph

1 In order to make a circle graph of this data, first find the percentage of each type of tree. To do this, divide the number of individual trees by the total number of trees and multiply by 100.

$$\frac{600 \text{ oak}}{3,000 \text{ trees}} \times 100 = 20\%$$

$$\frac{750 \text{ maple}}{3,000 \text{ trees}} \times 100 = 25\%$$

$$\frac{300 \text{ beech}}{3,000 \text{ trees}} \times 100 = 10\%$$

$$\frac{1,200 \text{ birch}}{3,000 \text{ trees}} \times 100 = 40\%$$

$$\frac{150 \text{ hickory}}{3,000 \text{ trees}} \times 100 = 5\%$$

2 Now determine the size of the pie shapes that make up the chart. Do this by multiplying each percentage by 360°. Remember that a circle contains 360°.

$20\% \times 360° = 72°$ $25\% \times 360° = 90°$
$10\% \times 360° = 36°$ $40\% \times 360° = 144°$
$5\% \times 360° = 18°$

3 Then check that the sum of the percentages is 100 and the sum of the degrees is 360.

$20\% + 25\% + 10\% + 40\% + 5\% = 100\%$
$72° + 90° + 36° + 144° + 18° = 360°$

4 Use a compass to draw a circle and mark its center.

5 Then use a protractor to draw angles of 72°, 90°, 36°, 144°, and 18° in the circle.

6 Finally, label each part of the graph, and choose an appropriate title.

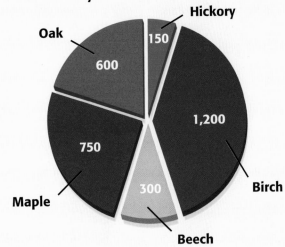

A Community of Wisconsin Hardwood Trees

Line Graphs

Population of Appleton, 1900–2000	
Year	Population
1900	1,800
1920	2,500
1940	3,200
1960	3,900
1980	4,600
2000	5,300

Line graphs are most often used to demonstrate continuous change. For example, Mr. Smith's science class analyzed the population records for their hometown, Appleton, between 1900 and 2000. Examine the data at left.

Because the year and the population change, they are the *variables*. The population is determined by, or dependent on, the year. Therefore, the population is called the **dependent variable**, and the year is called the **independent variable**. Each set of data is called a **data pair**. To prepare a line graph, data pairs must first be organized in a table like the one at left.

How to Make a Line Graph

1 Place the independent variable along the horizontal (*x*) axis. Place the dependent variable along the vertical (*y*) axis.

2 Label the *x*-axis "Year" and the *y*-axis "Population." Look at your largest and smallest values for the population. Determine a scale for the *y*-axis that will provide enough space to show these values. You must use the same scale for the entire length of the axis. Find an appropriate scale for the *x*-axis too.

3 Choose reasonable starting points for each axis.

4 Plot the data pairs as accurately as possible.

5 Choose a title that accurately represents the data.

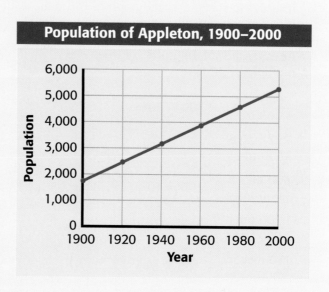

How to Determine Slope

Slope is the ratio of the change in the *y*-axis to the change in the *x*-axis, or "rise over run."

1 Choose two points on the line graph. For example, the population of Appleton in 2000 was 5,300 people. Therefore, you can define point *a* as (2000, 5,300). In 1900, the population was 1,800 people. Define point *b* as (1900, 1,800).

2 Find the change in the *y*-axis.
(*y* at point *a*) − (*y* at point *b*)
5,300 people − 1,800 people = 3,500 people

3 Find the change in the *x*-axis.
(*x* at point *a*) − (*x* at point *b*)
2000 − 1900 = 100 years

4 Calculate the slope of the graph by dividing the change in *y* by the change in *x*.

$$\text{slope} = \frac{\text{change in } y}{\text{change in } x}$$

$$\text{slope} = \frac{3{,}500 \text{ people}}{100 \text{ years}}$$

$$\text{slope} = 35 \text{ people per year}$$

In this example, the population in Appleton increased by a fixed amount each year. The graph of this data is a straight line. Therefore, the relationship is **linear.** When the graph of a set of data is not a straight line, the relationship is **nonlinear.**

Using Algebra to Determine Slope

The equation in step 4 may also be arranged to be:

$$y = kx$$

where y represents the change in the y-axis, k represents the slope, and x represents the change in the x-axis.

$$slope = \frac{change\ in\ y}{change\ in\ x}$$

$$k = \frac{y}{x}$$

$$k \times x = \frac{y \times x}{x}$$

$$kx = y$$

Bar Graphs

Bar graphs are used to demonstrate change that is not continuous. These graphs can be used to indicate trends when the data are taken over a long period of time. A meteorologist gathered the precipitation records at right for Hartford, Connecticut, for April 1–15, 1996, and used a bar graph to represent the data.

Precipitation in Hartford, Connecticut April 1–15, 1996

Date	Precipitation (cm)	Date	Precipitation (cm)
April 1	0.5	April 9	0.25
April 2	1.25	April 10	0.0
April 3	0.0	April 11	1.0
April 4	0.0	April 12	0.0
April 5	0.0	April 13	0.25
April 6	0.0	April 14	0.0
April 7	0.0	April 15	6.50
April 8	1.75		

How to Make a Bar Graph

❶ Use an appropriate scale and a reasonable starting point for each axis.

❷ Label the axes, and plot the data.

❸ Choose a title that accurately represents the data.

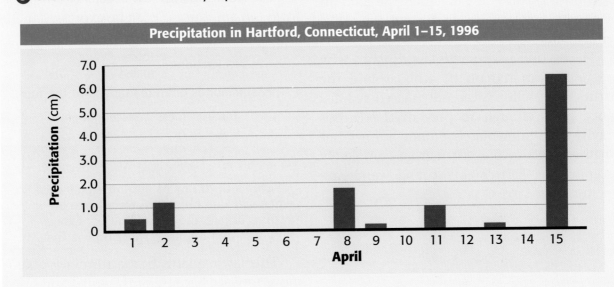

Physical Science Laws and Principles

Law of Conservation of Energy

The law of conservation of energy states that energy can be neither created nor destroyed.

The total amount of energy in a closed system is always the same. Energy can be changed from one form to another, but all the different forms of energy in a system always add up to the same total amount of energy, no matter how many energy conversions occur.

Law of Universal Gravitation

The law of universal gravitation states that all objects in the universe attract each other by a force called gravity. The size of the force depends on the masses of the objects and the distance between them.

The first part of the law explains why a bowling ball is much harder to lift than a table-tennis ball. Because the bowling ball has a much larger mass than the table-tennis ball, the amount of gravity between the Earth and the bowling ball is greater than the amount of gravity between the Earth and the table-tennis ball.

The second part of the law explains why a satellite can remain in orbit around the Earth. The satellite is carefully placed at a distance great enough to prevent the Earth's gravity from immediately pulling it down but small enough to prevent it from completely escaping the Earth's gravity and wandering off into space.

Newton's Laws of Motion

Newton's first law of motion states that an object at rest remains at rest and an object in motion remains in motion at constant speed and in a straight line unless acted on by an unbalanced force.

The first part of the law explains why a football will remain on a tee until it is kicked off or until a gust of wind blows it off.

The second part of the law explains why a bike's rider will continue moving forward after the bike tire runs into a crack in the sidewalk and the bike comes to an abrupt stop until gravity and the sidewalk stop the rider.

Newton's second law of motion states that the acceleration of an object depends on the mass of the object and the amount of force applied.

The first part of the law explains why the acceleration of a 4 kg bowling ball will be greater than the acceleration of a 6 kg bowling ball if the same force is applied to both.

The second part of the law explains why the acceleration of a bowling ball will be larger if a larger force is applied to it.

The relationship of acceleration (a) to mass (m) and force (F) can be expressed mathematically by the following equation:

$$\text{acceleration} = \frac{\text{force}}{\text{mass}}, \text{ or } a = \frac{F}{m}$$

This equation is often rearranged to the form:

$$\text{force} = \text{mass} \times \text{acceleration},$$
$$\text{or}$$
$$F = m \times a$$

Newton's third law of motion states that whenever one object exerts a force on a second object, the second object exerts an equal and opposite force on the first.

This law explains that a runner is able to move forward because of the equal and opposite force the ground exerts on the runner's foot after each step.

Law of Reflection

The law of reflection states that the angle of incidence is equal to the angle of reflection. This law explains why light reflects off of a surface at the same angle it strikes the surface.

A line perpendicular to the mirror's surface is called the *normal.*

The beam of light reflected off the mirror is called the *reflected beam.*

The beam of light traveling toward the mirror is called the *incident beam.*

The angle between the incident beam and the normal is called the *angle of incidence.*

The angle between the reflected beam and the normal is called the *angle of reflection.*

Charles's Law

Charles's law states that for a fixed amount of gas at a constant pressure, the volume of the gas increases as its temperature increases. Likewise, the volume of the gas decreases as its temperature decreases.

If a basketball that was inflated indoors is left outside on a cold winter day, the air particles inside of the ball will move more slowly. They will hit the sides of the basketball less often and with less force. The ball will get smaller as the volume of the air decreases. If a basketball that was inflated outdoors on a cold winter day is brought indoors, the air particles inside of the ball will move more rapidly. They will hit the sides of the basketball more often and with more force. The ball will get larger as the volume of the air increases.

Boyle's Law

Boyle's law states that for a fixed amount of gas at a constant temperature, the volume of a gas increases as its pressure decreases. Likewise, the volume of a gas decreases as its pressure increases.

This law explains why the pressure of the gas in a helium balloon decreases as the balloon rises from the Earth's surface.

Pascal's Principle

Pascal's principle states that a change in pressure at any point in an enclosed fluid will be transmitted equally to all parts of that fluid.

When a mechanic uses a hydraulic jack to raise an automobile off the ground, he or she increases the pressure on the fluid in the jack by pushing on the jack handle. The pressure is transmitted equally to all parts of the fluid-filled jacking system. The fluid presses the jack plate against the frame of the car, lifting the car off the ground.

Archimedes' Principle

Archimedes' principle states that the buoyant force on an object in a fluid is equal to the weight of the volume of fluid that the object displaces.

A person floating in a swimming pool displaces 20 L of water. The weight of that volume of water is about 200 N. Therefore, the buoyant force on the person is 200 N.

Glossary

A

absorption the transfer of energy carried by light waves to particles of matter (74)

amplitude the maximum distance a wave vibrates from its rest position (10, 39)

Archimedes' (ahr kuh MEE deez) **principle** the principle that states that the buoyant force on an object in a fluid is an upward force equal to the weight of the volume of fluid that the object displaces (145)

B

Boyle's law the law that states that for a fixed amount of gas at a constant temperature, the volume of a gas increases as its pressure decreases (145)

C

Charles's law the law that states that for a fixed amount of gas at a constant pressure, the volume of a gas increases as its temperature increases (145)

compression a region of higher density or pressure in a wave (8, 30)

concave lens a lens that is thinner in the middle than at the edges (104)

concave mirror a mirror that is curved inward like the inside of a spoon (100)

constructive interference interference that results in a wave that has a greater amplitude than that of the individual waves (17, 44, 77)

convex lens a lens that is thicker in the middle than at the edges (103)

convex mirror a mirror that is curved outward like the back of a spoon (102)

cornea a transparent membrane that protects the eye and refracts light (105)

crest the highest point of a transverse wave (7)

D

decibel (dB) the most common unit used to express loudness (39)

destructive interference interference that results in a wave that has a smaller amplitude than that of the individual waves (17, 44, 77)

diffraction
diffraction the bending of waves around a barrier or through an opening (15, 47, 77)

Doppler effect the apparent change in the frequency of a sound caused by the motion of either the listener or the source of the sound (refers to sound only) (38)

E

echo a reflected sound wave (14, 41)

echolocation the process of using reflected sound waves to find objects (42)

electromagnetic spectrum the entire range of electromagnetic waves (65)

electromagnetic wave a wave that can travel through space or matter and consists of changing electric and magnetic fields (6, 62)

F

fiber optics the use of optical fibers (thin, flexible glass wires) to transmit light over long distances (112)

fluorescent light visible light emitted by a phosphor particle when it absorbs energy such as ultraviolet light (96)

focal length the distance between a mirror or lens and its focal point (100)

focal point the point on the axis of a mirror or lens through which all incident parallel light rays are focused (100)

frequency the number of waves produced in a given amount of time (12, 36)

fundamental the lowest resonant frequency (46)

G

gamma rays EM waves with very high energy and no mass or charge; they are emitted by the nucleus of a radioactive atom (72)

H

hertz (Hz) the unit used to express frequency; one hertz is one cycle per second (12, 36)

hologram a piece of film on which an interference pattern produces a three-dimensional image of an object (111)

I

illuminated the term describing visible objects that are not a light source (94)

incandescent light light produced by hot objects (95)

infrared waves EM waves that are between microwaves and visible light in the electromagnetic spectrum (69)

infrasonic the term describing sounds with frequencies lower than 20 Hz (37)

inner ear the part of the ear where vibrations created by sound are changed into electrical signals for the brain to interpret (33)

interference a wave interaction that occurs when two or more waves overlap (16, 44, 77)

iris the colored part of the eye (105)

L

laser a device that produces intense light of only one wavelength and color (109)

law of reflection the law that states that the angle of incidence is equal to the angle of reflection (73)

lens a curved, transparent object that forms an image by refracting light (103); *also* the part of the eye that refracts light to focus an image on the retina (105)

longitudinal wave a wave in which the particles of the medium vibrate back and forth along the path that the wave travels (8)

loudness how loud or soft a sound is perceived to be (38)

luminous the term describing objects that produce visible light (94)

M

medium a substance through which a wave can travel (5, 32)

microwaves EM waves that are between radio waves and infrared waves in the electromagnetic spectrum (68)

middle ear the part of the ear where the amplitude of sound vibrations is increased (33)

N

neon light light emitted by atoms of certain gases, such as neon, when they absorb and then release energy (96)

noise any undesired sound, especially nonmusical sound, that includes a random mix of pitches (51)

O

opaque the term describing matter that does not transmit any light (80)

optical axis a straight line drawn outward from the center of a mirror or lens (100)

oscilloscope (uh SIL uh SKOHP) a device used to graph representations of sound waves (40)

outer ear the part of the ear that acts as a funnel to direct sound waves into the middle ear (33)

overtones resonant frequencies that are higher than the fundamental (46)

P

Pascal's principle the principle that states that a change in pressure at any point in an enclosed fluid is transmitted equally to all parts of that fluid (145)

perpendicular at right angles (7, 62)

photon a tiny "packet" of energy that is released by an electron that moves to a lower energy level in an atom (63)

pigment a material that gives a substance its color by absorbing some colors of light and reflecting others (82)

pitch how high or low a sound is perceived to be (36)

plane mirror a mirror with a flat surface (99)

polarized light consists of light waves that vibrate in only one plane (one direction) (112)

primary colors of light red, blue, and green; these colors of light can be combined in different ratios to produce all colors of light (82)

primary pigments yellow, cyan, and magenta; these pigments can be combined to produce any other pigment (83)

pupil the opening to the inside of the eye (105)

R

radiation the transfer of energy through matter or space as electromagnetic waves, such as visible light and infrared waves (63)

radio waves EM waves with long wavelengths and low frequencies (66)

rarefaction (RER uh FAK shuhn) a region of lower density or pressure in a wave (8, 30)

real image an image through which light passes (100)

reflection the bouncing back of a wave after it strikes a barrier or an object (14, 41, 73)

refraction the bending of a wave as it passes at an angle from one medium to another (15, 75)

resonance what occurs when an object vibrating at or near a resonant frequency of a second object causes the second object to vibrate (18, 46)

resonant frequencies the frequencies at which standing waves are made (18, 46)

retina the back surface of the eye (105)

S

scattering the release of light energy by particles of matter that have absorbed energy (75)

secondary color cyan, magenta, and yellow; a color of light produced when two primary colors of light are added together (82)

sonar (**so**und **na**vigation and **r**anging) a type of electronic echolocation (42)

sonic boom the explosive sound heard when a shock wave from an object traveling faster than the speed of sound reaches a person's ears (45)

sound quality the result of several pitches blending together through interference (48)

standing wave a wave that forms a stationary pattern in which portions of the wave do not move and other portions move with a large amplitude (18, 45)

surface wave a wave that occurs at or near the boundary of two media and that is a combination of transverse and longitudinal waves (9)

T

tinnitus hearing loss resulting from damage to the hair cells and nerve endings in the cochlea (34)

translucent the term describing matter that transmits light but also scatters the light as it passes through the matter (80)

transmission the passing of light through matter (79)

transparent the term describing matter through which light is easily transmitted (80)

transverse wave a wave in which the particles of the wave's medium vibrate perpendicular to the direction the wave is traveling (7)

trough the lowest point of a transverse wave (7)

U

ultrasonic the term describing sounds with frequencies higher than 20,000 Hz (37)

ultrasonography a medical procedure that uses echoes from ultrasonic waves to "see" inside a patient's body without performing surgery (43)

ultraviolet light EM waves that are between visible light and X rays in the electromagnetic spectrum (71)

V

vapor light light produced when electrons combine with gaseous metal atoms (97)

vibration the complete back-and-forth motion of an object (30)

virtual image an image through which light does not actually pass (99)

visible light the very narrow range of wavelengths and frequencies in the electromagnetic spectrum that humans can see (70)

W

wave a disturbance that transmits energy through matter or space (4, 31)

wavelength the distance between one point on a wave and the corresponding point on an adjacent wave in a series of waves (11)

wave speed the speed at which a wave travels (13)

X

X rays high-energy EM waves that are between ultraviolet light and gamma rays in the electromagnetic spectrum (72)

Index

Credits

Abbreviations used: (t) top, (c) center, (b) bottom, (l) left, (r) right, (bkgd) background

ILLUSTRATIONS

All illustrations, unless noted below, by Holt, Rinehart and Winston.

Table of Contents v, Gary Ferster; vii, Sidney Jablonski.

Scope and Sequence: T11, Paul DiMare, T13, Dan Stuckenschneider/Uhl Studios, Inc.

Chapter One Page 4, Will Nelson/Sweet Reps; 7(tr), Preface, Inc.; 7(b), 8(t,c), John White/The Neis Group; 8(b), Sidney Jablonski; 9(tl), Stephen Durke/Washington Artists; 9(r), Jared Schneidman/Wilkinson Studios; 10(t), Marty Roper/Planet Rep; 10(b), 11, 12, Sidney Jablonski; 12(cl, cr), 13(cl,cr), Mike Carroll/Steve Edsey & Sons; 13, 15, Will Nelson/Sweet Reps; 17(tl,tc,tr,cl,c,cr), John White/The Neis Group; 17(br), Terry Guyer; 22(b), John White/The Neis Group; 25(r), Sidney Jablonski.

Chapter Two Page 30, Annie Bissett; 31(l), Gary Ferster; 31(br), Terry Kovalcik; 32(tl), David Merrell/Suzanne Craig; 33, Keith Kasnot; 34 (tl), Terry Kovalcik; 35, Keith Locke/Suzanne Craig; 36, Annie Bissett; 37, Will Nelson/ Sweet Reps (dolphin, cat, dog), Rob Wood (whale), Michael Woods (bat, bird), John White/ The Neis Group (girl), and Preface, Inc.; 38, Gary Ferster; 40, Annie Bissett; 41(b), John White/The Neis Group; 42(t), Gary Ferster; 42(b), Terry Guyer; 44(t), Gary Ferster; 44(b), 45, Terry Guyer; 47, 48(c), Gary Ferster; 48(b), 51, Annie Bissett; 54(br), Keith Kasnot; 57(r), Annie Bissett; 58, Barbara Hoopes-Ambler.

Chapter Three Page 62, Sidney Jablonski; 63(tr), Blake Thornton/Rita Marie; 63(b), Stephen Durke/Washington Artists; 66(t), Blake Thornton/Rita Marie; 66(b), Preface, Inc.; 67(tl,tr), Terry Guyer; 67 (b), Preface, Inc.; 68, Dan Stuckenschneider/Uhl Studios Inc.; 70, Preface, Inc.; 71, Blake Thornton/Rita Marie; 72, 73, 74, Dan Stuckenschneider/Uhl Studios Inc.; 76, Stephen Durke/ Washington Artists; 78, Preface, Inc.; 80, Dave Joly; 81, Preface, Inc.; 86, Stephen Durke/Washington Artists.

Chapter Four Page 95, 96, 97, Dan Stuckenschneider/Uhl Studios Inc.; 98, Stephen Durke/Washington Artists; 99, Preface, Inc.; 101, 102, 103, 104, Will Nelson/Sweet Reps (flowers) and Preface, Inc.; 105, Keith Kasnot; 106, Keith Kasnot and Preface Inc.; 108, 109, Dan Stuckenschneider/Uhl Studios Inc.; 110(t), Digital Art; 110(b), Stephen Durke/Washington Artists; 111, Digital Art; 112, Stephen Durke/ Washington Artists; 116(t), Dan Stuckenschneider/Uhl Studios Inc.; 116(b), Keith Kasnot; 119, Stephen Durke/Washington Artists (rulers) and Preface, Inc.

LabBook Page 130, Blake Thornton/Rita Marie; 132, Terry Guyer; 134, John White/The Neis Group.

Appendix Page 140(b), Mark Mille/Sharon Langley Artist Rep.; 141, 142, 143, Preface, Inc.; 145(t), Dan Stuckenschneider/Uhl Studios Inc.

PHOTOGRAPHY

Front Cover and Title Page: Telegraph Colour Library/FPG

Table of Contents Page v(tr), Richard Megna/Fundamental Photographs; v(b), Sam Dudgeon/HRW Photo; vi(t), Richard Megna/Fundamental Photographs; vi(c), Matt Meadows/Photo Researchers, Inc.; vi(b), Robert Wolf; vii(t), James L. Amos/National Geographic Society; vii(c), Dr. E.R. Degginger/ColorPic, Inc.; vii(b), John Langford/HRW Photo.

Scope and Sequence: T8(l), Lee F. Snyder/Photo Researchers, Inc.; T8(r), Stephen Dalton/Photo Researchers, Inc.; T10, E. R. Degginger/Color-Pic, Inc., T12(l), Rob Matheson/The Stock Market

Master Materials List: T25(bl, bc), Image ©2001 PhotoDisc

Feature Borders Unless otherwise noted below, all images ©2001 PhotoDisc/HRW: "Across the Sciences" 27, all images by HRW; "Eureka" 91, ©2001 PhotoDisc/HRW; "Eye on the Environment" 121, clouds and sea in bkgd, HRW, bkgd grass and red eyed frog, Corbis Images, hawks and pelican, Animals Animals/Earth Scenes, rat, John Grelach/Visuals Unlimited, endangered flower, Dan Suzio/Photo Researchers, Inc.; "Science Fiction" 59, saucers, Ian Christopher/Greg Geisler, book, HRW, bkgd, Stock Illustration Source; "Science, Technology, and Society" 26, 58, 90, 120, robot, Greg Geisler.

Chapter One pp. 2-3 Jim Russi/Adventure Photo; p. 3 HRW Photo; p. 5(t), Phil Degginger/Color-Pic, Inc.; p. 5(b), Emil Muench/Photo Researchers, Inc.; p. 6, Norbert Wu; p. 14(b), Erich Schrempp/Photo Researchers, Inc. ; p. 14, Don Spiro/Stone; p. 16(tl,tr,), Richard Megna/Fundamental Photographs; p. 16(b), Richard Hamilton Smith/Corbis-Bettmann; p. 18(t), Richard Megna/ Fundamental Photographs; p. 19, AP/Wide World Photos; p. 21 Sam Dudgeon/HRW Photo; p. 22, Norbert Wu; p. 24, Richard Megna/Fundamental Photographs; p. 25, Martin Bough/Fundamental Photographs; p. 26, Pete Saloutos/The Stock Market; p. 27, Betty K. Bruce/Animals Animals/Earth Scenes.

Chapter Two pp. 28-29 Kim Westerskov/Stone; p. 29 HRW Photo; p. 34(c), Michael A. Keller/The Picture Cube; p. 39(cl), Art Wolfe/ Stone; p. 39(b), Tom Hannon/Picture Cube; p. 40, Charles D. Winters/Timeframe Photography Inc.; p. 41, Dr. E.R. Degginger/Color-Pic, Inc.; p. 42, Stephen Dalton/Photo Researchers, Inc.; p. 43(b), Matt Meadows/Photo Researchers, Inc.; p. 43(t), courtesy of Johann Borenstein; p. 46(b,c), Richard Megna/ Fundamental Photographs; p. 49(l), p. 50 (tl,tr), Image Club Graphics © 1998 Adobe Systems; p. 50(br), Bob Daemmrich/HRW Photo; p. 53 Sam Dudgeon/HRW Photo; p. 56, Ross Harrison Koty/Stone; p. 57, Dick Luria/Photo Researchers, Inc.

Chapter Three pp. 60-61 Matt Meadows/Peter Arnold, Inc..; p. 61 HRW Photo; p. 63, Photo Researchers, Inc.; p. 64, A.T. Willet/The Image Bank; p. 65(r,l), Leonard Lessing/Photo Researchers, Inc.; p. 65(c), Michael Fogden and Patricia Fogden/Corbis; p. 66(l), Robert Wolf; p. 67(c), Hugh Turvey/Science Photo Library/Photo Researchers, Inc.; p. 67(r), Blair Seitz/Photo Researchers, Inc.; p. 67(l), Leonide Principe/Photo Researchers, Inc.; p. 69(t), Bachmann/ Photo Researchers, Inc.; p. 69(b), The Stock Market; p. 70, Cameron Davidson/Stone; p. 72, Michael English/Custom Medical Stock Photo; p. 75, Richard Megna/Fundamental Photographs; p. 76, Robert Wolf; p. 77(t), Fundamental Photographs; p. 79(t), Robert Wolf; p. 79(b), Stephanie Morris/ HRW Photo; p. 81(t), Image copyright 2001 PhotoDisc, Inc.; p. 81(c), Renee Lynn/Davis/Lynn Images; p. 81(b), Robert Wolf; p. 82, Leonard Lessing/Peter Arnold, Inc.; p. 83, Index Stock Photography; p. 85 Sam Dudgeon/HRW Photo; p. 86, Leonard Lessing/ Photo Researchers, Inc.; p. 87, Robert Wolf; p. 89(tr), Charles Winters/Photo Researchers, Inc.; p. 89(cr), Mark E. Gibson; p. 89(br), Richard Megna/Fundamental Photographs; p. 90(t,b), Dr. E.R. Degginger/ Color-Pic, Inc.; p. 91, courtesy of the Raytheon Company.

Chapter Four pp. 92-93 The Purcell Team/CORBIS; p. 93 HRW Photo; p. 94 (b), Harry Rogers/Photo Researchers, Inc.; p. 94(r), Kindra Clinett/The Picture Cube; p. 96, Peter Van Steen/HRW Photo; p. 97, Alan Schein/The Stock Market; p. 98(tr), Yoav Levy/Phototake; p. 99(tr), Stephanie Morris/HRW Photo; p. 100(c), Richard Megna/Fundamental Photographs; p. 102, p. 103(b), Robert Wolf; p. 103(t,c), Dr. E.R. Degginger/Color-Pic, Inc.; p. 107(l,r), Leonard Lessing/Peter Arnold, Inc.; p. 112, Don Mason/The Stock Market; p. 113(l,r), Ken Lax; p. 114 Sam Dudgeon/HRW Photo; p. 118, James L. Amos/National Geographic Society; p. 120(b), US Patent and Trade Office; p. 120(t), Private collection of Garrett Morgan Family; p. 121(b), NASA; p. 121(t), SuperStock.

LabBook "LabBook Header": "L," Corbis Images, "a," Letraset Phototone, "b" and "B," HRW, "o" and "k," Images ©2001 PhotoDisc/HRW; 123(c), Michelle Bridwell/HRW Photo; 123(br), Image © 2001 PhotoDisc, Inc.; 124(cl), Victoria Smith/HRW Photo; 124(bl), Stephanie Morris/HRW Photo; 125(tl), Patti Murray/Animals Animals; 125(b), Peter Van Steen/HRW Photo; 125(tr), Jana Birchum/HRW Photo; 127, 128, Richard Megna/Fundamental Photographs.

Sam Dudgeon/HRW Photo Page viii-1; 12; 23; 31(b); 32; 34(r); 37(t); 46(t); 48; 54-55; 66(c); 88; 94(l); 100(b); 111; 122; 123(b); 124(br,t); 125(tl); 126; 129; 131; 133; 135.

John Langford/HRW Photo Page v(cr); vi(tr); 18(b); 31(t); 39(t,bc); 49(r); 66(r); 71; 74; 77(b); 80; 94(inset); 99(b); 100(tl); 101(b); 119; 123(t).

Scott Van Osdol/HRW Photo Page 89(bl).

Self-Check Answers

Chapter 1—The Energy of Waves

Page 6: Mechanical waves require a medium; electromagnetic waves do not.

Page 15: A light wave will not refract if it enters a new medium perpendicular to the surface because the entire wave enters the new medium at the same time.

Chapter 2—The Nature of Sound

Page 45: A person hears a sonic boom when a shock wave reaches his or her ears. If two people are standing a block or two apart, the shock wave will reach them at different times, so they will hear sonic booms at different times.

Page 49: Interference is the most important wave interaction for determining sound quality.

Chapter 3—The Nature of Light

Page 81: The paper will appear blue because only blue light is reflected from the paper.

Chapter 4—Light and Our World

Page 109: Concave lenses do not form real images. Only a real image can be magnified by another lens, such as the eyepiece lens.